I0605754

ULTRA

ULTRA

THE WORLD ATLAS OF ULTRA MARATHONS

JEN AND SIM BENSON

CASSELL

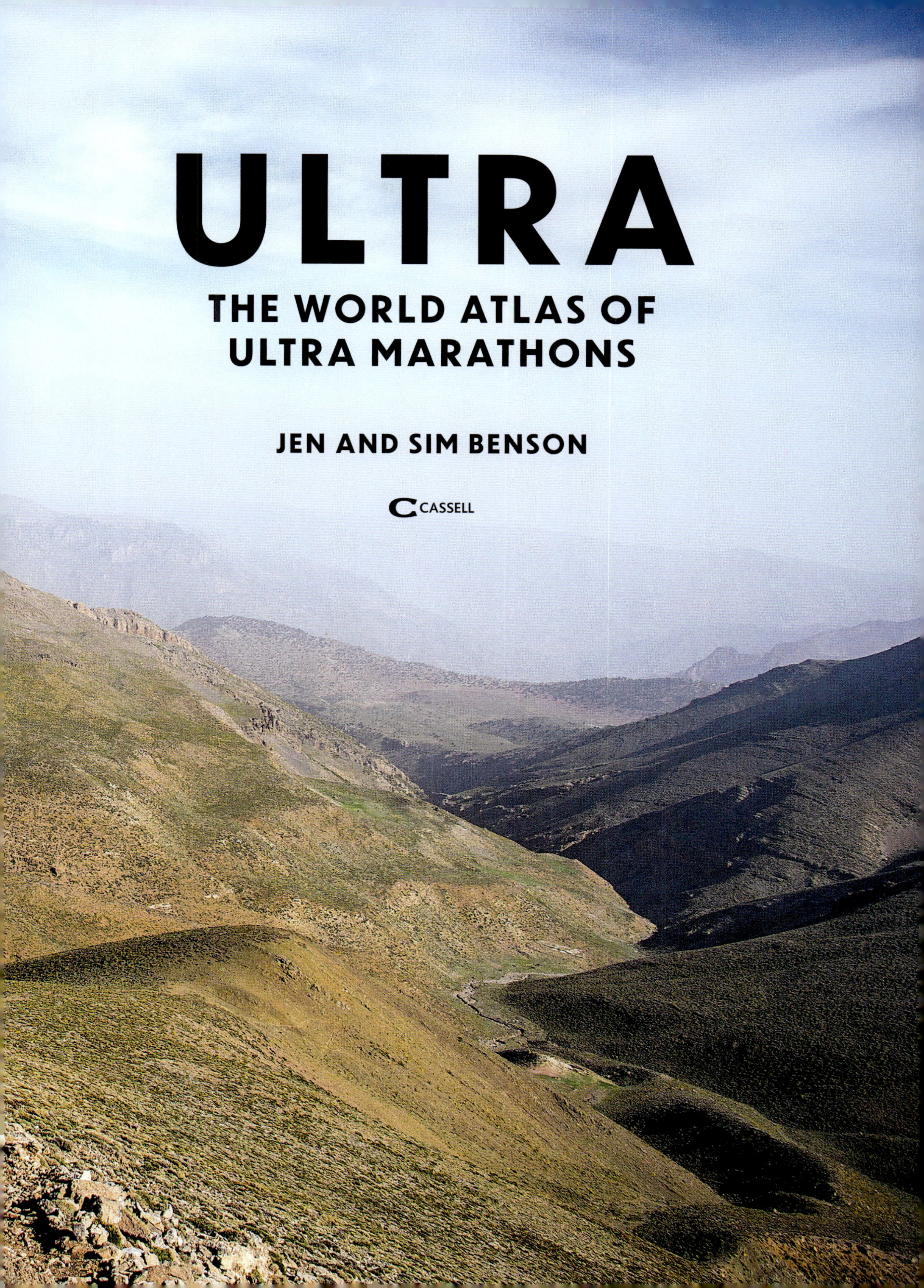

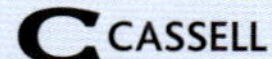

CONTENTS

PAGE 1 Lapland Arctic Ultra, Sweden; **PREVIOUS PAGES** Runners in the Mustang Trail Race, Nepal; **LEFT** Lac Combal on the TDS course, UTMB Mont-Blanc, France.

FOREWORD by Susie Chan

Ultrarunning – once the underground sport on the fringes of recreational sport, is now mainstream. If you know anything about running, or mix with the running community, then the chances are you have heard of the more famous ultra races, or perhaps know someone who runs further than a marathon or have completed one yourself. The growth in popularity has seen more races than ever before and, pleasingly, more people than ever before testing themselves, and seeing how far their resilience, will power and mindset can let them run.

When I started ultrarunning back in 2012, there were fewer than 20 ultramarathons in the UK. The internet threw up very little information about the races, how to take part, what to wear or what to expect. Noticeably, there were very few women at the start lines. How things have changed. I spent the first several years not realizing the popularity of ultramarathons was on the rise; I immersed myself in the community and tackled races myself – it took over my spare time, my social life, and eventually took over as my job. It is only now on reflection, that I can see that I, too, was part of the new wave of people who found running a long, long way one of the best ways to spend a weekend.

What a wonderful world it is to be part of. As an ultrarunner it can be hard to explain to others why you would want to run 50 miles in one go up a mountain. It was not the miles themselves that kept me coming back for more – it was the ultrarunning community who are infectious and inspiring. At each race there was always someone there who had a story about another race – a more extreme, longer, hotter, colder, wilder, rugged race. There was always more to do, to see and experience. The people who I met were ordinary people with ordinary jobs, doing something extraordinary for fun, and they made it all seem so doable!

I started with the Marathon des Sables, which I went on to complete four times. I thought completing the very first one would be the end of it, job done. Ultrarunning :TICK, back to half and full marathons. But getting that first MdS medal lit the touchpaper to wanting more and wondering if I could. What would it feel like to run 100 miles? To run through the hottest place on earth at the hottest time of the year? Could I do it? I found myself getting sucked into the world of ultrarunning, and revelling in just how enabling the community is. Running 50 miles up a mountain for fun is normal in this world.

For me (very much a mid-packer) the best thing these races offered was the afterglow. Each struggle deep into the race, each wave of nausea I overcame, each slow tired mile slogged out meant for a more rewarding finish line. The deeper I had to dig, the more golden the glow. The real happiness would be delayed, not coming immediately at the finish line, but in the morning and days after. It took years for me to realize the happiness was actually the gift of confidence gained from running a long way – not a brash, show-off confidence, but a quiet one that helps shape and build you. It lifts you up.

I favour the long, flatter ultramarathons (a fear of heights has lead me to straight lines of road for 100 miles), loops around a track for 24 hrs and I especially enjoy the challenges of hot environments. These are my own personal mountains. A particular triumph was to complete Badwater 135. It was stunning and truly savage at the same time. I will never forget that last mile, and the exhausted exhilaration I felt. I was forcing myself to be in the moment, to savour and remember it.

Now, with so many races in so many incredible places to choose from, this book is a bucket list from bright, mass-participation ultra races to the more infamous how-do-they-even-do-it event – the Barkley Marathons. Some iconic, some historic and all deserving of their place in these pages.

What also needs to be acknowledged are those who make ultramarathons happen. Behind these successful races are all the people who keep the ultrarunning scene thriving. The big name elites who are like famous rockstars to runners. The race directors, who we only see on the day of the race, and yet they have been working away for months behind the scenes, getting organized, doing endless admin, obtaining permits and making these races as safe and clear as they can be. The races would also not happen if it were not for the teams of volunteers, frequently ultrarunners themselves, giving back by marking the course, or standing behind the aid station for hours on end providing fuel, water and encouragement. Then, there are the participants – each person, from winner to last over the line, complete these races with an equal amount of grit to cover an equal amount of miles. The finish times may differ, but the personal glory does not. It is not just the elites who inspire – everyone in the field will have a story, and perhaps be the person who encourages another to lace up their trainers and embark on their own ultrarunning journey.

Hopefully, this upward trend will continue and start lines will have wider demographics of people, equal numbers of women to men, and be as accessible as they can be to anyone who wants to give it a go. Ultrarunning is the most accessible, extreme sport there is, and everyone is welcome.

INTRODUCTION

Welcome to the wonderful, wacky and sometimes downright weird world of ultrarunning. This is a unique sport that demands everything of its participants, with races often taking days to complete, reducing even the fittest and best-prepared runners to shadows of their former selves – not only during the event but often for weeks afterwards. Training and preparation takes many months, if not many years, of dedication specific to the demands of a race. But in return, ultrarunning gives us so much: views, camaraderie, multi-day picnics, the opportunity to take on a challenge where success is far from guaranteed... In a fast-paced world dominated by complex stressors far removed from our evolutionary past, it's also brutally simple: eat, drink and put one foot in front of the other.

Ultrarunning is a rapidly growing sport. According to a recent report by RunRepeat.com and the International Association of Ultrarunners, analysis of 5,010,730 results from 15,451 ultrarunning events spanning the past 23 years shows an increase in participation of 1,676 per cent overall, including an increase of 345 per cent in the last decade. Step into the ultrarunning world as a competitor, crew member, volunteer or spectator and it's soon obvious why: this is a sport that captures the imaginations of runners and non-runners alike in its toughness, its spirit of adventure, its scenic backdrops, and its quirky characters. Involving any distance longer than a marathon (26¼ miles/42km), every weekend, across the globe, runners line up to take on races of anything from 50km (31 miles) up to 200 miles (320km) and beyond – currently the longest organized ultramarathon is the Self-Transcendence 3,100-mile (4,989km) race in New York.

Recent technological advances mean ultrarunning has also become a popular spectator sport. While 'dot-watching' – tracking runners' locations and race positions via dots on a digital map as they make their way through hours or even days of running – has long been a popular pastime in the niche world of the competitors' partners, parents and other interested parties, today's biggest races are brought to viewers via livestream, chronicling the pain, tumbles and triumphs of the leading runners and the heart-warming (and sometimes heart-wrenching) stories of those chasing cut-off times.

Whether you're a seasoned endurance athlete, finding your feet in ultra, or prefer to watch the action unfold from somewhere warm, dry and comfortable, ultrarunning is a fascinating sport. The art of running such long distances brings together a complex intermeshing of physiology, biomechanics, psychology, kit, self-management and more than a little good luck in a way few other pastimes do. For most ultrarunners, racing is less a battle against others and more of a battle of will against an ever-increasing desire to stop. Success lies in the art of self-management, something even the best runners often forget at their peril.

RIGHT Quebec Mega Trail, Canada.

Ultrarunning has also become an arena for men and women competing on more equal terms, with women increasingly taking the top spots in many races. According to the analysis mentioned above, the longer the distance, the smaller the difference in finishing time is between genders. Over 5km (3 miles), men run 17.9 per cent faster than women; for marathons the difference is 11.1 per cent. At 100-mile (161km) races the difference shrinks to just .25 per cent, and above 195 miles (314km), women were found to be 0.6 per cent faster than men. Being a relatively new sport, in a mainstream context at least, and even newer in terms of women's participation, researchers are still puzzling out exactly why this is. But for most participants, taking part in an ultra is nothing to do with finishing times or places; instead, it's a voyage of discovery, uncovering new places and new strengths, meeting like-minded others and, in the words of one of the world's greatest ultrarunners Courtney Dauwalter, chipping away at your own, personal pain cave.

ABOUT THIS BOOK

This book takes you on a global tour through the world of ultramarathons. It's not intended as a tick list (although kudos if you do manage them all!) but as a source of inspiration and wonderment. It's a celebration of ultrarunning culture – the people, the places, the races. We share the history of the sport and its most intriguing events, and celebrate the incredible achievements and stories of those who've lined up to take on the challenge.

ULTRAMARATHON RACE SERIES

UTMB WORLD SERIES

Growing from – and still focused around – its flagship race, UTMB Mont-Blanc, the UTMB World Series aims to bring together trail running communities around the world through leading international events in stunning locations. The UTMB World Series offers trail runners the chance to experience the UTMB style of events, with professional organization and branded start/finish and checkpoint areas, yet each retaining its unique aspects that made it a great race in the first place. With events taking place across Asia, Oceania, Europe, Africa and the Americas, runners can find a race closer to them. It is also the only place where runners can begin their quest to reach UTMB Mont-Blanc, where the prestigious UTMB World Series Finals are held.

The UTMB World Series integrates three levels of event:

- UTMB World Series Finals
- UTMB World Series Majors
- UTMB World Series Events

ABOVE US ultrarunner Jim Walmsley tackles an ascent on his way to winning the 2021 Ultra Trail Cape Town 100km.

BELOW The start line, Four Sisters Ultra Tour on Mount Siguniang, China.

WORLD TRAIL MAJORS

worldtrailmajors.com

Created with the purpose of uniting a number of historic races based on a responsible environmental stance, historical heritage and natural beauty, the World Trail Majors series brings together some of the best trail and ultra races in the world, each with its own identity, personality and commitment to diversity and respect. For those keen to tick off races around the world, it's an appealing bucket list for both amateur and professional runners who want to challenge themselves across a range of unique racing experiences.

The World Trail Majors consist of:

1. Hong Kong 100 Ultramarathon (Hong Kong) – 102km (63 miles)
2. Black Canyon Ultras (Phoenix, Arizona, United States) – 100km (62 miles)
3. The North Face Transgrancanaria (Maspalomas, Gran Canaria) – 126km (78 miles)
4. Mt. Fuji 100 (Fujiyoshida, Japan) – 165km (102½ miles)
5. MIUT (Madeira Island Ultra Trail) (Machico, Madeira) – 115km (71½ miles)
6. Swiss Canyon Trail (Val de Travers, Jura Mountains, Switzerland) – 111km (69 miles)
7. South Downs Way 100 (Winchester, United Kingdom) – 161km (100 miles)
8. Quebec Mega Trail (Quebec, Canada) – 160km (99½ miles)
9. Grand Raid des Pyrénées (Hautes-Pyrénées, France) – 160km
10. RMB Ultra-Trail Cape Town (Cape Town, South Africa) – 166km (103 miles)
11. Vietnam Mountain Marathon (Sapa, Vietnam) – 102km (63 miles)
12. Grampians Peaks Trail 100 Miler (Halls Gap, Victoria, Australia) – 162km (100½ miles)

Other global race series include:

Golden Trail World Series, www.goldentrailseries.com
ÖTILLÖ world series, www.otilloswimrun.com
Ultra-X, www.ultra-x.co
Endurancelife, www.endurancelife.com
4 Deserts Ultramarathon Series, www.racingtheplanet.com
World Mountain Running, www.wmra.info
Skyrunning, www.skyrunning.com
TOR-X, www.torxtrail.com

RIGHT In the distance, Mount Buffalo is the highest point of the Buffalo Stampede 100km trail run in Australia.

WORLD MAP OF RACES

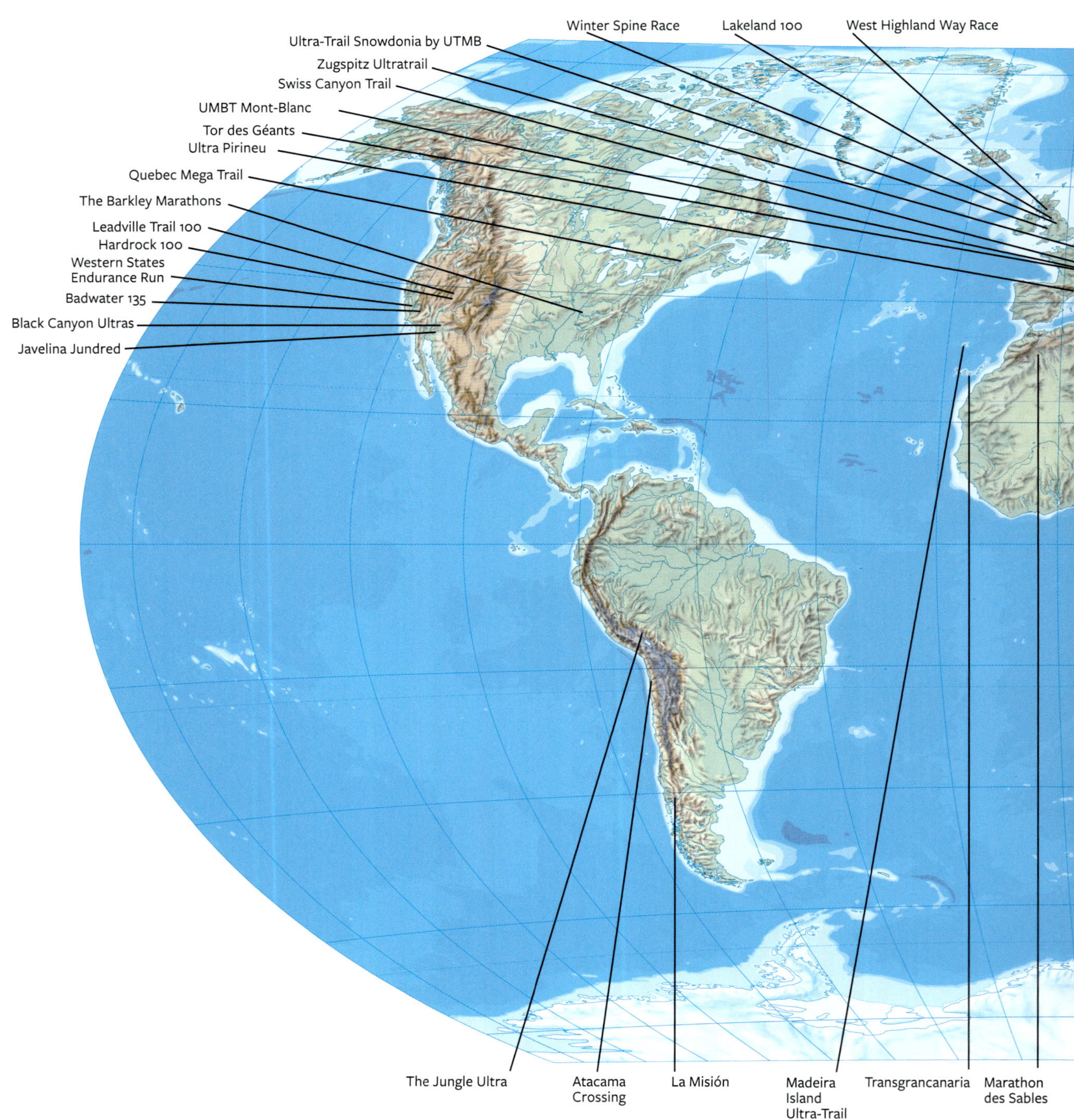

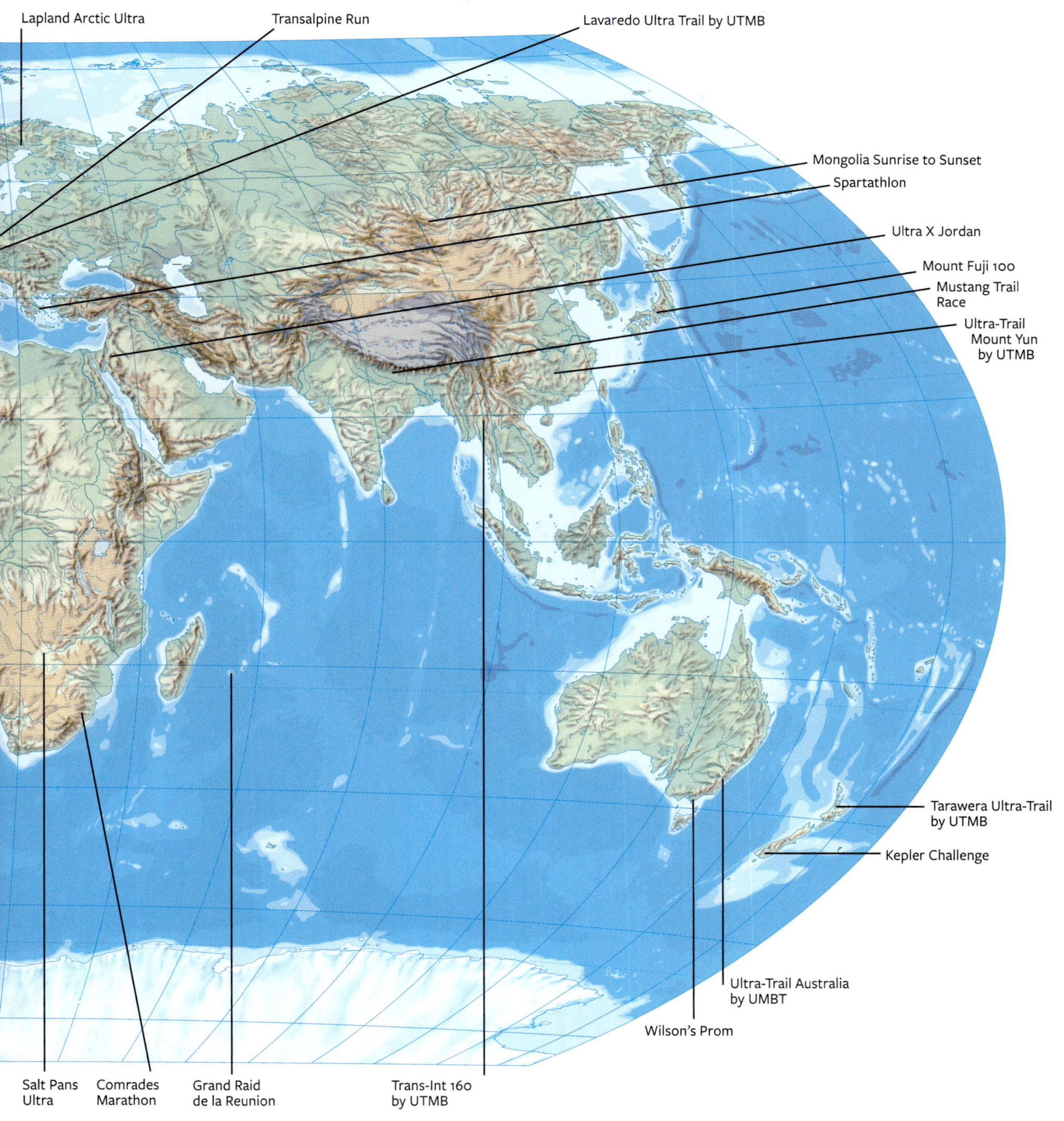
Lapland Arctic Ultra
Transalpine Run
Lavaredo Ultra Trail by UTMB
Mongolia Sunrise to Sunset
Spartathlon
Ultra X Jordan
Mount Fuji 100
Mustang Trail Race
Ultra-Trail Mount Yun by UTMB
Tarawera Ultra-Trail by UTMB
Kepler Challenge
Ultra-Trail Australia by UMBT
Wilson's Prom
Salt Pans Ultra
Comrades Marathon
Grand Raid de la Reunion
Trans-Int 160 by UTMB

HOLGER
232

EUROPE

EUROPE INTRODUCTION

Europe has one of the longest traditions of ultrarunning in the world, dating back to the foot-messengers of ancient Greece, of whom Pheidippides is the best-known. He famously dropped dead after running around 240km (150 miles) to Sparta and back to request help against the invading Persians, and then 40km (25 miles) to the battlefield near Marathon and back to Athens to announce the Greek victory in the Battle of Marathon in 490 BC. In the UK, Welsh shepherd Griffith Morgan, better known as Guto Nyth Brân, could herd sheep without the need for a dog and dominated long-distance footraces in the Welsh hills, while Scottish footmen, tasked with keeping up with their masters' carriages as well as with sending orders and bringing news, vied for the honour of being the swiftest. In the late 17th century, pedestrianism took off in Britain, with men and women taking part in races lasting up to six days in front of huge crowds of rowdy spectators. Running's popularity lulled in the first half of the 20th century but, after World War II, it gradually regained popularity, with ultra-distance races taking place both on the fells and hills of Scotland, Wales and northern England and on the roads and track.

During the running boom of the 1980s, some of the now-classic ultramarathons were founded. 1983 saw the first running of the 246km (153 miles) Spartathlon (see page 48), founded by British Royal Air Force (RAF) Wing Commander John Foden and won by ultrarunning legends Yiannis Kouros and Eleanor Adams (now Robinson), who was the first and only woman to take part that year. In 1985 the first West Highland Way Race (see page 88) took place in Scotland, following the waymarked trail between Milngavie, on the outskirts of Glasgow, and Fort William, at the foot of Ben Nevis.

With the rise of ultrarunning globally over the past decade, France has been at the forefront, boasting the largest number of ultrarunners of any country in the world, and the highest percentage of its population running ultras. UTMB Mont-Blanc (see page 20), probably the world's best-known and most competitive mountain ultramarathon, takes place in Chamonix in the French Alps each summer, the biggest race in a week-long celebration of ultrarunning. The Ultra Trail du Mont Blanc was first held in 2003 with 700 starters and now sees more than 2,700 tackling the roughly 170km (104 miles) route around the Tour du Mont Blanc hiking trail each year, visiting Italy and Switzerland along the way.

PREVIOUS PAGE Stage 5 of the 2023 Transalpine Rache in the Larein-Valley (Silvretta-Mountains).

ABOVE Runners in Transgrancanaria set out at midnight from Las Palmas.

Mountains dominate the European ultra scene, from Ultra-Trail Snowdonia (see page 82), held on the rugged mountains of Eryri in North Wales, the West Highland Way Race traversing nearly 160km (100 miles) of beautiful Scotland, the institution that is the Lakeland 100 in the English Lake District (see page 88) and the infamous Winter Spine Race along the Pennine Way – the backbone of England. Then down through the Alps via the Swiss Canyon Trail (see page 30) and the epic undertakings of the 336km (209 miles) Tor des Géants (see page 38) in Italy's Aosta Valley and the week-long Transalpine Run (see page 26). Italy's majestic Dolomites host Lavaredo Ultra Trail (see page 34) and Germany summons runners to its highest mountain, the Zugspitze (see page 44), while on the border between France and Spain, the Catalan Pyrenees offer a wilder option to the well-trodden trails of the Alps with Ultra Pirineu exploring the spectacular Cadí-Moixeró Natural Park (see page 64). Runners can experience the delights of running across the extraordinary islands of Madeira (see page 52) and Gran Canaria (see page 58). Or, for something completely different, the wintry expanses of Lapland host an annual Arctic Ultra (see page 92) – ten days of incredible non-stop, self-supported adventure.

UTMB MONT-BLANC

CHAMONIX, FRANCE

Every year in late August, the world of trail and ultrarunning descends on the Alpine town of Chamonix for a week of races, talks, networking and celebrations, also known as the UTMB World Series Finals. Originally the Ultra-Trail du Mont-Blanc, and now UTMB Mont-Blanc, it's one of the world's best-known mountain running events. It is responsible for catapulting this niche sport into the public consciousness through ground-breaking media coverage, the French love of the sport (France has more ultrarunners, and a higher percentage of the population runs ultras, than any other country worldwide) and an unbeatable setting – the grand arena of the Mont Blanc Massif.

Around 10,000 runners compete in seven different races held throughout the week, plus many more aspiring ultrarunners in the mini UTMB races, held in towns and villages around the iconic Tour du Mont Blanc route, which circles the massif through France, Italy and Switzerland.

UTMB Mont-Blanc begins in Chamonix and heads anticlockwise around Mont Blanc, the highest mountain in mainland Europe, passing through Saint Gervais, Les Contamines and La Balme. Les Chapieux and Lac Combal are checkpoints five and six before the race descends to Courmayeur, in Italy's Aosta Valley.

RACE STATISTICS

MONTH: August
DISTANCE: 176.6km (109¾ miles)
TOTAL ASCENT: 9,957m (32,667ft)
HIGHEST POINT: 2,575m (8,448ft)
STARTERS 2024: 2,761 (355 female, 2,406 male)
FINISHERS 2024: 1,760 (204 female, 1,556 male)
TIME ALLOWED: 46hr 30min
FEMALE COURSE RECORD: Katie Schide 22:09:31 (2024)
MALE COURSE RECORD: Jim Walmsley 19:37:43 (2023)
FIRST RUN: 2003
ENTRY FEE: €398

WEBSITE: montblanc.utmb.world/races/UTMB

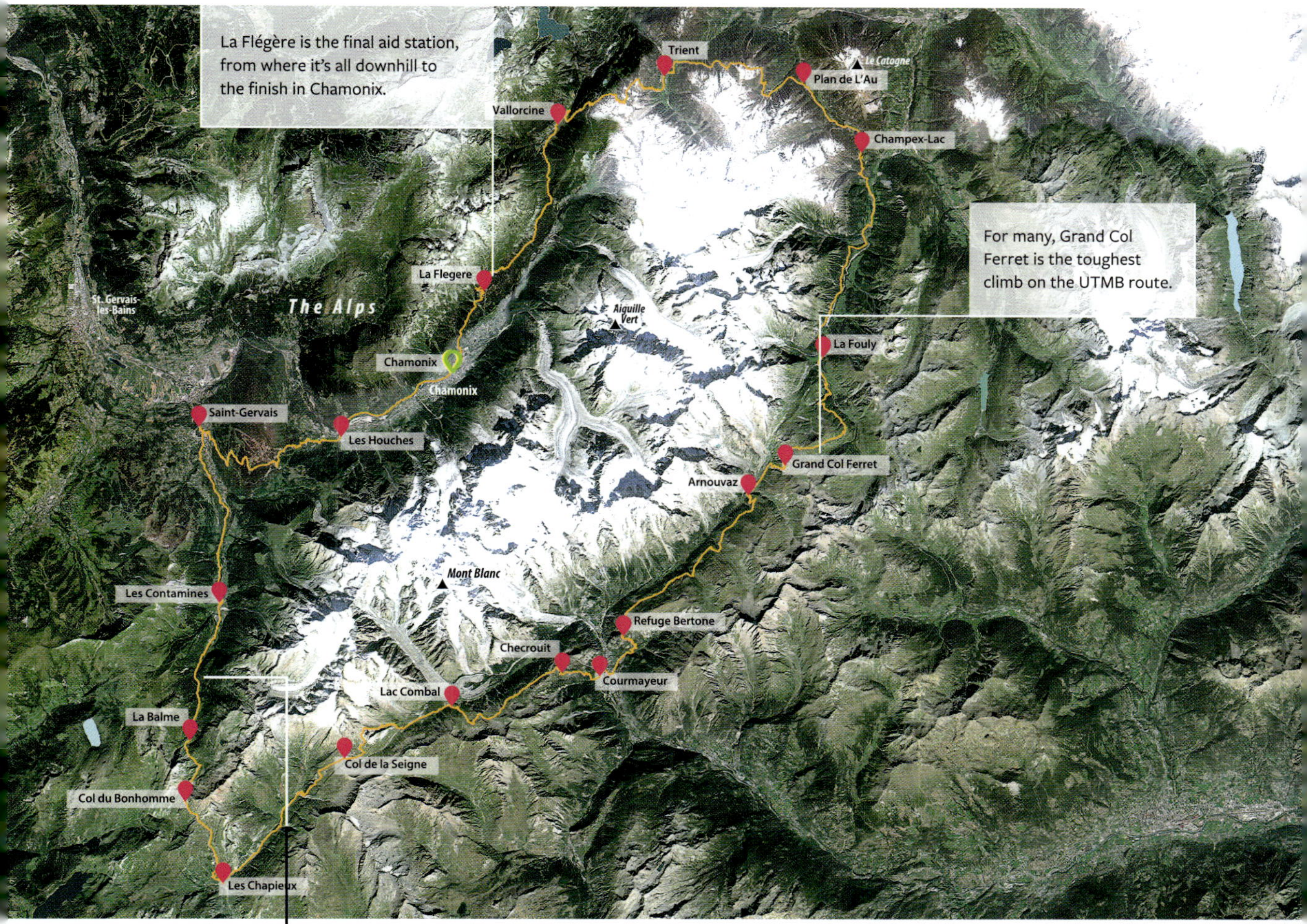

La Flégère is the final aid station, from where it's all downhill to the finish in Chamonix.
Trient
Le Catogne
Plan de L'Au
Vallorcine
Champex-Lac
For many, Grand Col Ferret is the toughest climb on the UTMB route.
La Flegere
St. Gervais-les-Bains
The Alps
Aiguille Vert
La Fouly
Chamonix
Chamonix
Saint-Gervais
Les Houches
Grand Col Ferret
Arnouvaz
Mont Blanc
Les Contamines
Refuge Bertone
Checrouit
Courmayeur
Lac Combal
La Balme
Col de la Seigne
Col du Bonhomme
Les Chapieux

Runners can expect a party atmosphere at Notre Dame de la Gorge, where crowds of supporters wait to cheer them through.

ELEVATION PROFILE

1,042M (3,418FT)
802M (2,631FT)
2,575M (8,448FT)
1,042M (3,418FT)
0.00km/miles
86.66km (53 miles)
176.61km (109¾ miles)

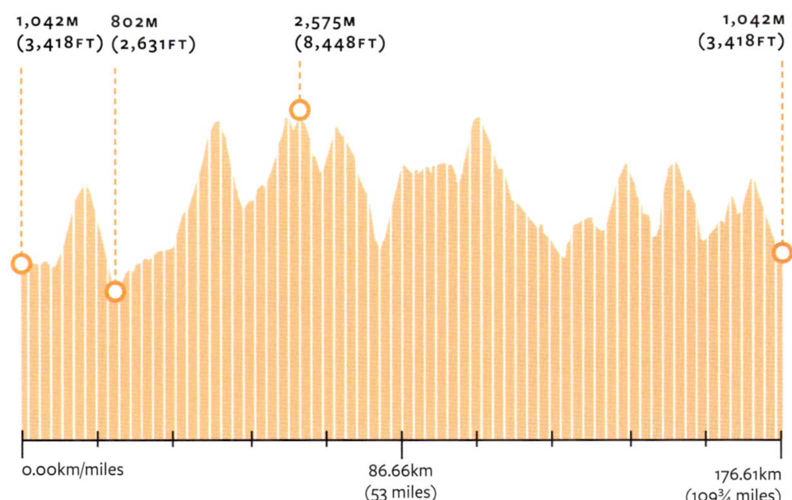

LEFT Stunning morning light for TDS runners heading for La Thuile.

KIPRUN

OTHER DISTANCES

YCC (Youth Chamonix Courmayeur) 20km (12½ miles) for youth athletes.

PTL (La Petite Trotte á Léon) 300km (186 miles) with 25,000m (82,000ft) ascent for teams of two

MCC (Martigny-Combe to Chamonix) 40km (25 miles) with 2,350m (7,700ft) ascent reserved primarily for UTMB volunteers, partners and local residents.

TDS (Sur les Traces des Ducs de Savoie) 148km (92 miles) with 9,300m (30,500ft) ascent, linking the Aosta Valley with the Savoie.

OCC (Orsières–Champex-Lac–Chamonix) 57km (35 miles) with 3,500m (11,500ft) ascent.

CCC (Courmayer–Champex-Lac–Chamonix) 101km (63 miles) with 6,050m (19,850ft) ascent.

Climbing once more, runners eventually reach Grand Col Ferret, the highest point in the race at 2,537m (8,324ft).

The route continues into Switzerland via La Fouly and Triente, then returns to France, with the final checkpoint being La Flégère, 166.3km (103¼ miles) into the course. From there it's all downhill, which sounds good until you add in rooty, rocky singletrack, extreme fatigue and legs that have already climbed considerably more than the height of Everest, resulting in an exciting finish as runners descend into Chamonix hoping to be inside the 46:30 cut-off time.

Many of the mountain passes exceed 2,400m (7,900ft) in altitude and the total cumulative ascent often tops 10,000m (33,000ft) – the route changes slightly from year to year. This savage terrain, combined with notoriously variable weather conditions – many years see changes to the route or kit requirements based on the weather – sets the stage for a highly challenging race that draws many of the world's best runners.

In 2003, when the UTMB Mont-Blanc was first held, only 67 runners completed the course. Tackling rain, hail and freezing temperatures at higher altitudes, the USA's Krissy Moehl took the women's win and Nepal's Dawa Sherpa the men's.

Jim Walmsley was the first US man to win, doing so in 2023 at his fifth attempt. Five US women – Courtney Dauwalter, Katie Schide, Rory Bosio, Nikki Kimball and Krissy Moehl – have won the race, clocking up nine victories between them.

France's François D'Haene and Spain's Kilian Jornet are the most successful male runners in UTMB history, having each won on four occasions. British runner Lizzy Hawker holds the record for the most female wins at five, also gaining a second place in 2009. Courtney Dauwalter (USA) set a new women's record in 2021, finishing seventh overall in 22:30:55, six minutes 42 seconds faster than the previous record set by fellow US runner Rory Bosio in 2013 over a course that was 3km (1¾ miles) longer.

LEFT Clémentine Geoffray on her way to 3rd place in the 2024 57km OCC, one of the championship races during UTMB finals week.

RIGHT Running past Lac du Verney in the TDS during UTMB finals week.

In 2023, Dauwalter took her third UTMB win, a feat made even more impressive by the fact that she had won both Western States and Hardrock 100-milers during the preceding ten weeks. 2024 saw the women's record change hands again, as France-based US runner Katie Schide knocked 21 minutes off the previous best, finishing in 22 hours, 9 minutes and 31 seconds.

Entry to UTMB Mont-Blanc requires a finish at a qualifying race plus at least one Running Stone, gained from a UTMB World Series event, with UTMB Mont-Blanc acting as the World Series Finals event for the 100-mile category. As it's a hugely popular race, entry is by lottery, with more Stones meaning more chances to earn a place. Generally, one Running Stone is earned for a 20km (12½ miles) index race, two for a 50km (31 miles), three for a 100km (62 miles) and four for a 161km (100 miles), with double Stones earned at UTMB World Series Majors.

ABOVE A stunning mountain backdrop for runners climbing from Lac Combal towards Arête du Mont Favre on UTMB Mont-Blanc.

RIGHT, ABOVE Gabriel Rueda in the 2024 UTMB Mont-Blanc.

RIGHT, BELOW Courtney Dauwalter wins the women's race in Chamonix at the UTMB 2023 Mont-Blanc.

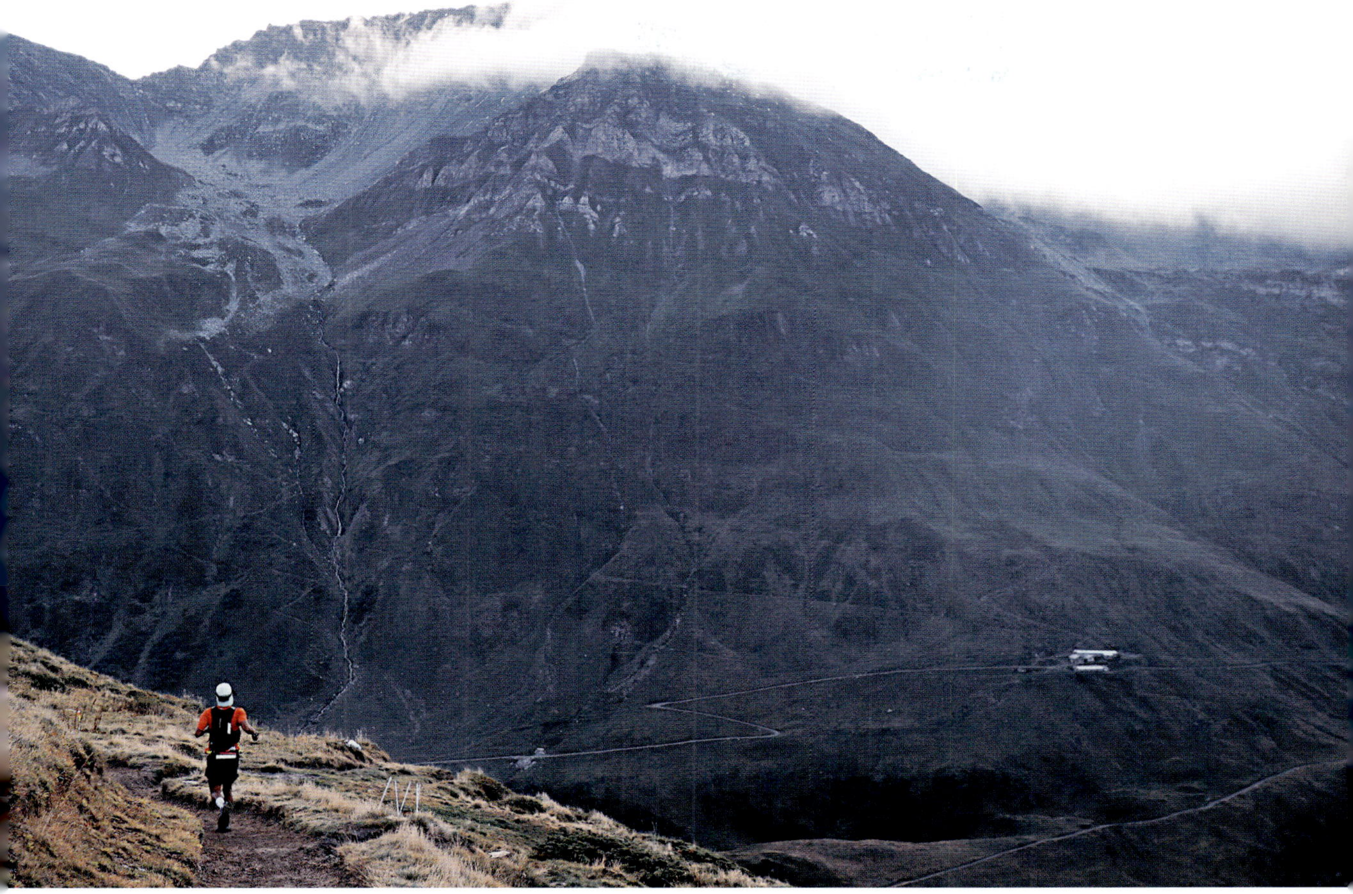

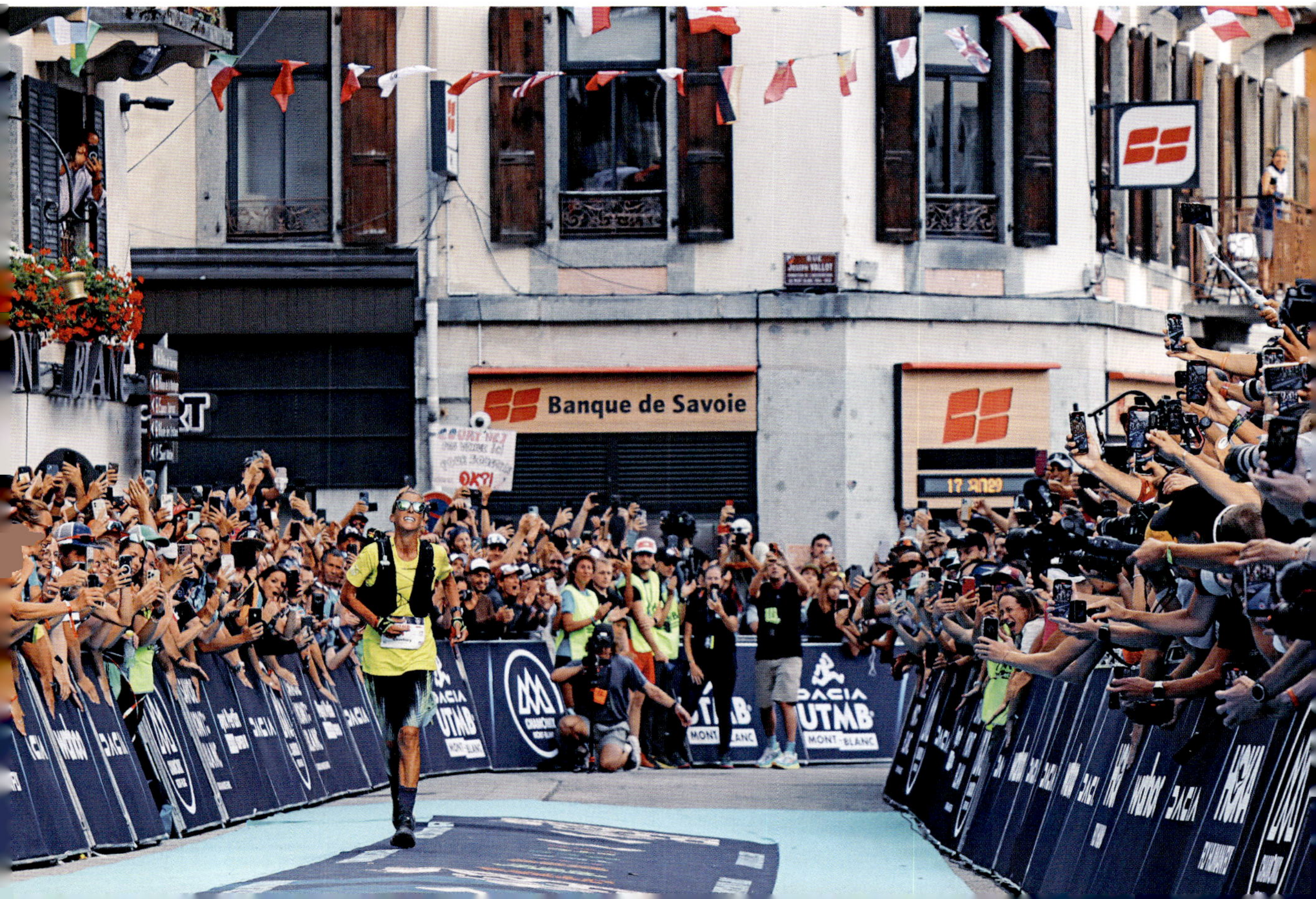
Banque de Savoie
DACIA
UTMB
MONT-BLANC

TRANSALPINE RUN

GERMANY, AUSTRIA, SWITZERLAND AND ITALY

In 218 BC, Carthaginian general Hannibal, along with his foot soldiers and elephants, crossed the Alps from Germany to Italy. Back then, there were no paths or mountain huts, and the feat went down in history as a tactical masterpiece. Over the centuries since, crossing the Alps on foot has evolved into an almost mythical challenge.

Following in these footsteps, the Transalpine Run is one of ultrarunning's best-known stage races. Over seven days, runners – alone or in teams of two – traverse the Alps, starting in Germany and running through Austria and often visiting Switzerland before finishing in Italy. While the route varies from year to year, alternating between an eastern and a western route, the TAR covers a distance of around 243km (151 miles) with 15,000m (49,000ft) of ascent, and passes through towns and villages, used as overnight base camps, along the way.

The first edition of TAR was held in 2005, when 74 teams set off from Oberstdorf to run across the Alps. Most walked, and the event was a relatively informal affair. Over the 20 years since, the field has grown to over 100 teams and individuals. Sponsors and partners have brought a bigger, more professional feel to the event and runners are well catered for.

RACE STATISTICS

MONTH: September
STAGE RACE: Seven stages over 7 days
DISTANCE: 243km (151 miles)
TOTAL ASCENT: 15,135m (49,655ft)
HIGHEST POINT: 2,941m (9,649ft)
STARTERS 2024: 553 (180 female, 373 male)
FINISHERS 2024: 410 (120 female, 290 male)
TIME ALLOWED: 56hr 30min
FEMALE COURSE RECORD: Tanja Löwenhagen 28:08:13 (2023)
MALE COURSE RECORD: Fabian Gering 23:08:47 (2023)
FIRST RUN: 2005
ENTRY FEE: €1,200

WEBSITE:
www.transalpine-run.com

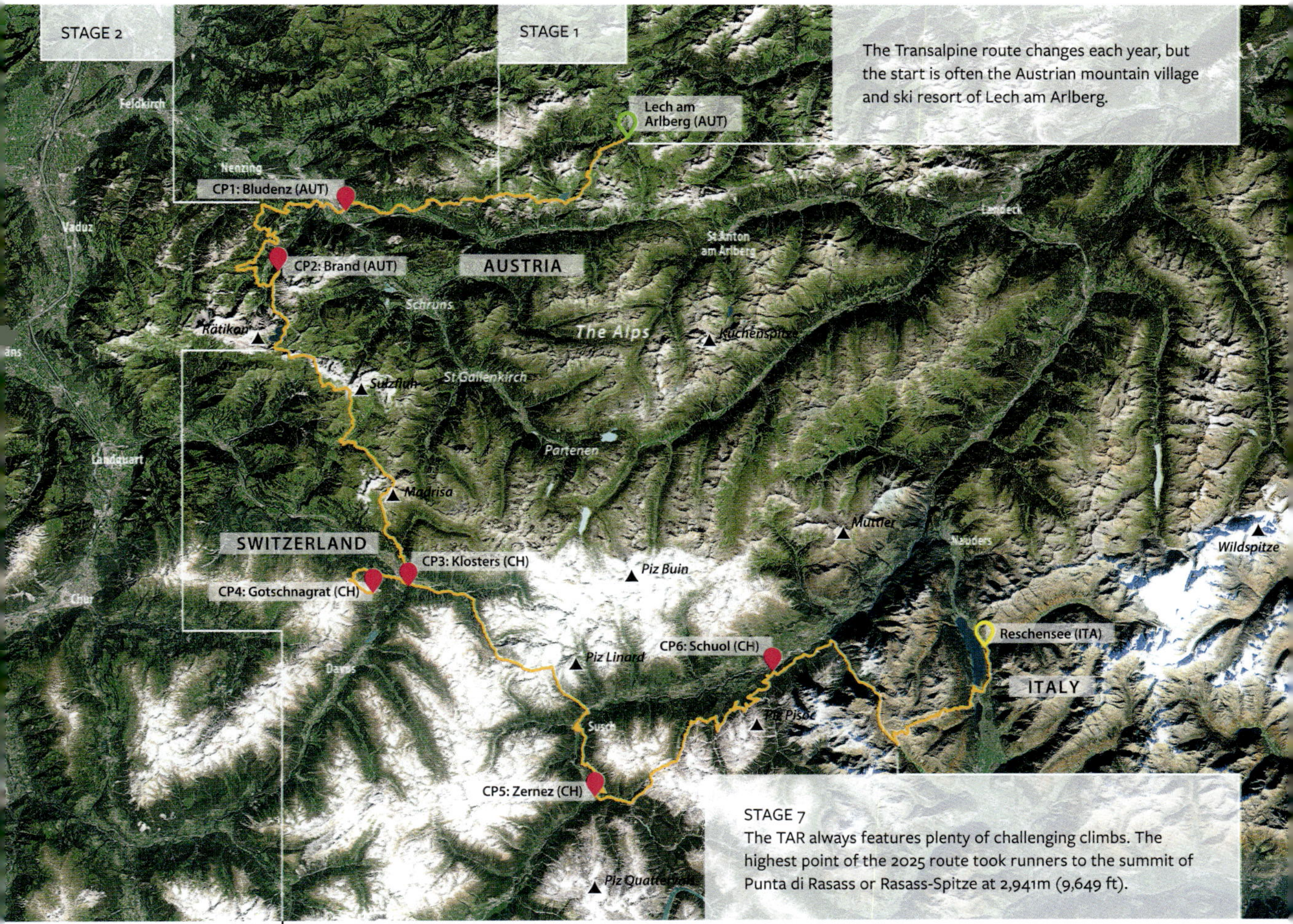

STAGE 2
STAGE 1
The Transalpine route changes each year, but the start is often the Austrian mountain village and ski resort of Lech am Arlberg.
Lech am Arlberg (AUT)
Feldkirch
Nenzing
CP1: Bludenz (AUT)
Vaduz
CP2: Brand (AUT)
AUSTRIA
Landeck
St Anton am Arlberg
Schruns
Rätikon
The Alps
Sulzfluh
St Gallenkirch
Landquart
Partenen
Madrisa
SWITZERLAND
Nauders
Wildspitze
CP3: Klosters (CH)
CP4: Gotschnagrat (CH)
Piz Buin
Chur
Davos
Piz Linard
CP6: Schuol (CH)
Reschensee (ITA)
ITALY
Susch
CP5: Zernez (CH)
STAGE 7
The TAR always features plenty of challenging climbs. The highest point of the 2025 route took runners to the summit of Punta di Rasass or Rasass-Spitze at 2,941m (9,649 ft).

STAGE 4
The longest stage is known as the Queen Stage, usually falling on Day 3 of the race.

ELEVATION PROFILE

698M (2,290FT)
2,941M (9,649FT)
1,500M (4,921FT)
0.00km/miles
128.18km (79½ miles)
243km (151 miles)

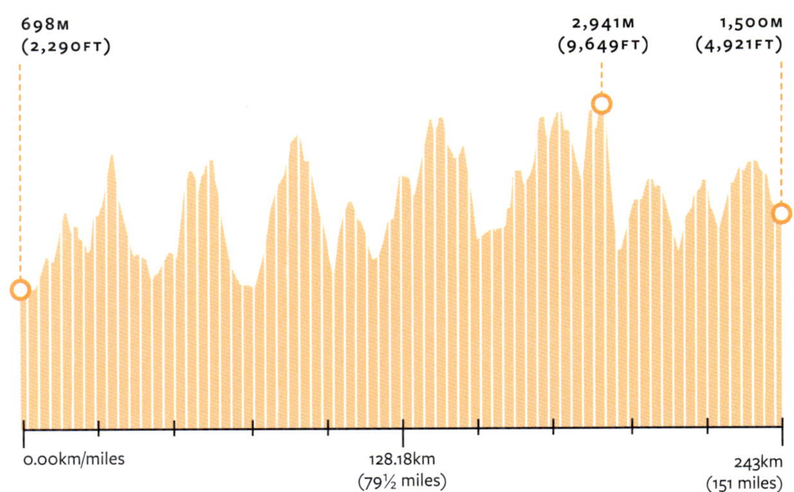

LEFT Ritzenjoch in the Silvretta-Mountains, during Stage 5.

OTHER DISTANCES

For those not yet ready to take on the full seven days, TAR is now offering the RUN2, allowing runners to take part in the first two days of the event – a combined 69.2km (43 miles), with 4,040m (13,255ft) ascent. This is a great way to take your first steps in stage racing.

The trails are now better-maintained and easier to run on. Everything including food stops, marking and labelling, managing runners en route, luggage transport, briefings and media coverage has improved. Times have dropped dramatically as many aim to run as much of the route as possible. But the friendly, supportive nature of those early years is still very much in evidence, and the challenge of running across the Alps over the course of a week remains one of the greatest adventures out there.

While the route and towns visited vary year on year, the mountain village and ski resort of Lech am Arlberg in the Bludenz district in the westernmost Austrian state of Vorarlberg often serves as the start point. Participants have the option of arranging their own accommodation close to the start/finish points of each stage, or paying for an all-inclusive package with race fees and accommodation included. Stages vary in distance, with one shorter day of around 10km (6¼ miles), the 'Queen' stage on day three, usually around 50km (31 miles), and the remaining days between 30–40km (18½–25 miles).

Runners can expect stunning alpine scenery and often vastly varying conditions – the 2024 event featured temperatures ranging from 28° to -4°C (82–25°F), with competitors finishing the final day in snow. Regardless of the specifics of the route, TAR competitors will discover alpine meadows and forests, glacial lakes and high mountain summits and passes. There's plenty of technical rocky terrain, often with ropes or cables alongside, and even sections that cross glaciers. TAR is a fully supported race, with organizers transporting supplies and baggage daily from town to town and overnight base camps in hotels that are famous for their hospitality, with a fun and friendly atmosphere and plenty of good food. Prizes are awarded to the top women's, men's and mixed teams and individuals.

ABOVE Runners during Stage 2 on the Tschirgant ridge with views to the Gurgl valley.

BELOW Descending technical terrain in Stage 4 at Schmalzgruben-Scharte in the Paznaun valley.

SWISS CANYON TRAIL

JURA REGION, SWITZERLAND

Held in the Neuchâtel canton of Switzerland, the Swiss Canyon Trail races cover a variety of distances, taking runners through the beautiful and rugged landscapes of the Jura Alps. This is a place of spectacular natural landscape features, including the dramatic limestone Gorges de l'Areuse, and the most famous canyon in Switzerland, the Creux du Van, where sheer limestone cliffs drop into deep, lushly wooded canyons. In fact, it's said that each twist and turn of the Swiss Canyon Trail route could bring you face-to-face with a mythical green fairy, ready to give you a helping hand when the climbs are needed. Underfoot is a mix of technical trails, forest paths and rocky ridgelines, with steep and often technical climbs and descents.

The 114km (71 miles) 'Queen' race is the main attraction for many of the world's elite ultrarunners. Its climbs and descents are unrelenting, with the four biggest ascents coming in the first half of the race. Le Soliat, at 1,460m (4,790ft), is 15km (9¼ miles) in, from where runners drop all the way into the valley at Carrière de Môtiers before heading straight up again, gaining nearly 1,000m (3,280ft) in the ascent to the highest point of the race – Le Chasseron at 1,606m (5,269ft), one of Switzerland's most isolated peaks. The mountain is forested up to a height of around 1,500m (4,900ft), the trail winding through trees before emerging from the treeline to vast mountain pastures.

RACE STATISTICS

MONTH: June
DISTANCE: 114.8km (71¼ miles)
TOTAL ASCENT: 5,294m (17,369ft)
HIGHEST POINT: 1,606m (5,269ft)
STARTERS 2024: 415 (44 female, 371 male)
FINISHERS 2024: 336 (38 female, 298 male)
TIME ALLOWED: 28hr
FEMALE COURSE RECORD: Camille Bruyas 12:14:50 (2019)
MALE COURSE RECORD: Miguel Arsenio 10:24:09 (2024)
FIRST RUN: 1994
ENTRY FEE: 220 CHF

WEBSITE:
www.swisscanyontrail.com

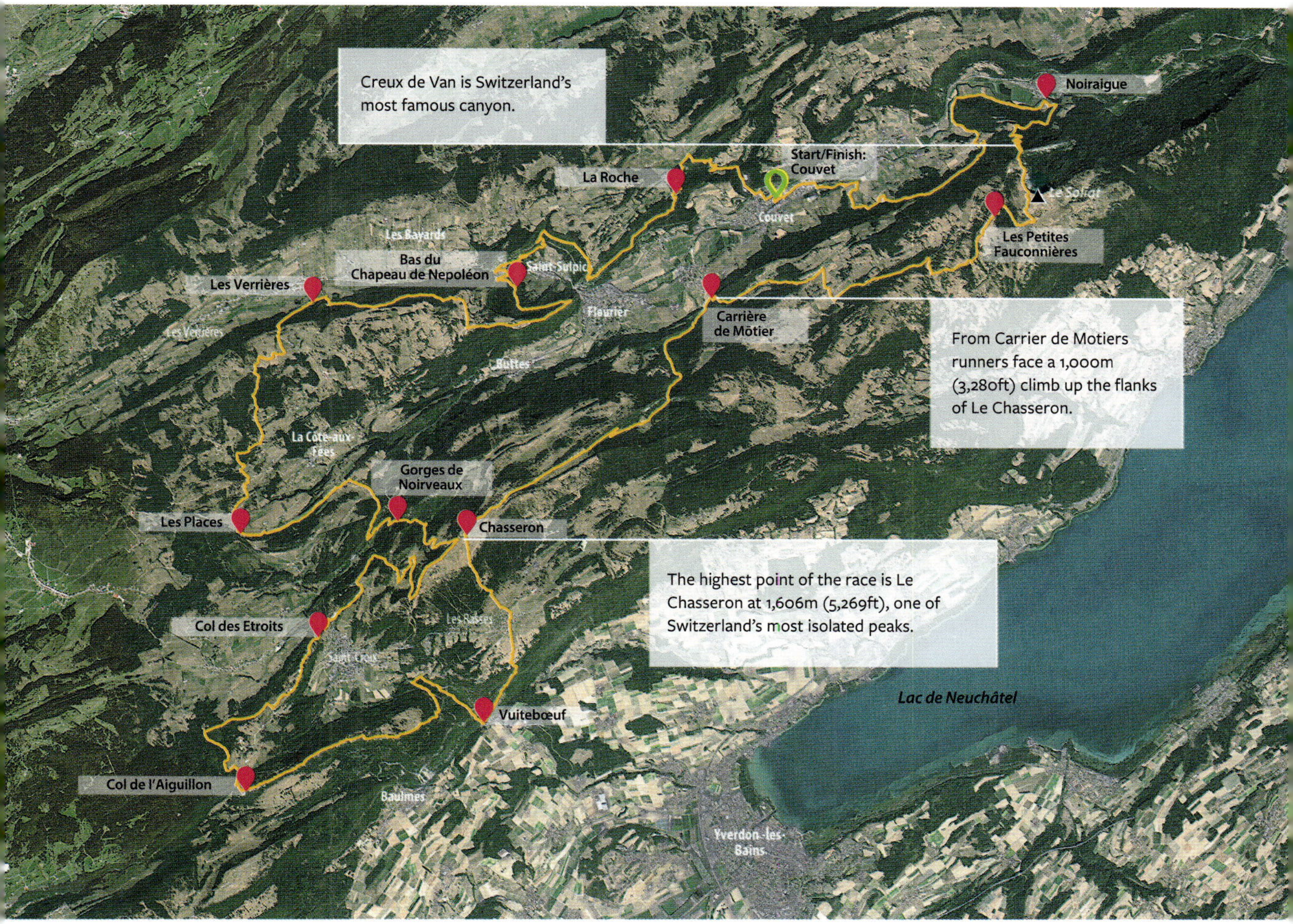

Creux de Van is Switzerland's most famous canyon.

From Carrier de Motiers runners face a 1,000m (3,280ft) climb up the flanks of Le Chasseron.

The highest point of the race is Le Chasseron at 1,606m (5,269ft), one of Switzerland's most isolated peaks.

ELEVATION PROFILE

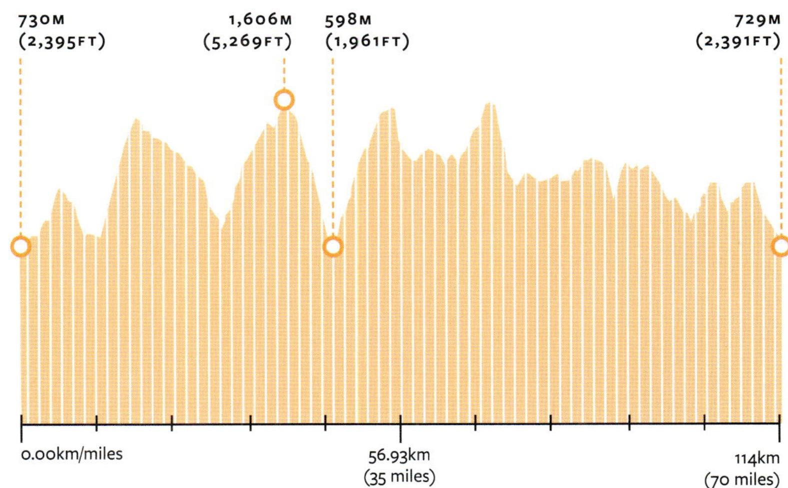

FAR LEFT AND LEFT Runners tackling the savage, stepped ascents and descents in the Swiss Canyon Trail.

OTHER DISTANCES

Alongside the 'queen' race, the Swiss Canyon Trail offers a range of shorter distance events, as well as a youth event for teams of five.

81km (50¼ miles); 3,491m (11,453ft) ascent

51km (31¾ miles); 2,632m (8,636ft) ascent

31km (19¼ miles); 1,380m (4,528ft) ascent

16km (10 miles); 577m (1,893ft) ascent

The southeastern slope of Le Chasseron is used for skiing in winter and runners pass several ski lifts and the famous mountain restaurant, perched on the summit, which hosts an aid station on race day. On a clear day, runners are afforded panoramic views of the Savoy Alps, Valais Alps, Bernese Alps and all the way to the Säntis.

The 5am race start makes the most of the daylight hours, important given the fierceness and technicality of the initial miles.

2024 saw hard-fought races on both the men's and women's sides in the Queen race, with Portuguese runner Miguel Arsenio breaking the men's record while Canada's Marianne Hogan took the crown for the women, getting close to Camille Bruyas's 2019 record, despite running a slightly longer course.

The race starts in Couvet in the Val-de-Travers district of Neuchâtel, said to be where Absinthe was invented in the late 18th century by French physician Pierre Ordinaire. The famous green drink is still made here, and the distillery offers tours to visitors. In fact, when the race was first held in 1994, it was under the name Trail de l'Absinthe. Over the years it's evolved to welcome more than 3,000 runners spread over five distances, the shortest of which (16km/10 miles) is also open to Nordic Walking enthusiasts.

The Swiss Canyon Trail's race organizers pride themselves on offering the best possible experience to runners. They believe this is much more than just a race; it's an immersive adventure, taking in the heart of the Val-de-Travers area. Race President, Patrick Christinat, says the 'Swiss Canyon Family embodies the spirit of trail running, today and for the future. Swiss Canyon Trail is driven by a commitment to showcasing our incredible regions.' An extraordinary total of 6,000 dedicated volunteers help make the event special every year.

New for 2025, to celebrate the race's 30th anniversary, a 160km (100 miles) event was held at the Swiss Canyon Trail for the first time. Adding an extra loop of the mountains to the southern end of the existing 100km (62 miles) route, the race takes in over 7,000m (23,000ft) of climbing.

LEFT Stunning waterfalls and lush canyons are some of the scenic highlights of this race.

LAVAREDO ULTRA TRAIL BY UTMB

DOLOMITES, CORTINA D'AMPEZZO, ITALY

Lavaredo Ultra Trail runs through the jagged pinnacles and moonscape plateaus of Italy's Dolomite mountains, a UNESCO World Heritage Site. It starts and finishes in the town of Cortina d'Ampezzo, hosts of the 2026 Winter Olympics and the hub and party venue for race week.

OTHER DISTANCES
Alongside the main event there are four other distance races, the most recent of which is a 10km (6¼ miles) night run. This is perfect for those new to mountain running wanting to experience the thrill of running through the darkness, with the trails illuminated by a snaking line of head torches.
80km (52¾ miles); 4,600m (15,092ft) ascent
50km (31 miles); 2,600m (8,530ft) ascent
20km (12½ miles); 1,000m (3,281ft) ascent
10km (6¼ miles); 200m (656ft) ascent

RACE STATISTICS

MONTH: June
DISTANCE: 120km (74½ miles)
TOTAL ASCENT: 5,800m (19,029ft)
HIGHEST POINT: 2,456m (8,058ft)
STARTERS 2024: 1,614
(203 female, 1,411 male)
FINISHERS 2024: 1,240
(156 female, 1,084 male)
TIME ALLOWED: 30hr
FEMALE COURSE RECORD:
Caroline Chaverot 14:05:45 (2017)
MALE COURSE RECORD:
Hannes Namberger 11:56:28 (2022)
FIRST RUN: 2007
ENTRY FEE: €169

WEBSITE:
lavaredo.utmb.world

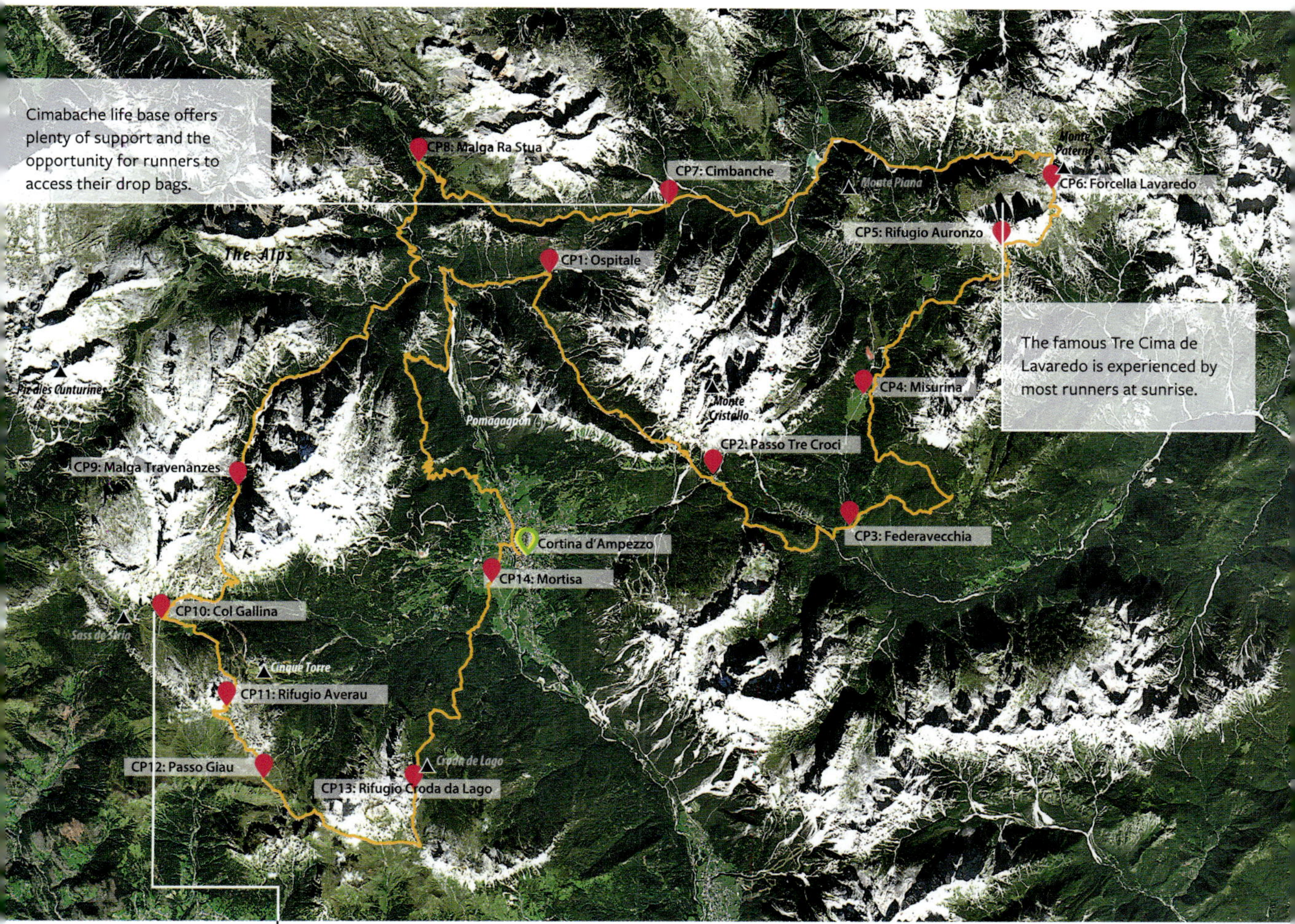

Cimabache life base offers plenty of support and the opportunity for runners to access their drop bags.
CP8: Malga Ra Stua
CP7: Cimbanche
Monte Paterno
CP6: Forcella Lavaredo
Monte Piana
CP5: Rifugio Auronzo
The Alps
CP1: Ospitale
The famous Tre Cima de Lavaredo is experienced by most runners at sunrise.
Piz dles Cunturines
CP4: Misurina
Monte Cristallo
Pomagagnon
CP2: Passo Tre Croci
CP9: Malga Travenanzes
CP3: Federavecchia
Cortina d'Ampezzo
CP14: Mortisa
CP10: Col Gallina
Sass de Stria
Cinque Torre
CP11: Rifugio Averau
Croda de Lago
CP12: Passo Giau
CP13: Rifugio Croda da Lago

A brutal section of the race takes runners over Forcella Nuvolau at 2,413m (7,916ft).

ELEVATION PROFILE

1,217M
(3,992FT)
2,456M
(8,057FT)
1,218M (3,996FT)
1,197M (3,927FT)
0.00km/miles
59.91km
(37 miles)
120km
(74½ miles)

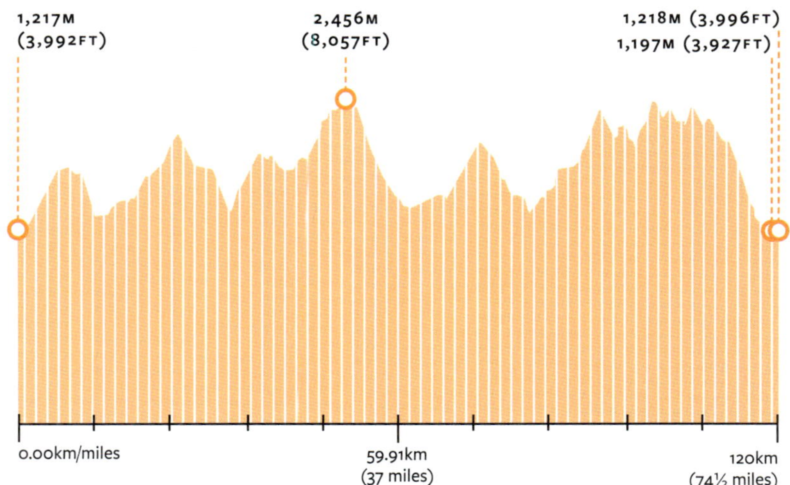

LEFT It's a tough race, but underfoot several sections are very runnable on the excellent gravelly mountain trails.

The Queen race is the main draw for many elite ultrarunners, which packs 5,800m (19,000ft) of ascent into a 120km (74½ miles) route that's also very technical underfoot. A UTMB classification of 161km (100 miles) despite being 20km short highlights the difficulty of the race.

Runners gather at the tower of Basilica Minore dei Santi Filippo e Giacomo in the centre of Cortina, ready for the 11pm start, live music ramping up the atmosphere. After making their way through the narrow streets and up a zigzagging trail into the Dolomites, runners continue through the night to reach the Tre Cime di Lavaredo and its three dramatic, battlement-like summits – Cima Piccola, Cima Grande and Cima Ovest – in time for sunrise, some six hours later. Right from the start there's a climb to an altitude of 1,700m (5,577ft), and the race stays at an average altitude of around 2,000m (6,500ft) throughout. The highest point is the pass of Forcella Lavaredo at 2,420m (7,939ft), with the famous jagged summits of the Tre Cima rising above, followed by a welcome 15km (9¼ miles) of downhill and relatively flat terrain. Being held in June in Italy means temperatures often top 30°C (86°F) in the valleys, and thunderstorms are also common, but the temperatures can fall below zero on the summits.

Anyone who has completed Lavaredo knows the real race doesn't start until 80km (49¾ miles) in, with a 20km (12½ miles) climb and 1,300m (4,265ft) of gain, all through the longest stretch between aid stations. This is the sting in the tail, crossing Col Piombin and several other passes at well over 2,300m (7,500ft) in altitude. For those who successfully cross this final section, however, the finish line is just one, 18km (11 miles) long, leg-sapping descent away.

First run in 2007, Lavaredo and its magnificent setting holds a special place in the hearts of Italian ultrarunners. The race was the brainchild of Simone Brogioni and Cristina Murgia, who right from the start had the dream of making it one of the world's biggest and best-known ultras. Just 200 runners, most of whom were Italian, took part in the first edition. By 2015, when the race moved from Auronzo di Cadore to Cortina d'Ampezzo and affiliated with the Ultra-Trail World Tour series, this had risen to 750. The growth has been exponential every year since, from 6,800 pre-registered in 2019 to over 14,000 in 2024. The Race Directors acknowledge they've now reached the maximum capacity for the race, intending to switch their efforts from generating publicity to an even better athlete experience and more sustainable organization.

Lavaredo Ultra Trail is one of the world's most popular mountain ultras, up there with Western States (see page 112) and UTMB Mont Blanc (see page 20) – it is a qualifier for both, and managed under the UTMB umbrella – but with a unique twist that means it never feels overly branded or mass-produced. Entry is via a draw, with numbers oversubscribed and sold out within hours every year.

ABOVE Passing the famous Tre Cima at Lavaredo.

BELOW The imposing Tofana di Rozes.

TOR DES GÉANTS

COURMAYEUR, VALLE D'AOSTA, ITALY

Considered one of the hardest trail races in the world, Tor des Géants (also known as TOR330) is a non-stop, 330km (205 miles) race with over 24,000m (78,740ft) of elevation gain. Starting and finishing in Courmayeur, at the foot of the Italian side of Mont Blanc, runners take in an anticlockwise loop traversing the mountainous western side of the Aosta Valley, crossing the valley at Donnas, then returning via the equally rugged eastern side. The route weaves its way through some of the highest peaks in the Alps, including several over 4,000m (13,100ft), going over 25 mountain passes and visiting Gran Paradiso National Park and Mont Avic Regional Park.

The TOR330 route is waymarked with yellow flags, as are other distances other than the 450 – the Tor des Glaciers – which is self-navigated and competitors must download the route onto a device to follow as they go.

Support along the way takes the form of regular refreshment points at *refuggios* and mobile aid stations, and seven Life Bases, where runners can sleep, eat, shower and receive massages, taping and other medical treatment. Life Bases are about 50km (31 miles) apart, at Valgrisenche, Cogne, Donnas, Gressoney-Saint-Jean, Valtournenche, Oyace and Ollomont. They're famous for taking in weary, disorientated runners and reviving them, ready to continue onwards.

RACE STATISTICS

MONTH: September
DISTANCE: 336km (209 miles)
TOTAL ASCENT: 24,000m (78,740ft)
HIGHEST POINT: 3,299m (10,813ft)
STARTERS 2024: 1,050 (161 female, 894 male)
FINISHERS 2024: 533 (66 female, 467 male)
TIME ALLOWED: 150hr
FEMALE COURSE RECORD: Katharina Hartmuth 79:10:40 (2024)
MALE COURSE RECORD: Franco Leo Colle 66:39:16 (2023)
FIRST RUN: 2010
ENTRY FEE: €900

WEBSITE:
www.torxtrail.com

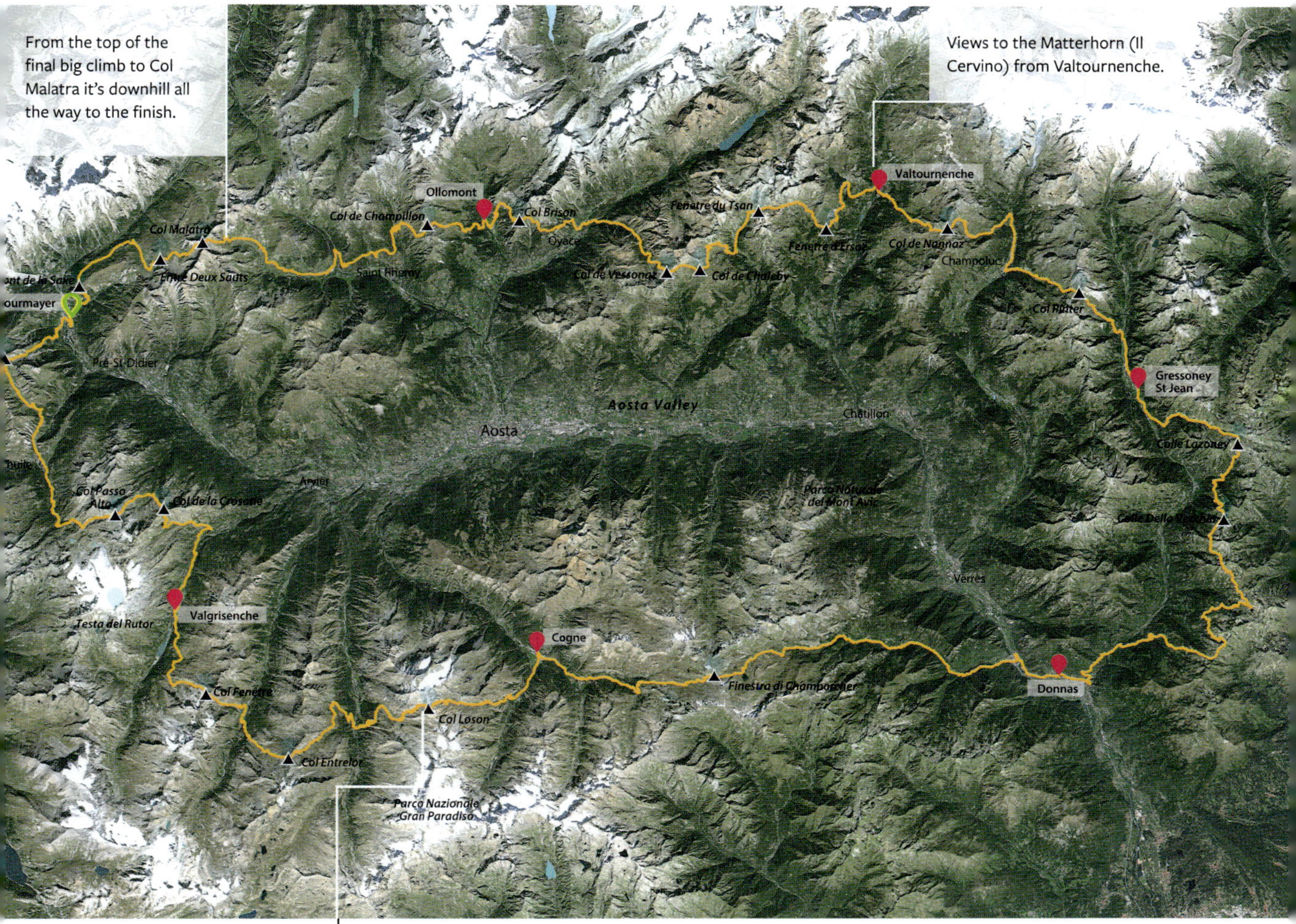

From the top of the final big climb to Col Malatra it's downhill all the way to the finish.

Views to the Matterhorn (Il Cervino) from Valtournenche.

Col Loson, at 3,299m (10,813ft), is the highest point on the TdG route.

ELEVATION PROFILE

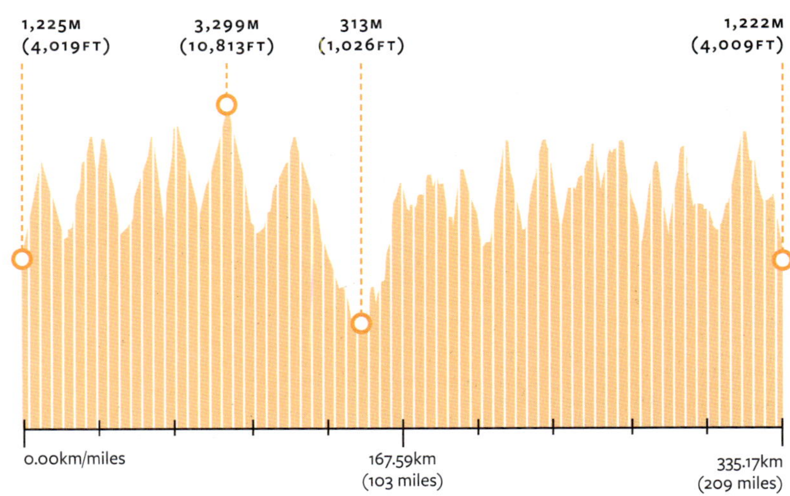

FAR LEFT Eventual men's race winner François D'Haene at the 2024 Tor des Géants.

LEFT Runners set out at the start of the race at Courmayeur.

LEFT ABOVE A runner near the Rifugio Bezzi during the second day of the Tor des Géants.

LEFT BELOW It can be hard to keep an eye on the trails with the distracting view of the Matterhorn in the background.

ABOVE Entre-Deux-Sauts bivouac point near the end of the course.

There's famously very little level ground on the TOR route, meaning runners are usually on a savagely steep ascent or descent, sometimes so steep there are ropes or chains to hold onto for safety. Many participants take close to the full 150-hour time limit – just over six days – to complete, and about half of the 1,000 starters drop out each year. Many top class runners are among those who DNF including, in 2024, Barkley Marathons finishers Jasmin Paris and John Kelly.

Conditions can vary dramatically during the event, with temperatures well into the 30s in the valleys and cold enough for snow on the summits. Huge thunderstorms are common, adding to the atmosphere of the race.

TOR330 has been described as more a psychedelic journey than a race, with many runners reporting hallucinations and other tricks of the mind, particularly in the later stages. A mythology has grown up around the race, central to which is an experience shared by many: Meeting the Dragon. Described as a moment of reckoning, an existential crisis, a total stripping-back of everything other than raw, moment-to-moment being, this phrase, borrowed from Buddhism, captures that sense of letting go of ego and external validation and simply existing; in the case of ultrarunning, simply carrying on. Ivan Parasacco, long-time commentator at TOR who has been involved with the event since it started, has seen thousands of people finish, and just as many fail, and views the dragon as an opportunity – a crossroads – where they can continue or quit.

Tor des Géants and its concurrent races are popular in the Aosta region, with local people and mountain refuges providing support to the often deeply sleep-deprived runners. Many who have taken on the race reflect on crazy hallucinations, and having no idea where they are or why they're there, but also how well they're looked after – and the quality of the Italian food, too!

The 2024 edition of the race saw Germany's Katharina Hartmuth break the women's record, previously held by GB ultrarunner Sabrina Verjee, with Verjee coming in second. On the men's side, legendary French runner François D'Haene – who, along with Kilian Jornet, holds the joint record for the most number of UTMB Mont-Blanc wins at four – won his first attempt at TOR330, it was a hard-won and well-deserved victory for the French runner who lives and trains in the French Alps and had, at the time of his win, returned from a long absence with a skiing injury.

> 'TdG was incredible. Surpassed my expectations in every way – especially difficulty! The main challenges were the altitude (some days you were up and down to altitude, others you were up and stayed up and both had their difficulties in terms of nutrition), the sleep, fuelling and just the difficulty of the terrain. You'd be absolutely exhausted, trying to get to the next refuge in the middle of the night, then suddenly there would be a *ferrata* section with sheer drops. It was relentless!'
>
> KIRSTY READE, TDG 2024 FINISHER.

> 'TOR is just incredible from start to finish. The scenery is spectacular but what makes it really special are the people – the volunteers, the medics and the spectators. The support is just unbelievable. Everybody goes out of their way to help you in whatever way they can. I was just so appreciative of that and it really can lift you when you're feeling tired or low.'
>
> EMMA STUART, TOR 2023 CHAMPION

OTHER DISTANCES

In recent years, organizers Tor-X have launched a series of alternatives to the main 330 event, offering different levels of challenge to suit more runners. These range from the 30km Passage au Malatrà to the utterly bonkers Tor des Glaciers, which gives runners 190 hours to cover 450km with 32,000m (105,000ft) of elevation gain.

Tor 450 Tor des Glaciers 450km; 32,000m (105,000ft) ascent

Tor 130 Tot Dret 130km; 12,000m (39,370ft) ascent

Tor 100 Cervino-Monte Bianco 100km; 8,000m (26,247ft) ascent

Tor 30 Passage au Malatrà 30km; 2,000m (6,562ft) ascent

RIGHT Descending passage Lago Chiaro (Clear Lake passage).

ZUGSPITZ ULTRATRAIL

GARMISCH-PARTENKIRCHEN, GERMANY

Germany's largest and best-known trail running event, Zugspitz Ultratrail (ZUT), draws runners from across the globe (59 countries were represented in 2024) to circumnavigate Germany's highest mountain, the Zugspitze. Standing at 2,962m (9,718ft) above sea level in the Wetterstein range on the German/Austrian border, the mountain guards two of Germany's last-remaining glaciers.

The first ZUT was held in 2011 in Grainau with 676 participants, and the race has steadily grown in popularity, with more than 3,850 runners participating across races of varying distances. In 2019, the start/finish moved to the ski resort of Garmisch-Partenkirchen, where it remains today.

Runners leave the Richard-Strauss-Platz at 10:15pm, heading out into the night. Garmisch-Partenkirchen is a traditional Bavarian town, with cobbled streets, and runners are given a rapturous welcome as they make their way out towards the mountains. It's easy to be lulled into a false sense of security as the first 6km (3¾ miles) are flat and fast, but long, steep climbs and descents on technical terrain await, offering no allowances for those who've gone out too hard. As compensation for the night-time start, many runners reach the highest point of the race at 2,200m (7,218ft) just as the sun rises over the mountains. And, throughout the race, even the longest, steepest climbs are tempered by views up to the snow-capped peaks of the Wetterstein.

RACE STATISTICS

MONTH: June
DISTANCE: 106km (66 miles)
TOTAL ASCENT: 5,080m (16,667ft)
HIGHEST POINT: 2,200m (7,218ft)
STARTERS 2024: 674 (92 female, 582 male)
FINISHERS 2024: 552 (76 female, 476 male)
TIME ALLOWED: 27hr
FEMALE COURSE RECORD: Esther Fellhofer 13:56:51 (2024)
MALE COURSE RECORD: Pierre-Emmanuel Alexandre 10:59:12 (2024)
FIRST RUN: 2011
ENTRY FEE: €180

WEBSITE:
www.zugspitz-ultratrail.com

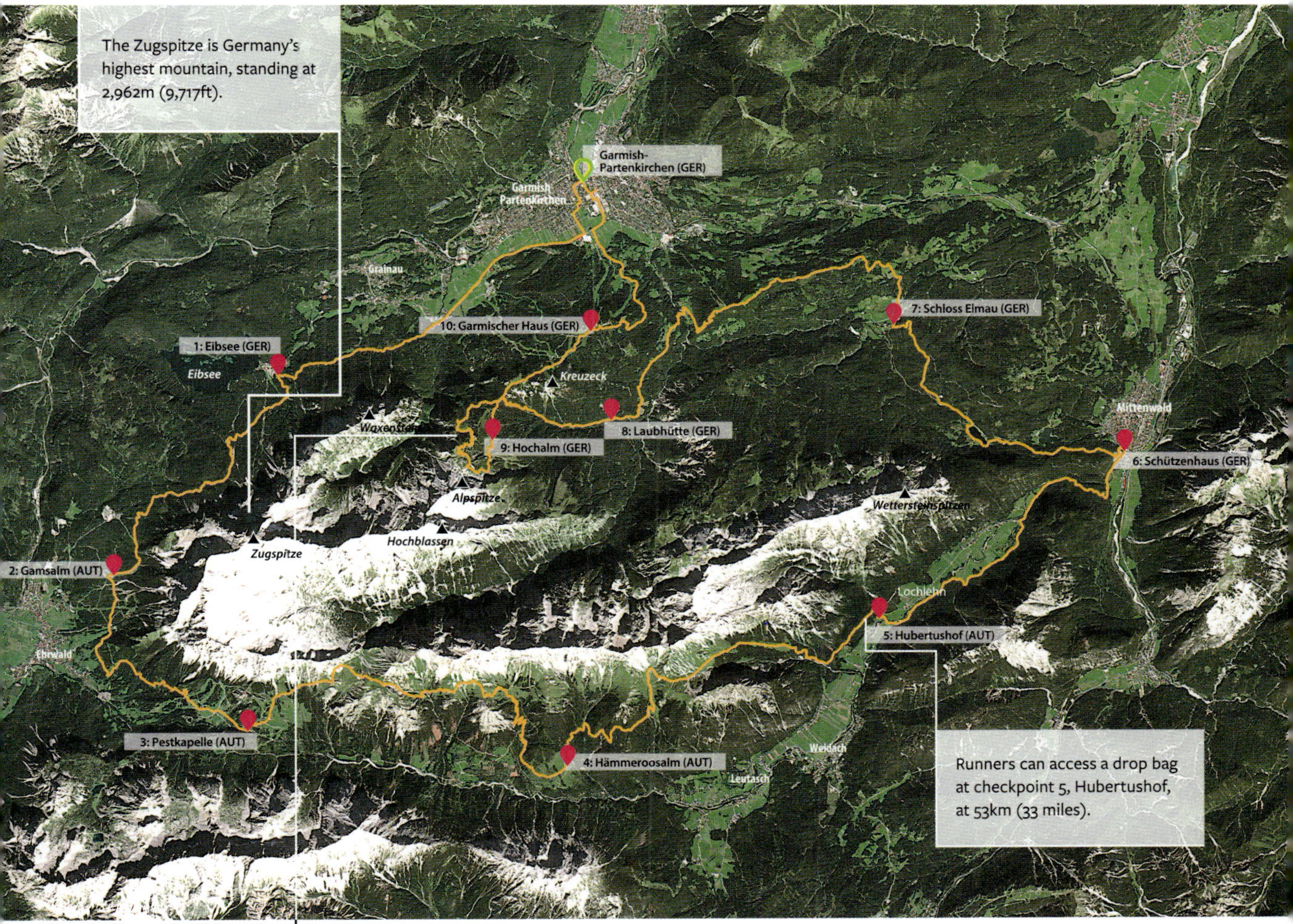

The Zugspitze is Germany's highest mountain, standing at 2,962m (9,717ft).

Runners can access a drop bag at checkpoint 5, Hubertushof, at 53km (33 miles).

The sting in the tail is the final 1,000m (3,280ft) climb to Osterfelderkopf.

ELEVATION PROFILE

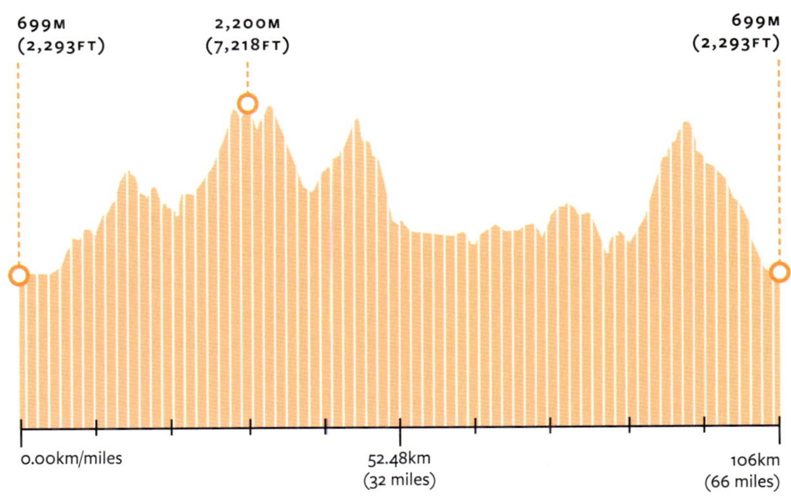

LEFT Descent of Scharnitzjoch in the Puit-Valley, Wetterstein-Mountains.

OTHER DISTANCES

For those keen to explore even more of the beautiful Zugspitz trails, a new 100-mile (161km) distance – ZUT100 – was introduced for 2025.

ZUT100: 161km (100 miles); 8,302m (27,238ft) ascent

Ehrwald Trail: 86km (53½ miles); 4,080m (13,386ft) ascent

Leutasch Trail: 68km (42¼ miles); 2,870m (9,416ft) ascent

Mittenwald Trail: 44km (27¼ miles); 1,860m (6,102ft) ascent

Garmisch-Partenkirchen Trail: 29km (18 miles); 1,440m (4,724ft) ascent

Grainau Trail: 16km (10 miles); 760m (2,493ft) ascent

Underfoot the terrain is varied, with twisty mountain trails, gravel paths, forest tracks, alpine meadows, grassy pistes and even snowfields at higher altitudes at times. Those who know leave something in the tank for the sting in the tail of the ZUT: the 1,000-m (3,280ft) climb at the 85km (53 mile) mark. The top of the climb is at the 100km (62 mile) point, from where it's all downhill to the finish – not as easy as it sounds on steep, slippery trails after a full day's running.

> 'I chose to run the Zugspitz Ultratrail Leutasch race in 2023 because Garmisch is a really special place for both Tom [Chrissie's husband] and I and somewhere we've been going for many years. We love the place in all its incredible seasons – in fact Tom proposed to me in one of our favourite spots in 2014, making it even more special. Having developed a deep love for trail running and the mountains, it made total sense to combine a race with visiting such an incredible place and have a chance to explore the area on foot. And it didn't disappoint – it was the most well organized, beautiful, heartwarming and uplifting event. It was just incredible from start to finish – not that my body necessarily felt incredible! But it was absolutely mind-blowingly stunning, with vistas that took my breath away if I had any breath left. The downhills were technical – for me at least! – but the course was nevertheless runnable almost in its entirety. I loved every minute, and to win the race was the icing on a phenomenal cake and I was so grateful that Tom and friends were at the finish to celebrate with. All in all it's an event I would highly recommend and an event that's enabled me to create memories that I'll never forget.'
>
> CHRISSIE WELLINGTON, FOUR TIMES IRONMAN WORLD CHAMPION AND WINNER OF THE 2023 ZUGSPITZ ULTRATRAIL LEUTASCH.

LEFT Negotiating the technical trails at the Zugspitz Ultratrail.

SPARTATHLON

ATHENS TO SPARTA, GREECE

Herodotus' account of the Battle of Marathon in 490 BC describes the incredible endurance feat of Athenian messenger, Pheidippides, who was sent by his generals to Sparta to request help for the Athenian forces against an invasion by the Persians. According to Herodotus, Pheidippides arrived in Sparta the day following his departure from Athens, a distance of 250km (155 miles) within 36 hours.

Whether this feat might actually be possible by modern runners captured the imagination of John Foden, a British RAF Wing Commander and ancient Greek history scholar. As an accomplished ultrarunner himself, he decided the only way to find out was to give it a go.

In October 1982, Foden – then aged 56 – and four of his RAF colleagues set out from Athens, supported by an RAF crew. The following day, three of the men finished, with John Scholten arriving in Sparta in 34:30, Foden in 37:37, and John McCarthy in 39 hours. The British team proved Herodotus was right – for people called John, at least. The following year, the Spartathlon became an official race, with 44 men and one woman from twelve countries lining up at the start. Legendary Greek ultrarunner, Yiannis Kouros, won the race in 20:25. Another legend, British ultrarunner Eleanor Adams (now Robinson), who was the only female competitor, finished in 32:37:52.

RACE STATISTICS

MONTH: September
DISTANCE: 246km (152¾ miles)
TOTAL ASCENT: 3,579m (11,742ft)
HIGHEST POINT: 1,200m (3,937ft)
STARTERS 2024: 395 (80 female, 315 male)
FINISHERS 2024: 194 (35 female, 159 male)
TIME ALLOWED: 36hr
FEMALE COURSE RECORD: Camille Herron 22:35:31 (2023)
MALE COURSE RECORD: Fotis Zisimopoulos 19:55:09 (2023)
FIRST RUN: 1983
ENTRY FEE: €950

WEBSITE:
www.spartathlon.gr

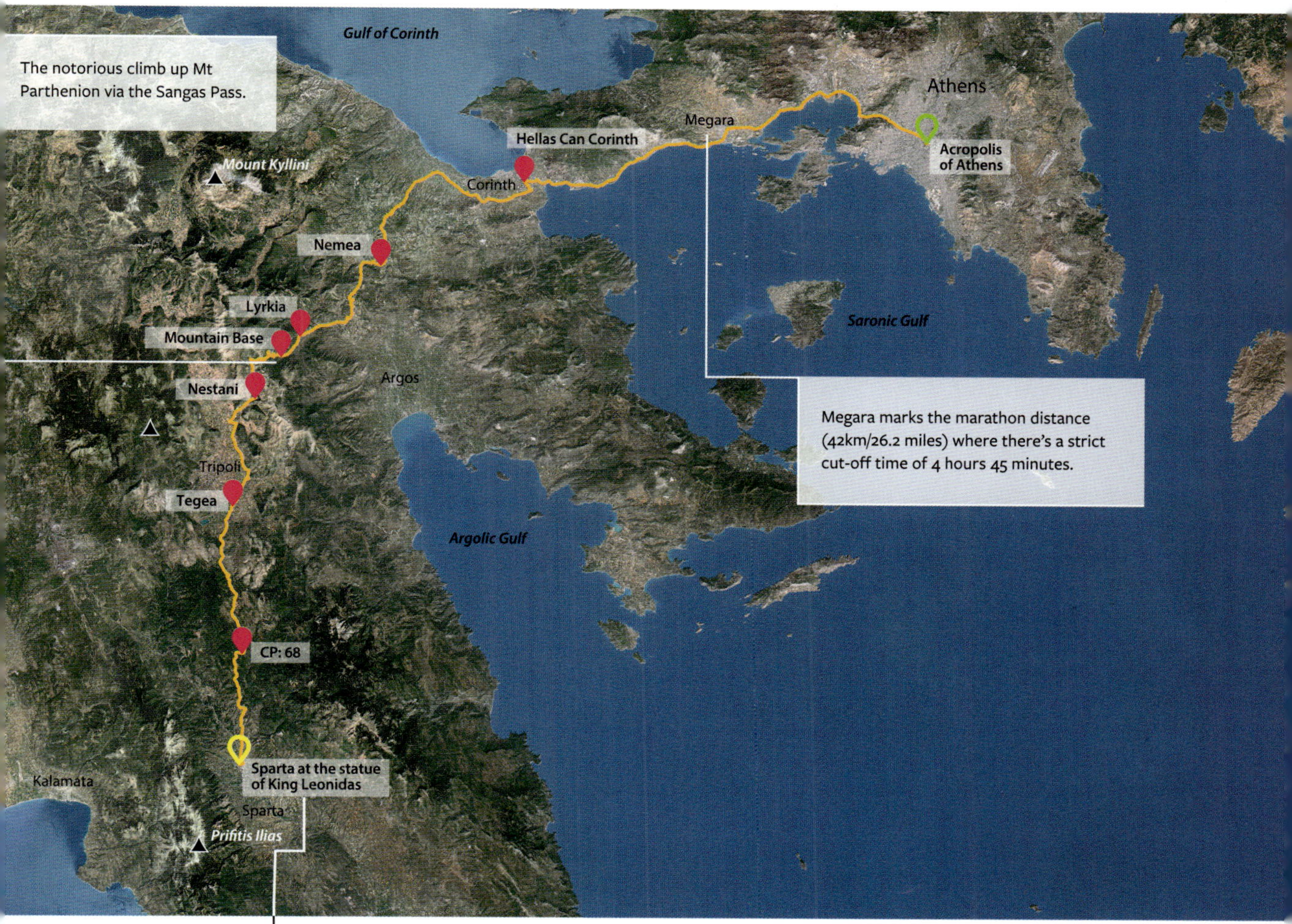

The notorious climb up Mt Parthenion via the Sangas Pass.

Megara marks the marathon distance (42km/26.2 miles) where there's a strict cut-off time of 4 hours 45 minutes.

The famous race finish at the statue of King Leonidas in Sparta.

FAR LEFT Runners coping with the sun at Kakia Skala, between Megara and Corinth.

LEFT Nervous runners waiting for the 7am start at the 2024 race.

ELEVATION PROFILE

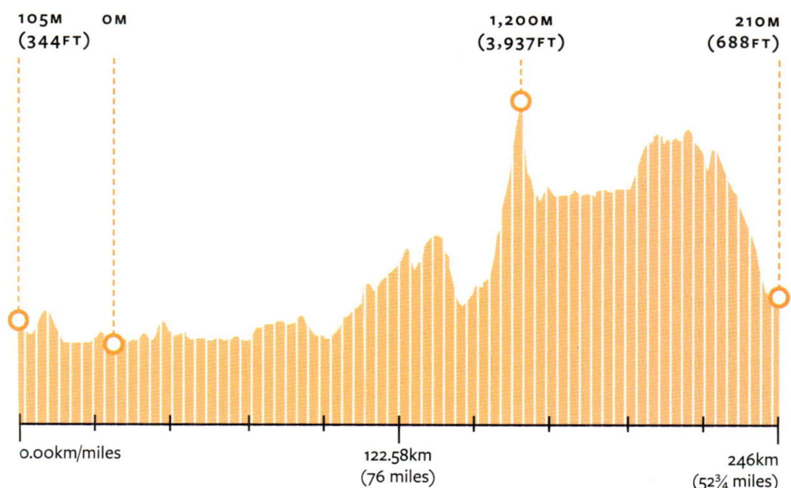

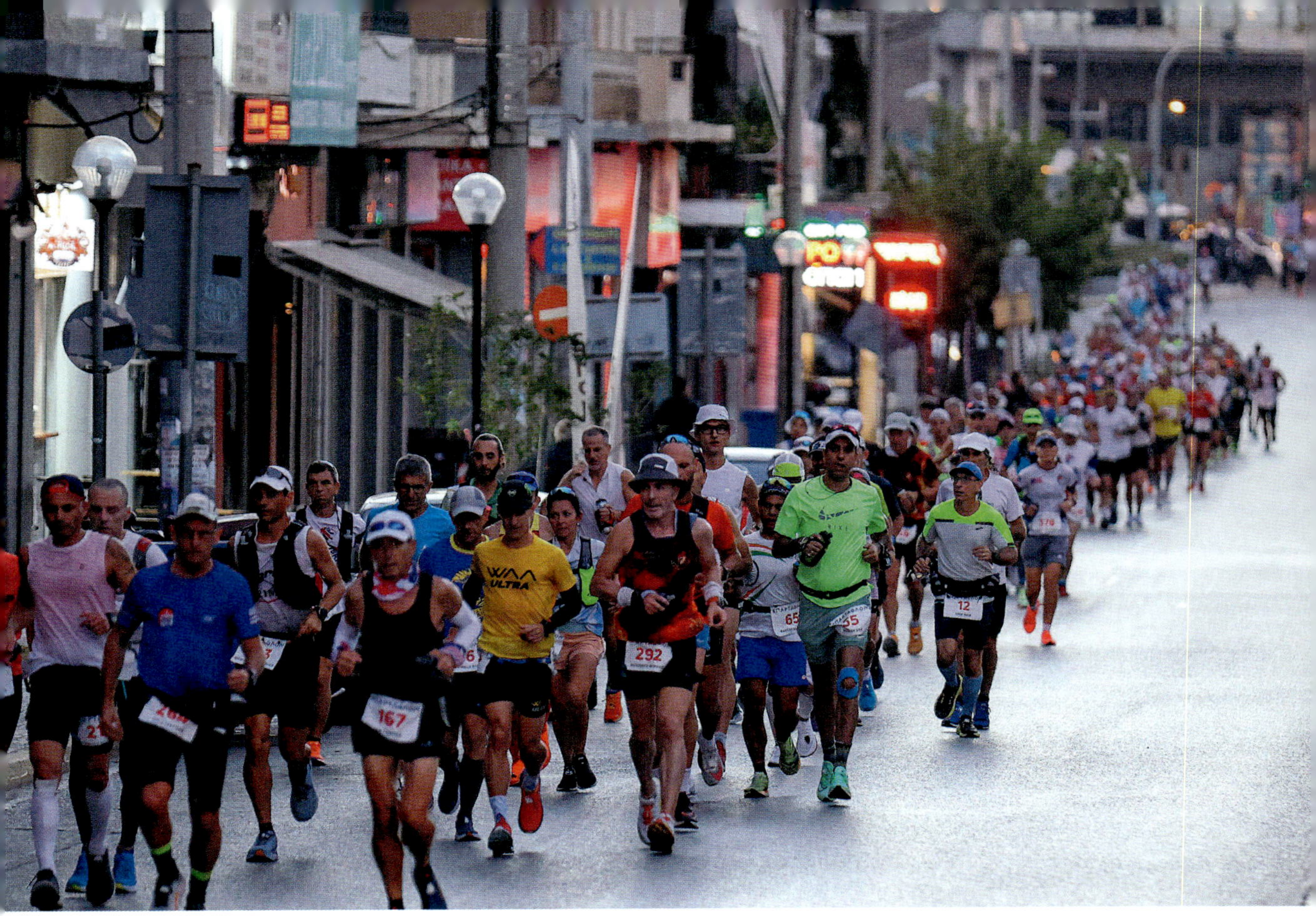
ULTRA
292
167
12

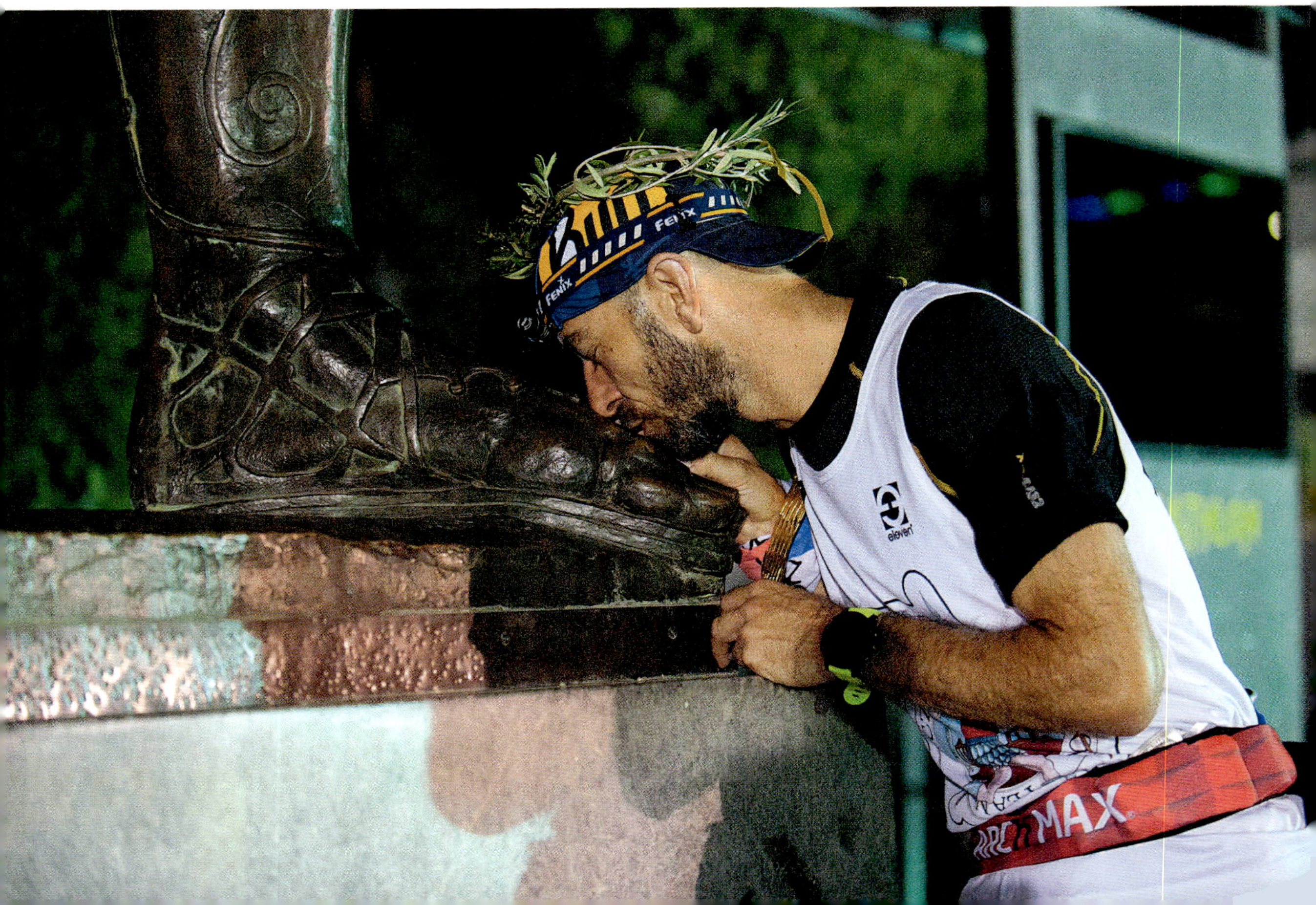
Fenix
MAX

John Foden would go on to organize the race in its early years, as well as being a key figure in British ultrarunning right up until his death in 2016 at the age of 90. Today, Spartathlon remains one of the world's most prestigious ultramarathons, and places are hard to come by, with strict eligibility criteria and a finisher rate around 50 per cent. Runners from a number of international teams tackle the 246km (153 miles) linear route from Athens to Sparta in September each year, often battling searing heat and heavy traffic. Away from the main road, the route is often peaceful and scenic, with Greek villages and hamlets guaranteeing a warm welcome for runners en route.

Waiting 150km (93 miles) into the race is the notorious climb up Mount Parthenion via the Sangas Pass at 1,100m (3,609ft). This legendary mountain was the place where Pheidippides is said to have met the god Pan during his run. Pan promised he would help the Athenians at Marathon if they agreed to worship him as they had done in the past. Narrow trails wind through its rocky, scrubby landscape adding technicality to the challenge. The final 28km (17½ miles) is predominantly downhill, and it's said that those who make it over the mountain almost always make it to the finish.

After challenging beginnings – Eleanor Robinson had to fight to line up at the start line of the first Spartathlon, with male entrants joining in to argue for her place – women now make up more than a quarter of starters, far higher than most races of 100+ miles. In 2012, five-time UTMB Mont-Blanc winner Lizzy Hawker won the women's race, finishing third overall.

'I've never known an ultrarunner to talk about hitting the wall, which is the favourite topic of conversation among marathon runners,' remarked John Foden, the Spartathlon founder. 'The art of it is to learn what is the fastest speed you can run at so that you don't get to 70km and simply run out of all forms of energy as that's when you just flap around.'

ABOVE Running through the streets of Athens at the 2022 Spartathlon.

BELOW Second-placed Radek Brunner of the Czech Republic kisses the foot of the statue of ancient Spartan king Leonidas at the finish of the 2017 Spartathlon.

MADEIRA ISLAND ULTRA-TRAIL

PORTO MONIZ, MADEIRA ISLAND

'Madeira is one of the most remarkable places in the world in terms of orography (the branch of physical geography dealing with the formation and features of mountains) and all of this is packed into just a 60km² island in the middle of the Atlantic. Running the MIUT is like retracing the steps of our ancestors, who once had to conquer this rugged terrain as they journeyed from one end of the island to the other. Along the way, you'll experience a breathtaking variety of landscapes – from ancient, endemic forests to quaint villages nestled in deep valleys, towering mountain peaks, and a striking final scene that resembles what Mars might look like if it had oceans.'

JOAO FARIA – MIUT CREW

Madeira is an archipelago of four islands off the northwest coast of Africa. An autonomous region of Portugal, it is known for its sweet namesake wine and subtropical climate. The main island is volcanic, with a mountainous interior, dense forests and, at its edges, high cliffs, pebbly beaches and settlements along deltas of the Fajã River. Madeira's capital, Funchal, is known for its beautiful botanic gardens and colourful harbour.

RACE STATISTICS

MONTH: April
DISTANCE: 115km (71½ miles)
TOTAL ASCENT: 7,090m (23,261ft)
HIGHEST POINT: 1,760m (5,774ft)
STARTERS 2024: 1,019 (109 female, 910 male)
FINISHERS 2024: 697 (72 female, 625 male)
TIME ALLOWED: 32hr
FEMALE COURSE RECORD: Martina Valmassoi 16:14:10 (2024)
MALE COURSE RECORD: Ben Dhiman 13:52:46 (2024)
FIRST RUN: 2008
ENTRY FEE: €180

WEBSITE:
www.miutmadeira.com

s race is known for the variety of
erfoot terrain; the descent to
o da Ribeira is considered to be
of the most technical sections.

The stunning PR1 is a technical, high-level trail which links some of the highest points on Madeira. It finishes at Pico Ruivo, the highest point on the island and on the race route.

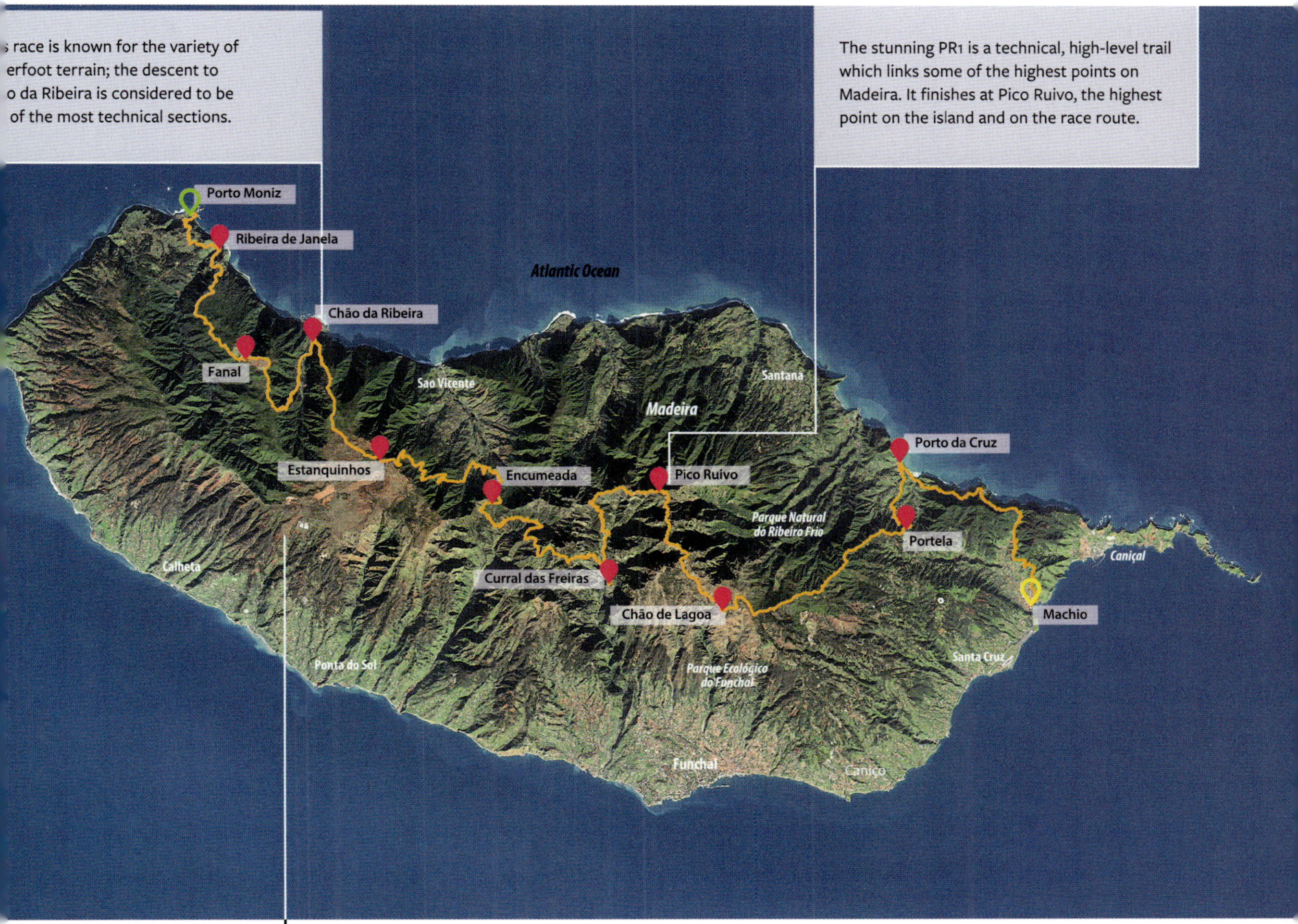

Porto Moniz
Ribeira de Janela
Atlantic Ocean
Chão da Ribeira
Fanal
Sao Vicente
Santana
Madeira
Estanquinhos
Encumeada
Pico Ruivo
Porto da Cruz
Parque Natural do Ribeiro Frio
Portela
Caniçal
Calheta
Curral das Freiras
Chão de Lagoa
Machio
Santa Cruz
Ponta do Sol
Parque Ecológico do Funchal
Funchal
Caniço

During August 2024 wildfires devastated a large area of forest in the centre of the island. A temporary route is in place until the race is able to return to its original course, shown here.

ELEVATION PROFILE

14M (45FT)
1,760M (5,774FT)
0M
9M (29FT)
0.00km/miles
56.66km (35 miles)
115km (70½ miles)

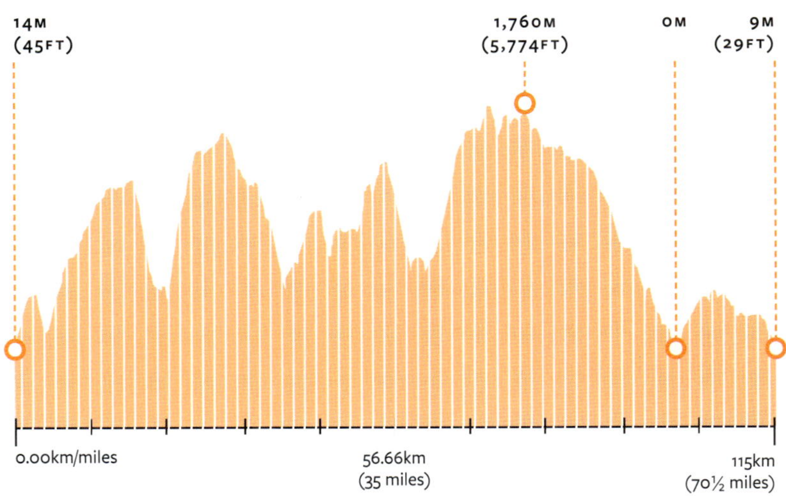

LEFT Courtney Dauwalter on the famous Pedra Rija ridgeline, part of the legendary PR1 trail, a breathtaking traverse connecting Madeira's highest peaks.

The first MIUT was held in 2008 – the first trail race ever organized in Madeira. But its origins date to 2004, when members of the Clube de Montanha do Funchal began attempting to cross the island in less than 24 hours. Some of those original runners are still part of the executive team of MIUT.

The 2008 race saw 141 runners linking the lighthouse of Ponta do Pargo with the city of Machico. The following year, the start was moved to Porto Moniz, where it remains today. In 2013, the race became part of the National Ultra-Trail Circuit and was also chosen as Portugal's Ultra-Trail Championship with 449 participants battling it out for the opportunity to compete in the Ultra-Trail World Championship. By 2016, MIUT had joined the Ultra-Trail World Tour circuit, with 2,041 runners representing 41 countries. Today, MIUT is one of the ten Gran Canaria World Trail Majors, and runners have five different distances to choose from (see box, opposite).

The main event – the 115km (71½ miles) race – sets out at midnight, with runners streaming out of Porto Moniz and heading into the darkness of the mountainous massif. Relentless climbs and descents include two highly challenging ascents at Fanal and Estanquinhos, and a particularly technical descent to Chão da Ribeira. Crowds of supporters await at the bridge over the Ribeira da Janela, cheering runners on as they make the

PREVIOUS PAGES The last runners making their way up the final major climb of the original route. As a reward for pushing their limits to beat the cut-offs, they are rewarded with a breathtaking sunset at one of Madeira's most stunning viewpoints.

ABOVE The famous 'Pedra Rija' ridgeline, part of the legendary PR1 trail, a breathtaking traverse connecting Madeira's highest peaks. The final stretch of the climb leads to the famous radar.

OTHER DISTANCES

Race week includes a range of shorter distances as alternatives to the full island crossing.
85km (52¾ miles); 4,000m (13,100ft)
60km (37¼ miles); 3,000m (9,850ft)
42km (26 miles); 1,400m (4,600ft)
16km (10 miles); 390m (1,280ft)

long ascent towards Fanal, a Reserve of Rest and Silence. A long descent to São Vicente followed by a climb to Encumeada takes runners through the lush Laurissilva forest and the forest park of Chão dos Louros, part of a European Network of Sites of Community Importance – Natura 2000.

From Encumeada, participants tackle Madeira's highest peaks: Ruivo and Areeiro. On a clear day the leg-sapping ascents are rewarded with stunning views of the valleys, ridges and plateaus, cut through by countless streams. Zino's petrel (*Pterodroma madeira*), an endemic species of the island and considered the most endangered seabird of Europe, is known to nest here.

From Pico do Areeiro, the race enters its final phase, crossing the Eastern massif, mainly descending but still with some good climbs in between. Leaving the mountains behind, the terrain becomes more rolling and, after passing through Portela, an ancient footpath descends towards Porto da Cruz and the ocean. The race finishes in the beautiful valley of Machico, just 17km (10½ miles) from Funchal.

Running right across an island that has changing weather and varying landscapes means MIUT is a proper adventure that draws some of ultrarunning's biggest names. Hot sunshine, rain or disorientating mists are all common, and runners must negotiate savage climbs and leg-breaking descents in the island's mountainous interior, along with dense forest and rocky, technical trails.

RIGHT The steep stairway connecting Porto da Cruz to Larano. At this stage, runners have just 10km to go, finally reaching a flatter section with breathtaking ocean views.

TRANSGRANCANARIA

LAS PALMAS DE GRAN CANARIA–MASPALOMAS

Gran Canaria is one of Spain's Canary Islands, surrounded by the vast Atlantic Ocean to the north of Morocco. Sandy beaches and clear seas edge the island, known for its year-round sunshine. But face away from the sea, and a rugged mountain range rises abruptly at the island's centre – sleeping volcanoes climbed by steep, winding trails.

Gran Canarians describe their island as a miniature continent – and what better way to explore it than on foot. Each February, Gran Canaria welcomes a deep field of elite and recreational runners. The longest of the races on offer, the Transgrancanaria Classic takes on 126km (78¼ miles) and almost 7,000m (23,000ft) of ascent, making a full crossing of the island from north to south on a route that can vary from year to year. Starting at midnight in the city of Las Palmas, runners trace the edge of the ocean, crossing soft, leg-sapping sand. The route then links towns, villages and refuges via deep valleys and long, mountainous ridgelines, finishing back at the ocean in Maspalomas.

Ten well-stocked aid stations await runners as they make their crossing. A notorious climb from the start sees the lead competitors arriving into the aptly named Teror aid station in total darkness, having ascended more than 1,500m (4,900ft) from sea level in 30km (18½ miles).

RACE STATISTICS

MONTH: February
DISTANCE: 126km (78¼ miles)
TOTAL ASCENT: 6,866m (22,526ft)
HIGHEST POINT: 1,850m (6,070ft)
STARTERS 2024: 753 (90 female, 663 male)
FINISHERS 2024: 498 (58 female, 440 male)
TIME ALLOWED: 30hr
FEMALE COURSE RECORD: Courtney Dauwalter 15:14:54 (2024)
MALE COURSE RECORD: Raul Octaviu Butaci 13:22:32 (2024)
FIRST RUN: 2003
ENTRY FEE: €195

WEBSITE:
www.transgrancanaria.net

Many runners catch sunrise at El Hornillo.

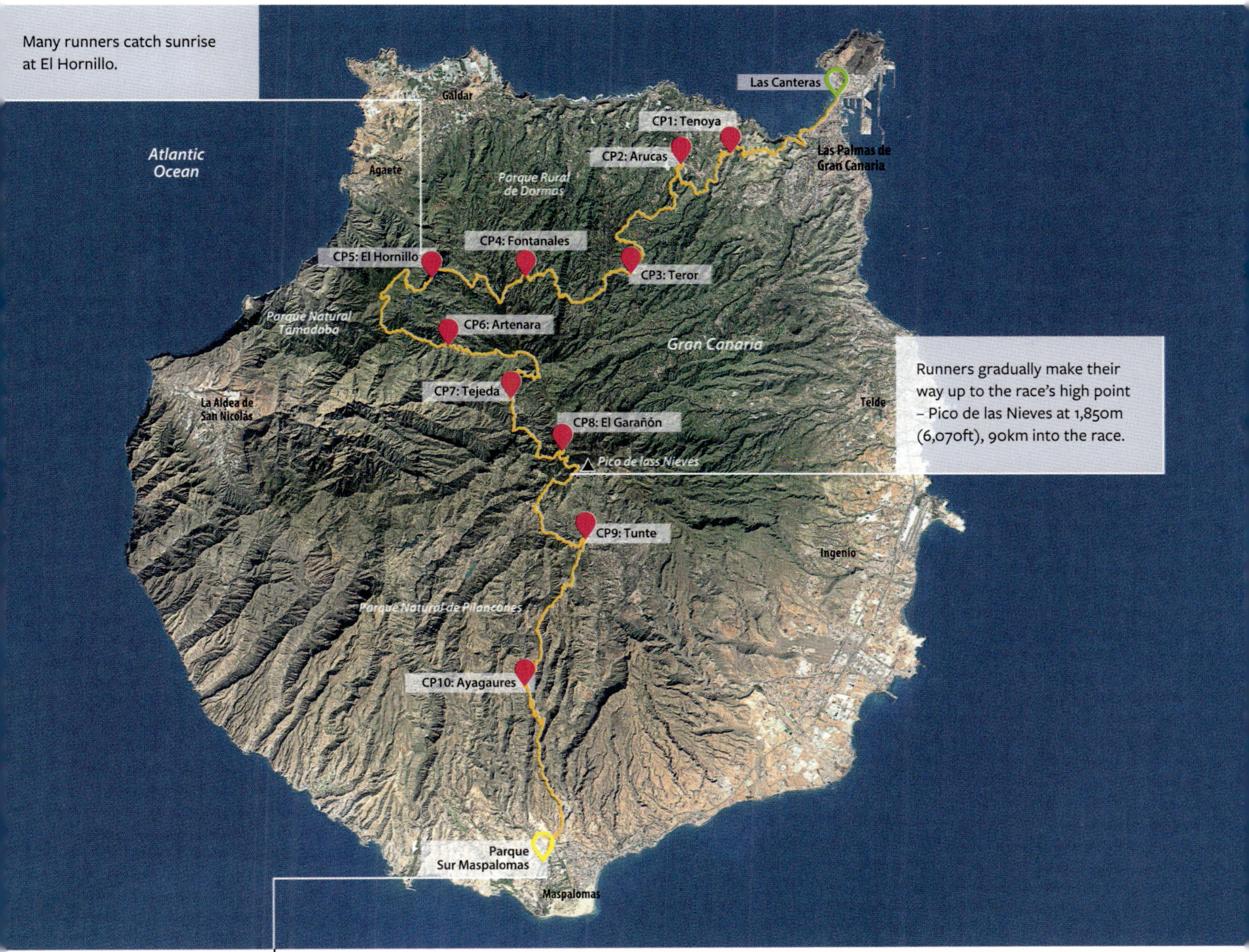

Las Canteras
Gáldar
CP1: Tenoya
CP2: Arucas
Las Palmas de Gran Canaria
Atlantic Ocean
Agaete
Parque Rural de Doramas
CP4: Fontanales
CP5: El Hornillo
CP3: Teror
Parque Natural Tamadaba
CP6: Artenara
Gran Canaria
La Aldea de San Nicolás
CP7: Tejeda
Telde
CP8: El Garañón
Pico de lass Nieves
CP9: Tunte
Ingenio
Parque Natural de Pilancones
CP10: Ayagaures
Parque Sur Maspalomas
Maspalomas

Runners gradually make their way up to the race's high point – Pico de las Nieves at 1,850m (6,070ft), 90km into the race.

Trail Zone event at race HQ ensures a warm welcome for runners at the finish.

ELEVATION PROFILE

9M (29FT)
0M
1,850M (6,070FT)
35M (114FT)
0.00km/miles
62.63km (39 miles)
126km (78¼ miles)

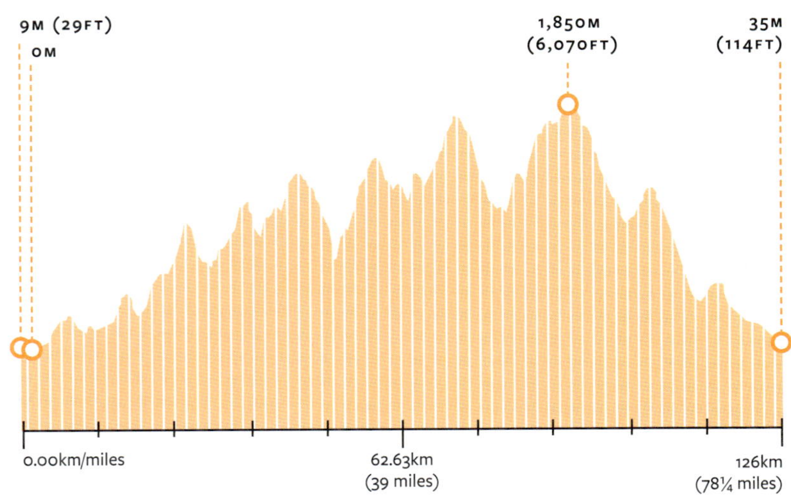

LEFT Technical rocky trails on the Paso de la Plata.

The climbing continues, crossing many of the highest points in the centre of the island including, some years, a visit to the surroundings of the stratovolcano and Gran Canaria's highest point, El Pico de Las Nieves. The views from the top will hopefully go some way towards distracting runners from the effort of the climb, featuring the rock formations Roque Nublo, Roque Bentayga, as well as panoramic views across the island and across to Teide, the highest summit on the neighbouring island of Tenerife.

Despite being in the sun-drenched Canaries, good weather is far from guaranteed, and an optional cold kit list includes warm gloves, windproof trousers, a thermal t-shirt and long thermal leg coverings on top of the usual kit required for long, mountain ultras.

Runners in the 2024 edition of the Classic faced particularly harsh conditions, with heavy rain and strong winds overnight giving way to hot sun during the day. A star-studded lineup in that race included US ultrarunning legends Courtney Dauwalter and Zach Miller. In the women's race, Courtney would go on to lead from the start, finishing in a new course record of 15:14:54. Spanish favourite Claudia Temps took second place, while Ireland's Emma Stuart, whose previous notable wins include UTS100 (see page 82), Tor des Géants (see page 38) and Lakeland 100 (see page 76), embraced the weather and finished third. The men's race unfolded in a similarly exciting manner, with Zach Miller characteristically taking the early lead. In the end, he finished back in seventh, while the relatively unknown Romanian runner

PREVIOUS PAGES Breathtaking views on the Paso de la Plata.

ABOVE Roque Nublo is an iconic landmark in the centre of the island.

OTHER DISTANCES

Advanced: 82km (51 miles); 4,265m (13,993ft) ascent
Marathon: 47km (29¼ miles); 1,840m (6,037ft) ascent
Half: 21km (13 miles); 1,372m (4,501ft) ascent
Promo: 12km (7½ miles); 730m (2,395ft) ascent
VK El Gigante: 5.5km (3½ miles); 1,060m (3,478ft) ascent

Raul Butaci took the win, also setting a new course record of 13:22:32. Miguel Heras, a long-time Spanish ultrarunning legend, finished second, a formidable feat at the age of 48.

TGC was Spain's first ultramarathon, with its inaugural running in 2003 attracting 60 entrants. Since then it has grown year-on-year, becoming one of the premier events on the ultrarunning calendar, and one of the ten global Gran Canaria World Trail Majors – an association of independent and emblematic races with the aim of promoting diversity, identity and respect in trail running. Youth and family events have been added, bringing the occasion to runners of all ages (see box). With a big race feel, mandatory kit list, and specific bib collection times, these races are a wonderful way to introduce younger runners to the world of mountain ultras. They also ensure everyone feels involved in a sport that can, with its lengthy hours of training and racing, be considered a solitary pastime. For many, as well as being an opportunity to join the annual celebration of ultrarunning that unfolds on the island, starting with a huge beach party at the start at Las Palmas, for those based in the northern hemisphere it's a welcome chance to soak up some winter sunshine.

Alongside a top-class elite field, TGC is known for its warm welcome to runners all the way through the pack, with great support crews championing runners at the back with no less enthusiasm than those fighting for podium places. This makes the TGC races ideal first mountain ultras for those considering moving into mountainous 100-milers.

In the words of the race organizers: 'It's tough, but as our claim says, "A goal, A dream." Maspalomas awaits with open arms to welcome you after 12, 15, 20, or 30 hours that seem like a lifetime.'

RIGHT Women's race winner Courtney Dauwalter at Transgrancanaria.

ULTRA PIRINEU

PARC NATURAL DEL CADÍ-MOIXERÓ, SPAIN

'Ultra Pirineu is an amazing race: a spectacular route on the Catalan Pyrenees, the international atmosphere, the best elite runners, impeccable organization, etc. But what makes it special is the people; the soul of Ultra Pirineu. Thanks to them, Ultra Pirineu is more than a race. It's a life experience.' DAVID PRIETO, RACE DIRECTOR

With a distance of 100km (62 miles) and more than 6,550m (21,490ft) of ascent, Ultra Pirineu crosses the high mountains of Catalonia's Parc Natural del Cadí-Moixeró. Part of the Skyrunner World Series, it has a reputation as one of the most demanding mountain ultramarathons in Europe, attracting elite runners from around the globe and participants from more than 50 countries. First held in 2009, when it was called the Cavalls del Vent (the horses of the wind) after the famous hiking route crossing the Catalan Pyrenees, it has since grown in popularity and rebranded to become Ultra Pirineu.

Cadí-Moixeró Natural Park is a place of rugged mountain trails, high-altitude passes and steep, technical ascents and descents. The route takes runners through spectacular mountain landscapes, the terrain varying from flowy forest singletrack and open alpine meadows to dramatic, knife-edge ridgelines. Race HQ is in Bagà, a small and (for the rest of the year, at least) peaceful village in the Berguedà region, which transforms into a lively hub during the race weekend as athletes, supporters and spectators arrive.

RACE STATISTICS

MONTH: October
DISTANCE: 100.2km (62¼ miles)
TOTAL ASCENT: 6,550m (21,490ft)
HIGHEST POINT: 2,520m (8,268ft)
STARTERS 2024: 1,061 (110 female, 951 male)
FINISHERS 2024: 800 (81 female, 719 male)
TIME ALLOWED: 26hr 30min
FEMALE COURSE RECORD: Núria Picas 12:12:00 (2022)
MALE COURSE RECORD: Kilian Jornet 10:25:00 (2021)
FIRST RUN: 2014
ENTRY FEE: €184.99

WEBSITE:
www.ultrapirineu.com

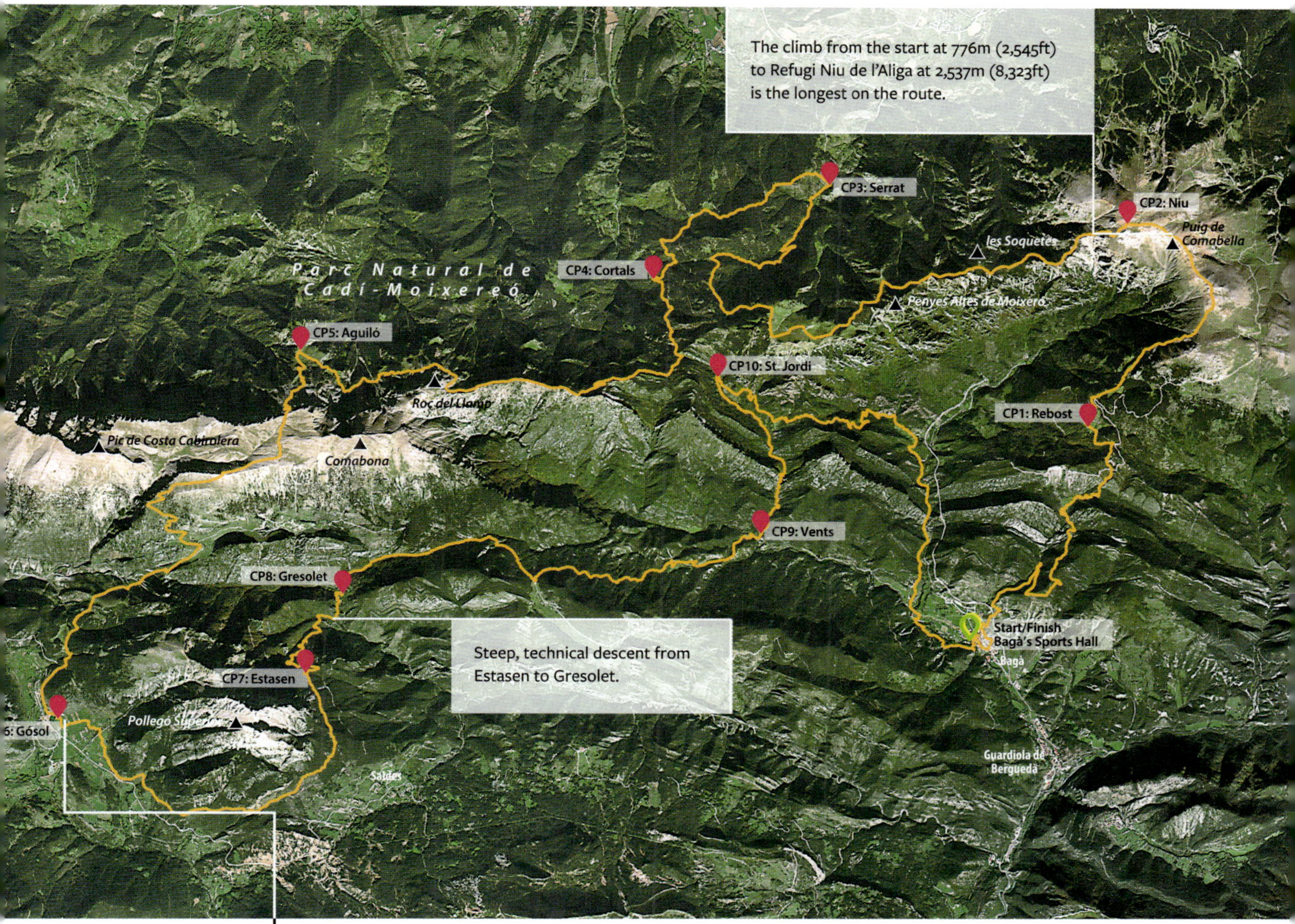

The climb from the start at 776m (2,545ft) to Refugi Niu de l'Aliga at 2,537m (8,323ft) is the longest on the route.

Steep, technical descent from Estasen to Gresolet.

Runners can expect a magnificent Catalan feast at Gósol aid station, 61.4km (38 miles) into the race.

ELEVATION PROFILE

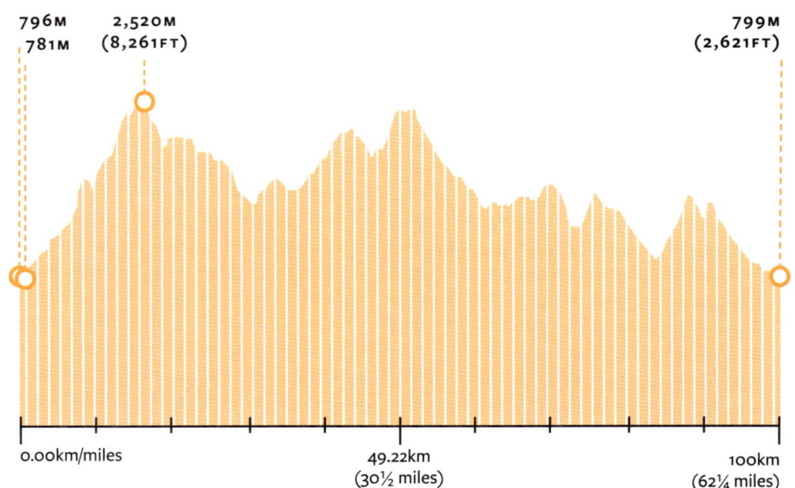

LEFT The 5:30am start at Ultra Pirineu in Baga.

OTHER DISTANCES

Alongside Ultra Pirineu's flagship 100km (62 miles) ultramarathon, the event offers these additional four races.

Martó Pirineu: 42km (26 miles); 2,700m (8,858ft) ascent

Mitja Pirineu: 21km (13 miles); 1,200m (3,937ft) ascent

La Molina Nit Pirineu: KV 5km (3 miles); 860m (2,822ft) ascent

Junior Pirineu: 12km (7½ miles); 920m (3,018ft) ascent

Ultrarunning is popular here, and support along the route is lively and enthusiastic, giving runners moments of party atmosphere interspersed by long, wild stretches through the mountains.

Runners set off from Bagà's Placa Porxada at 5:30am, streaming through the town's narrow streets in darkness to rapturous support and traditional Catalan music. Steep trails lead up into the mountains – rooty singletrack weaving between pine trees – the rising sun greeting runners as they reach the top. Much of the higher ground takes in out-of-season ski areas, wild and windswept above the treeline.

Ultra Pirineu's aid stations are legendary for their generous and varied offerings. Runners can expect fruit, organic nuts, soup, pasta, burgers (including veggie options); local delicacies such as bread with tomato and Catalonian sausage; sweet and savoury pastries; and even beer!

Taking place in early autumn in the high mountains, the weather conditions are notoriously variable. Past races have seen everything from warm sunshine to cold rain or even snow at higher altitudes. Mandatory equipment includes a full layer of warm clothing, as well as insulated, windproof and waterproof jackets, preparing runners for any eventuality even if they need to stop in the mountains at night. The combination of technical difficulty, unpredictable weather and demanding elevation profile make this a complex race but an outstanding adventure for the well prepared.

It's precisely this combination that means Ultra Pirineu draws some of the world's greatest ultrarunners to its start line. Both the women's and men's record holders – Nuria Picas and Kilian Jornet – are Catalan born and bred. Jornet grew up in a mountain refuge in the Pyrenees, climbing his first 3,000m (9,850ft) peak at the age of three. The Pyrenees, which straddle the border between France and Spain, have been his playground since, despite moving to Norway with wife and ultrarunner Emilie Forsberg in 2016. In 2023 he completed a challenge to summit all 177 peaks over 3,000m in the Pyrenees in a single push, a distance of 486km (302 miles) that took him just over eight days to complete.

ABOVE The brilliant supporters cheering on runners near the refuge of 'Niu de l'Aliga', the highest point of the race (2520m) at around 16km.

BELOW Dimitry Mityaev (eventual 2nd place in 2022) and Miguel Hera (eventual winner in 2022) racing near the refuge of 'Prat d'Aguiló' at around 48km. The mountain in the background is 'El Comabona'.

WINTER SPINE RACE

PENNINE WAY, UK

The Winter Spine is billed as Britain's most brutal endurance race. Taking place in the depths of the British winter, this non-stop, self-navigated, 431km (268 miles) race follows the full length of the Pennine Way National Trail along the rugged and often remote 'spine' of northern England – The Pennines.

Beginning in Edale, in Derbyshire's Hope Valley, runners have 168 hours to reach Kirk Yetholm, just over the border into Scotland. On the way, they'll experience dramatic Pennine landscapes, including the Peak District, Yorkshire Dales and Northumberland national parks; Hadrian's Wall and the Cheviots; along with bog, flagstone, rocky scrambles and bleak, open moorland. Five mandatory checkpoints, where participants are provided with hot food and drink, toilets and showers, somewhere to sleep, and access to their drop bag (which is transported from checkpoint to checkpoint for them), are at the following locations:

- Hebden Hey at 74km (46 miles)
- Hawes at 182km (113 miles)
- Middleton in Teesdale at 250km (155 miles)
- Alston at 300km (186 miles)
- Bellingham at 367km (228 miles)

RACE STATISTICS

MONTH: January
DISTANCE: 431km (268 miles)
TOTAL ASCENT: 10,732m (35,210ft)
HIGHEST POINT: 893m (2,930ft)
STARTERS 2024: 164 (32 female, 132 male)
FINISHERS 2024: 91 (16 female, 75 male)
TIME ALLOWED: 168hr
FEMALE COURSE RECORD: Jasmin Paris 83:12:23 (2019)
MALE COURSE RECORD: Jack Scott 72:55:05 (2024)
FIRST RUN: 2012
ENTRY FEE: £1,195

WEBSITE: www.thespinerace.com/race/montane-winter-spine

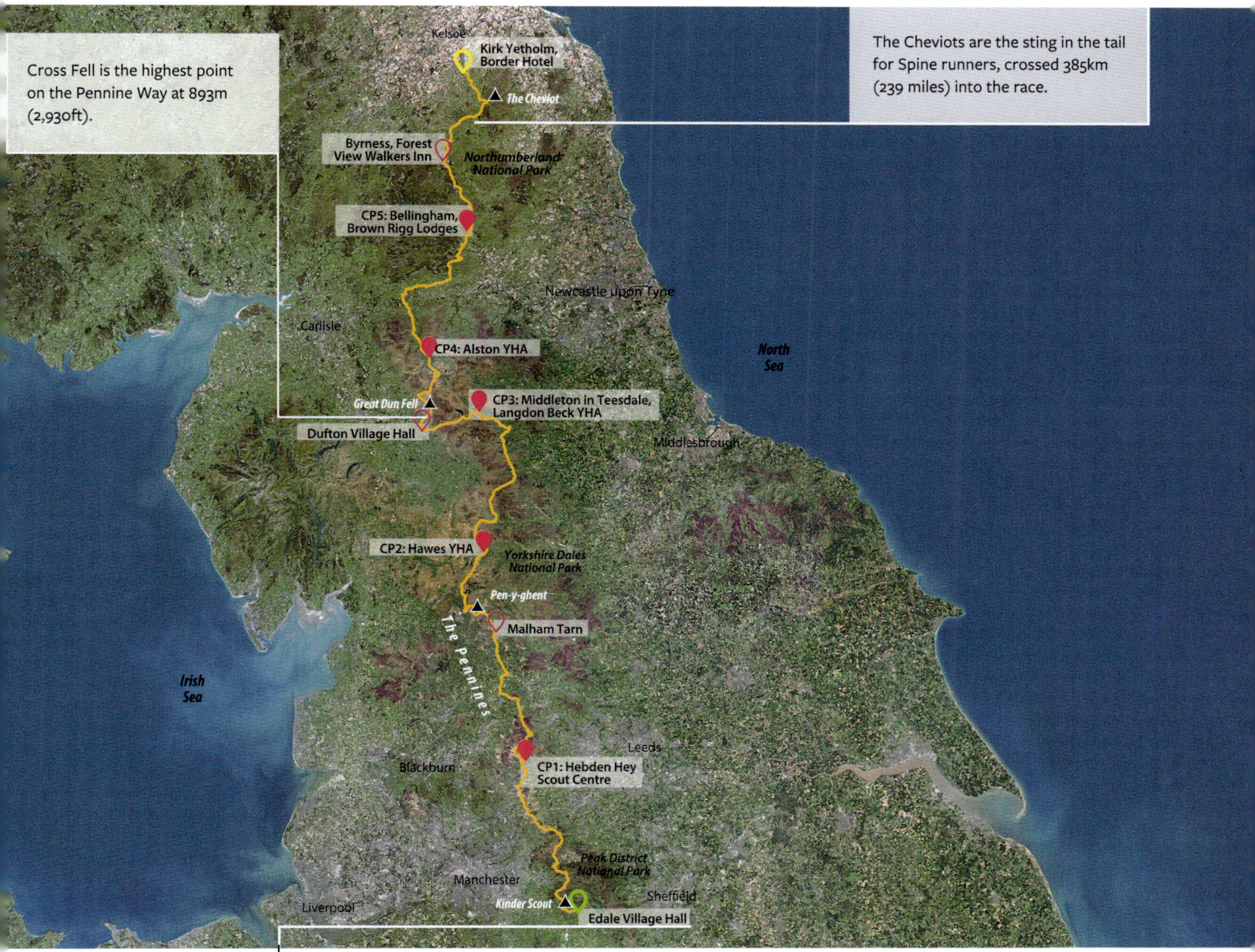

Kelsoe
Kirk Yetholm, Border Hotel
The Cheviot
Byrness, Forest View Walkers Inn
Northumberland National Park
CP5: Bellingham, Brown Rigg Lodges
Newcastle upon Tyne
Carlisle
CP4: Alston YHA
North Sea
Great Dun Fell
CP3: Middleton in Teesdale, Langdon Beck YHA
Dufton Village Hall
Middlesbrough
CP2: Hawes YHA
Yorkshire Dales National Park
Pen-y-ghent
Malham Tarn
The Pennines
Irish Sea
Leeds
Blackburn
CP1: Hebden Hey Scout Centre
Peak District National Park
Manchester
Sheffield
Liverpool
Kinder Scout
Edale Village Hall

Cross Fell is the highest point on the Pennine Way at 893m (2,930ft).

The Cheviots are the sting in the tail for Spine runners, crossed 385km (239 miles) into the race.

Kinder Scout is the highest point in the Peak District and the site of the 1932 Mass Trespass, paving the way for the National Parks Act in 1949.

ELEVATION PROFILE

236M (774FT)
106M (347FT)
893M (2,930FT)
114M (374FT)
0.00km/miles
212.56km (132 miles)
431km (268 miles)

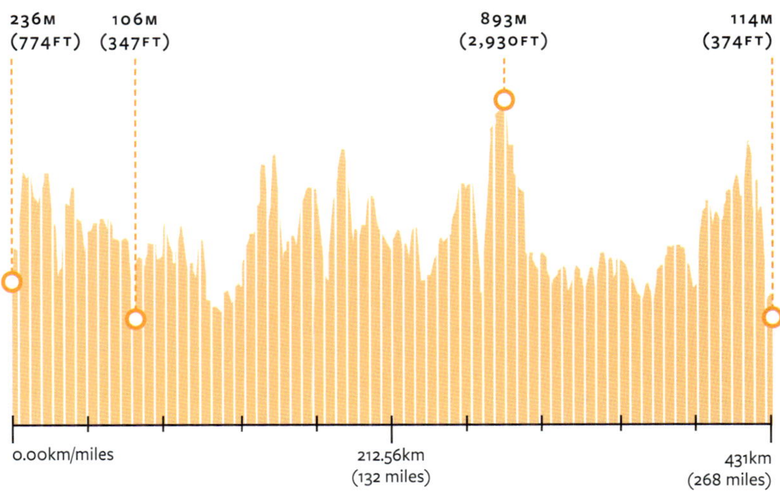

LEFT Runners cross moorland at Standedge during the 2025 Winter Spine Race.

PREVIOUS PAGES John Kelly leads the elite men's race early in the 2025 Winter Spine Race – eventual race winner Kim Collison follows in 4th place.

LEFT Hannah Rickman early on in the 2025 Winter Spine Race.

ABOVE Jayson Cavill at Cow Green Reservoir, Upper Teesdale, in the 2020 Race.

Designed to test runners to their physical and psychological limits, checkpoints are widely spaced, meaning the ability to be self-reliant for long periods of time is essential. Runners carry their own kit, including a sleeping mat and sleeping bag, so they're free to choose when and where to sleep – either at checkpoints, where they also have access to a drop bag, or simply out on the trail. Some Spine racers have even been caught napping in public toilets . . .

The race has an ethos of non-stop, day and night racing, meaning it's those with the best self-reliance and self-management, including navigating, fuelling and sleep strategy, who often prevail over those who can simply run fast for a long way. Participants are expected to possess the knowledge, experience, skills, fitness and preparedness to overcome any challenge they meet on the 431km (268 miles) journey – one which will take some an entire week to complete. Qualification criteria include having previously completed a minimum of an 80-mile (129km) ultra, or similar level of experience.

As in any ultra, but particularly one involving the distance and conditions encountered in the Winter Spine, some eventualities cannot be planned for, so all runners carry a GPS tracker with an emergency SOS button, and a team of dedicated race crew are constantly monitoring runners' progress, ready to contact them if they've been stationary for longer than expected, or to despatch help if required.

To keep runners safe out on the trail, an extensive list of mandatory kit is required, and the stringent pre-race kit check is feared by many. The following list (see box on page 74) offers a glimpse into the extent of the Winter Spine kit list. While all elements are mandatory, and runners are not permitted to start the race without them, items are divided into red, amber and green categories.

Runners found during en-route kit checks without green items receive a 30-minute penalty; those without amber items receive a 1-hour penalty; those without red items cannot continue unless they are at a checkpoint and able to replace the item, in which case they receive a 3-hour penalty. Detailed pass and fail parameters are provided for each item to ensure it is of a sufficient standard to be effective in case of need. One note reminds competitors that their spork (a spoon/fork combo used for eating) cannot be used as a trowel (included in toilet kit) or vice versa.

WINTER SPINE RACE KIT LIST

- Knife
- Medical Kit
- Spork
- Mug
- Rear Pack Red Light
- Toilet Kit
- Compass
- GPS
- Paper Maps
- Whistle
- Goggles
- Head Torch
- Waterproof Jacket
- Waterproof Trousers
- Hat
- Gloves
- Spare Socks
- Neck Gaiter
- Ice Spikes
- Cooking Stove
- Matches
- Lighter or Fire Steel
- 2L (3½ pints) water carrying capacity
- Food
- Mobile Phone
- Backpack
- Spare Base Layer, Top and Bottom layer
- Spare Cold Weather Mid Layer
- Appropriate Footwear
- Sleeping Bag
- Sleeping Mat
- Shelter
- Bivvy bag or Tent

OTHER DISTANCES

Sprint: 74km (46 miles); 2,017m (6,617ft) ascent
Challenger North: 258km (160¼ miles); 5,290m (17,356ft) ascent
Challenger South: 174km (108 miles); 5,451m (17,884ft) ascent

On top of the epic distance, the non-stop format and the toughness of the terrain, the mid-winter timing and northern latitude of the Spine ensure runners are exposed to, in the organizers' words, 'the full intensity and ferocity of the British Winter including deep snow, storm force winds and driving rain.'

In 2019 Jasmin Paris made ultrarunning history by winning the Spine outright, beating the second-placed runner (and first-placed man, Eoin Keith) by more than 12 hours, all while stopping to express milk for her 14-month-old daughter at checkpoints. In his 11 January 2019 blog entry, Eoin wrote, somewhat prophetically, 'There is a reasonable chance the race could be won outright by a female this year, as Jasmin Paris is competing.'

The Pennine Way holds a celebrated place in the history of ultrarunning aside from the Spine races, hosting epic battles for the record – or Fastest Known Time. Most notable are the rivalries between Mike Hartley and Mike Cudahy in the 1980s. Mike's book, *Wild Trails to Far Horizons*, details this time brilliantly. Hartley's time of 2 days, 17 hours and 20 minutes stood for 31 years before being broken by US ultrarunner and Barkley Marathons finisher John Kelly, who set a new record of 2 days, 16 hours and 46 minutes in July 2020. Just a week later, the UK's Damian Hall again broke the record, lowering it to 2 days, 13 hours and 35 minutes. The following spring, Kelly returned to reclaim the record, finishing in 2 days, 10 hours, 4 minutes and 53 seconds. The current women's record is held by Anna Troup, who completed the trail in 3 days and 46 minutes in August 2021, breaking Sabrina Verjee's previous record.

ABOVE Runners finish by kissing the wall of the Border Hotel in Kirk Yetholm.

LAKELAND 100

LAKE DISTRICT NATIONAL PARK, UK

The Lakeland 100 'Ultra Tour of the Lake District' is an establishment in its own right in the English Lake District. Taking in a circumnavigation of the lakeland fells, the route weaves through the National Park's valleys, almost entirely on footpaths and bridleways.

Runners set out from Coniston at 6pm amid a party atmosphere, heading into the evening. The self-navigated route travels south, then takes in a clockwise loop of the Dunnerdale fells, Eskdale, Wasdale and Buttermere to reach the town of Keswick. Matterdale and Haweswater follow, before the home stretch via Kentmere, Ambleside and Elterwater to the finish back in Coniston. Avoiding the busiest tourist hotspots, and exploring many lesser-visited parts of the Lake District National Park, the full route as of 2025 is 164km (102 miles) with around 6,300m (20,669ft) of ascent, a highest point of 664m (2,178ft) at High Kop, and a 40-hour cut-off. Despite the fact that the route doesn't summit any of the high fells, some of the terrain is extremely challenging, including Scarth Gap Pass and Blacksail Pass, considered two of the Lake District's toughest passes.

Entry to the ever-popular Lakeland 100 is by ballot, with the ballot opening for just 48 hours in early September and filling more than enough places for the race the following summer.

RACE STATISTICS

MONTH: July
DISTANCE: 164km (102 miles)
TOTAL ASCENT: 6,300m (20,669ft)
HIGHEST POINT: 664m (2,178ft)
STARTERS 2024: 735 (165 female, 570 male)
FINISHERS 2024: 457 (96 female, 361 male)
TIME ALLOWED: 40hr
FEMALE COURSE RECORD: Beth Pascall 21:29:36 (2016)
MALE COURSE RECORD: Mark Darbyshire 18:45:19 (2024)
FIRST RUN: 2008
ENTRY FEE: £180

WEBSITE:
www.lakeland100.com

Black Sail Pass is considered one of the toughest climbs in the Lakes

Dalemain is the start of the Lakeland 50 race.

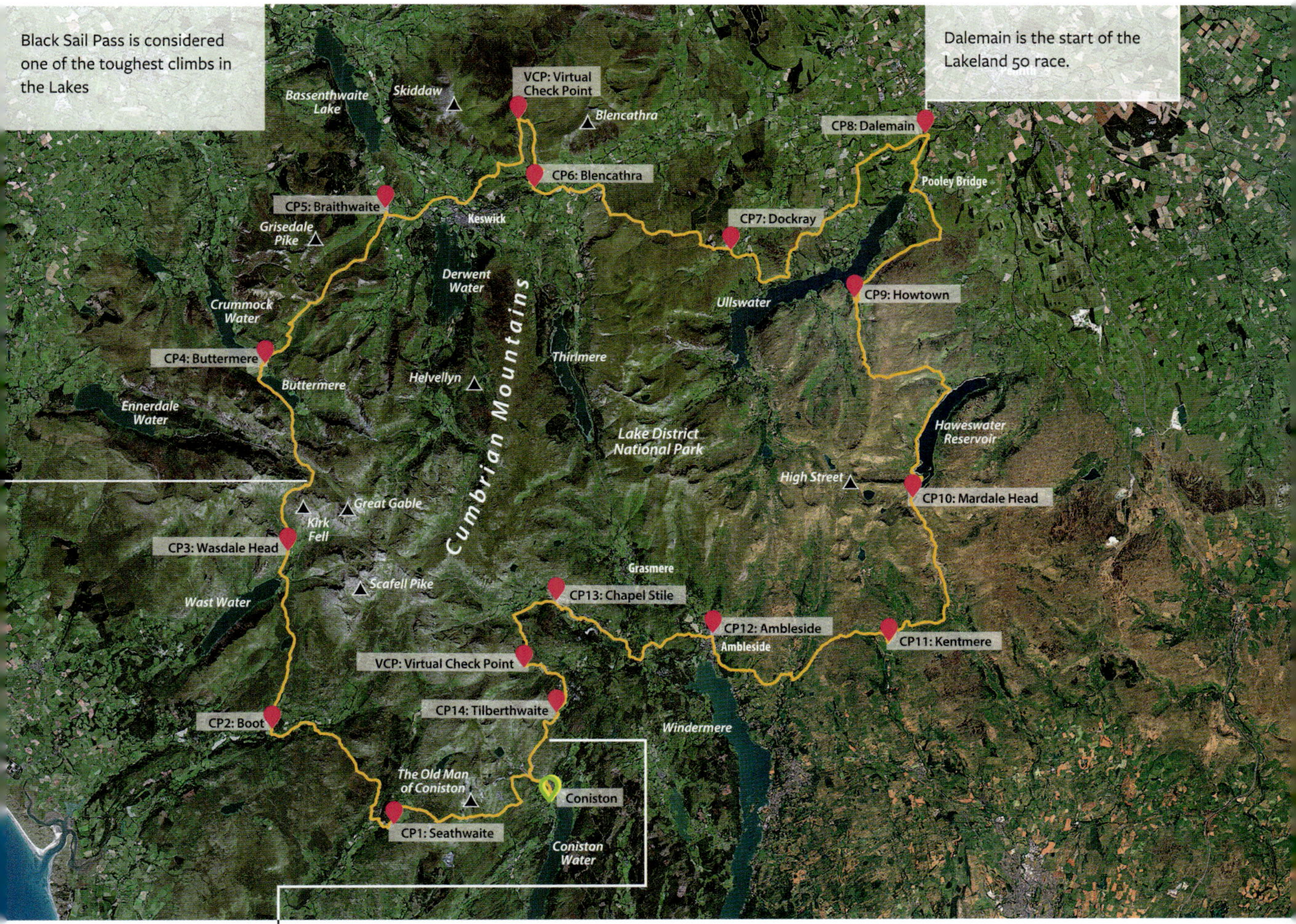

Bassenthwaite Lake
Skiddaw
VCP: Virtual Check Point
Blencathra
CP8: Dalemain
CP6: Blencathra
Pooley Bridge
CP5: Braithwaite
Keswick
CP7: Dockray
Grisedale Pike
Derwent Water
Cumbrian Mountains
Ullswater
CP9: Howtown
Crummock Water
CP4: Buttermere
Thirlmere
Buttermere
Helvellyn
Ennerdale Water
Haweswater Reservoir
Lake District National Park
High Street
CP10: Mardale Head
Great Gable
Kirk Fell
CP3: Wasdale Head
Grasmere
Scafell Pike
CP13: Chapel Stile
Wast Water
CP12: Ambleside
Ambleside
CP11: Kentmere
VCP: Virtual Check Point
CP14: Tilberthwaite
CP2: Boot
Windermere
The Old Man of Coniston
Coniston
CP1: Seathwaite
Coniston Water

Jacob's Ladder – the steps out of the final checkpoint – are named in memory of a runner's son and runners traditionally drop a pound in a bucket here to raise money for the Cancer Trust.

ELEVATION PROFILE

53M (173FT)
664M (2,178FT)
44M (114FT)
53M (173FT)
0.00km/miles
82.37km (51 miles)
164.73km (102 miles)

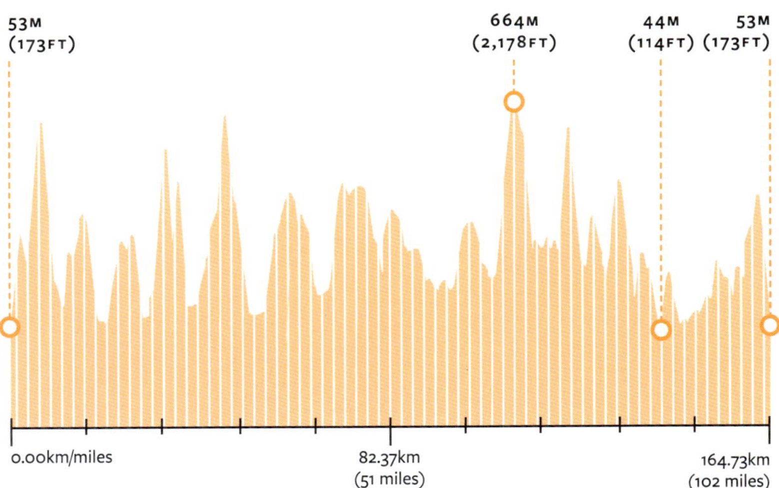

LEFT Andy Berry on his way to winning the 2023 Lakeland 100.

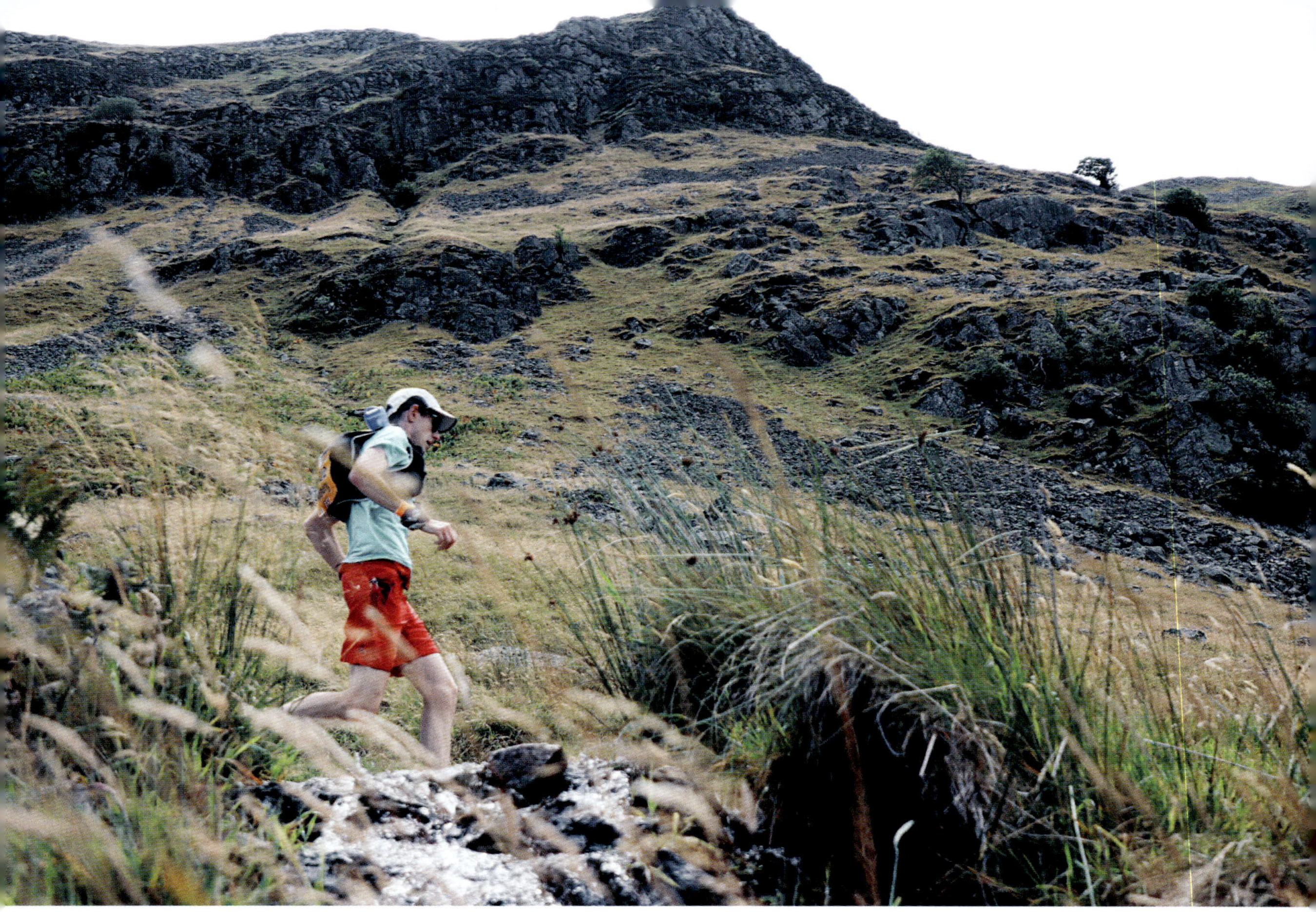

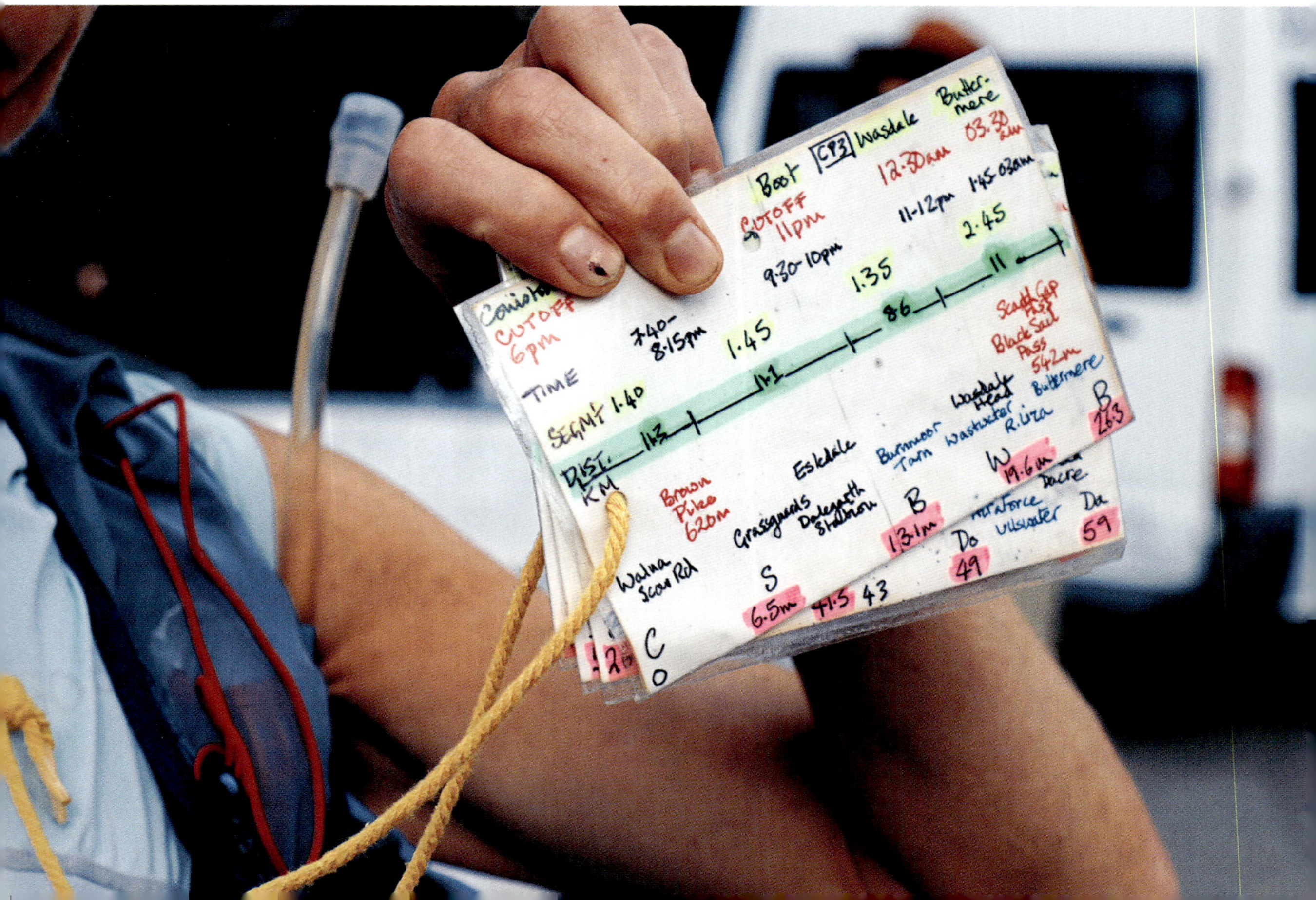
Boot
CP3
Wasdale
Butter-mere
12.30am
03.30am
CUTOFF 11pm
11-12pm
1.45-03am
2.45
9.30-10pm
1.35
86
11
CUTOFF 6pm
7.40-8.15pm
1.45
TIME
SEGMT 1.40
DIST. KM
Brown Pike 620m
Eskdale
Grassguards
Dalegarth Station
Walna Scar Rd
S
6.5m
41.5 43
C
B
13.1m
Burnmoor Tarn
Wasdale Head
Wastwater
W
19.6m
Black Sail Pass 542m
Buttermere
B
26.3
Do
49
Ullswater
Dacre
Da
59

LEFT On the descent to Haweswater during the Lakeland 50.

BELOW LEFT Pace cards at Lakeland 100.

Strict entry criteria mean only runners with sufficient 100-mile and/or mountain ultra experience line up at the start, but still only around 50 per cent of runners finish.

The Lakeland 100 is an unmarked, self-navigated event, meaning no unsightly waymarkers or plastic tape around the route. Digital navigation devices (GPS watches, handheld devices, smartphones) are permitted. Each runner receives a waterproof Road Book to be used in conjunction with their race map. This provides a clear description of the route, with specific guidance on route details and advice on detours around farm buildings or specific points on the course where the track is faint and hard to follow. Fourteen friendly and well-stocked checkpoints offer food, drink, rest and encouragement along the way. As far as mountain 100-milers go, entry to the Lakeland 100 is great value. The entry fee includes:

1. Two nights' camping at race HQ
2. Detailed waterproof Road Book
3. Waterproof Harvey (1:40,000) map of the Lake District with the route and checkpoints pre-marked
4. Well-stocked checkpoints
5. Multi-functional head scarf
6. Car sticker
7. Finishers' t-shirt
8. Quality finishers' medal
9. Free race photo downloads
10. Finishers' meal at race HQ
11. For 50-mile competitors, coach transport to the start at Dalemain
12. Medical support from race medics and physio team
13. Live event monitoring and GPS tracking throughout the event
14. The opportunity to attend the pre-event recce days
15. The chance to be a legend

Founded and run by Marc Laithwaite, a former sports science teacher and multiple Ironman Kona qualifier, the event has an annual theme. In 2024 this was *Top Gun*, with folk decked out, Tom Cruise-style, in jumpsuits and shades. Checkpoints also have their own themes, with volunteers getting creative to give the runners a boost out on the course. Many a sleep-deprived runner has been left wondering whether that was a real unicorn . . .

Checkpoint 14, the final stop, which is located at Tilberthwaite quarry, 4.8km (3 miles) from the finish in Coniston, is a particularly special place. As well as an incredible atmosphere, runners are often rewarded with hot snacks including the legendary cheese toasties. A set of steps leads out of the checkpoint, known as 'Jacob's ladder' in memory of a runner's son, who sadly passed away from cancer. It has become a mark of respect and a race tradition for every runner to place a pound in the bucket, which continues to raise essential funds for the Cancer Trust.

Back in the mid-2000s, Laithwaite was a trail runner himself and also a member of the Achille Ratti climbing club based in Langdale, in the Lake District. Along with some local running friends, he plotted a circular race route that missed out the obvious landmarks and celebrated the National Park's lesser-known gems. In 2008, the first official race was held, with just 60 competitors. Despite not being a financial success, the feedback from runners was so positive the race had to continue, and the following year saw 200 entrants. Today, nearly 2,500 people stand on the start line, and the race has become an institution in ultrarunning, drawing some of the biggest names in the sport. In 2024, top-three men Mark Darbyshire, Gavin Dale and Kim Collison all finished in under 20 hours, with Darbyshire's time of 18:45 setting a new course record. Beth Pascall's women's record of 21:29 has remained untouched since the Western States winner set it in 2016.

OTHER DISTANCES
The Lakeland 50 starts on the day after the 100, taking in the second half of the 100-mile route.
Lakeland 50: 80.5km (50 miles); 2,965m (9,728ft) ascent

ABOVE The checkpoint at Kentmere for both the Lakeland 100 and 50 races.

RIGHT Tom Nicholson went on to finish 2nd in the 2023 Lakeland 50.

50
2153
Tom

ULTRA-TRAIL SNOWDONIA BY UTMB

ERYRI NATIONAL PARK, WALES, UK

Ultra-Trail Snowdonia was first held in 2018 with the aim of creating a UK-based alternative to the big alpine ultras. That first year, of the 46 runners who entered the 100-mile race, only 13 finished– a testament to the race tagline 'beautiful beyond belief, savage beyond reason'. Acquired by UTMB in 2021, the race has grown year-on-year, and is now a celebration of mountain trail running set amidst the spectacular arena of Eryri (Snowdonia) National Park. Drawing around 2,500 runners from across the world, and with a choice of four distances from 25km (15½ miles) to 100 miles, runners have the opportunity to collect Running Stones to aid entry into the main events at UTMB Mont-Blanc in Chamonix, with the top runners in each distance securing a guaranteed place.

Starting at midday on the Friday of race weekend, runners in the 100-mile race are introduced to Eryri with an ascent of the mighty Yr Wyddfa (Snowdon) almost from the start. From the fingerstone, just short of the summit of Wales's highest mountain, the route descends the steep, stepped Pyg Track to Pen-y-Pass, before climbing over the Glyder and Carneddau ranges in a series of steep, rocky climbs, often bordering on scrambles, and technical bouldery or scree-filled descents. There's a short stretch of easier running alongside Llyn Cowlyd before competitors tackle Moel Siabod, Moelwyn Mawr and the Welsh Matterhorn – Cnicht.

RACE STATISTICS

MONTH: May
DISTANCE: 168km (104 miles)
TOTAL ASCENT: 9,500m (31,168ft)
HIGHEST POINT: 1,066m (3,497ft)
STARTERS 2024: 260 (21 female, 239 male)
FINISHERS 2024: 99 (8 female, 91 male)
TIME ALLOWED: 48hr
FEMALE COURSE RECORD: Emma Stuart 28:23:29 (2023)
MALE COURSE RECORD: Mark Darbyshire 23:41:13 (2024)
FIRST RUN: 2018
ENTRY FEE: £279

WEBSITE:
snowdonia.utmb.world

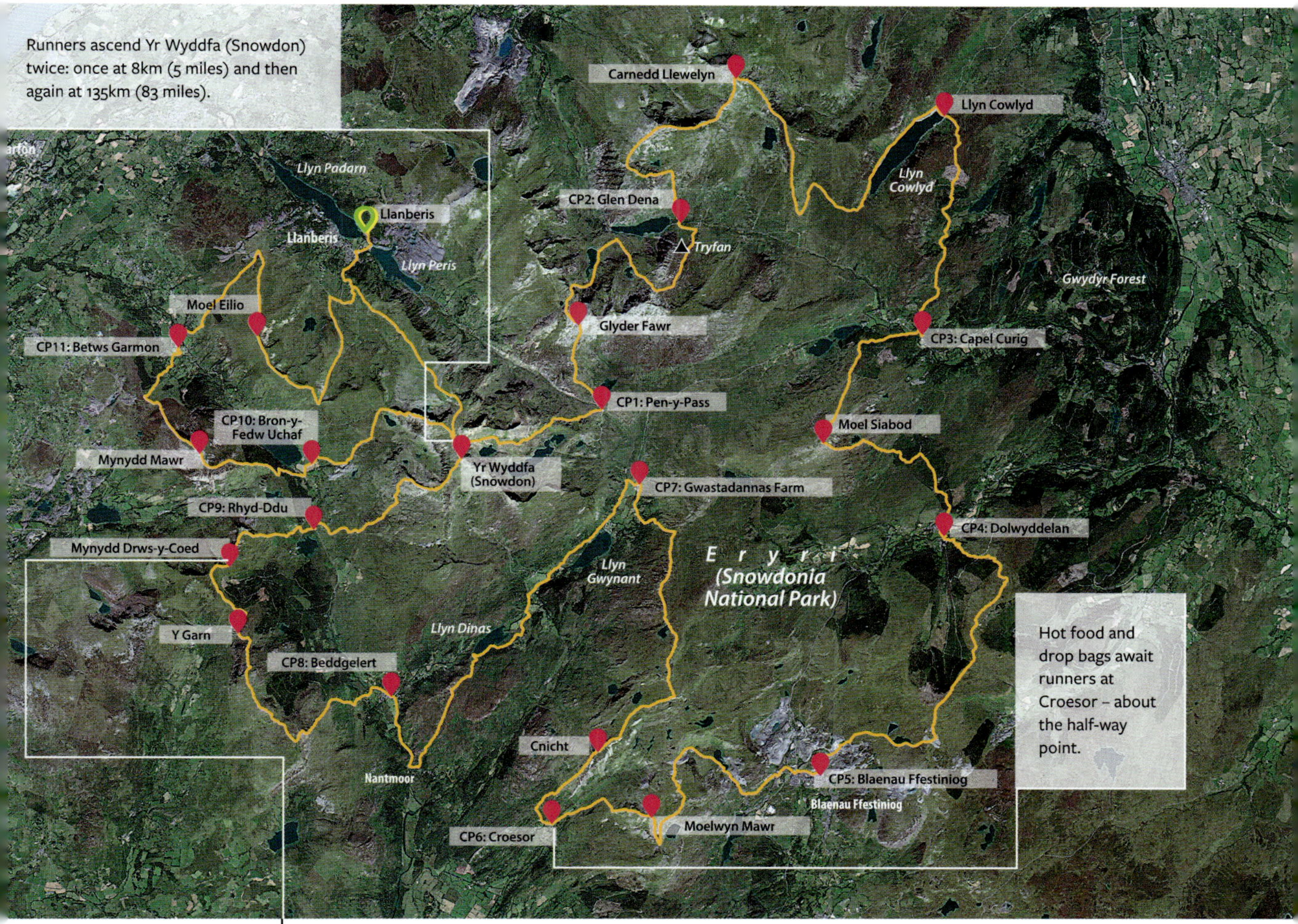

Runners ascend Yr Wyddfa (Snowdon) twice: once at 8km (5 miles) and then again at 135km (83 miles).
Carnedd Llewelyn
Llyn Cowlyd
Llyn Cowlyd
Llyn Padarn
Llanberis
Llanberis
Llyn Peris
CP2: Glen Dena
Tryfan
Gwydyr Forest
Moel Eilio
CP11: Betws Garmon
Glyder Fawr
CP3: Capel Curig
CP1: Pen-y-Pass
CP10: Bron-y-Fedw Uchaf
Moel Siabod
Mynydd Mawr
Yr Wyddfa (Snowdon)
CP7: Gwastadannas Farm
CP9: Rhyd-Ddu
CP4: Dolwyddelan
Mynydd Drws-y-Coed
Llyn Gwynant
Eryri (Snowdonia National Park)
Y Garn
Llyn Dinas
Hot food and drop bags await runners at Croesor – about the half-way point.
CP8: Beddgelert
Cnicht
Nantmoor
CP5: Blaenau Ffestiniog
Blaenau Ffestiniog
CP6: Croesor
Moelwyn Mawr

Knife-edge scramble along the Nantlle Ridge above Clogwyn Marchnad.

ELEVATION PROFILE

105M (344FT)
14M (45FT)
1,066M (3,497FT)
105M (344FT)
0.00km/miles
80.80km (50 miles)
168km (104 miles)

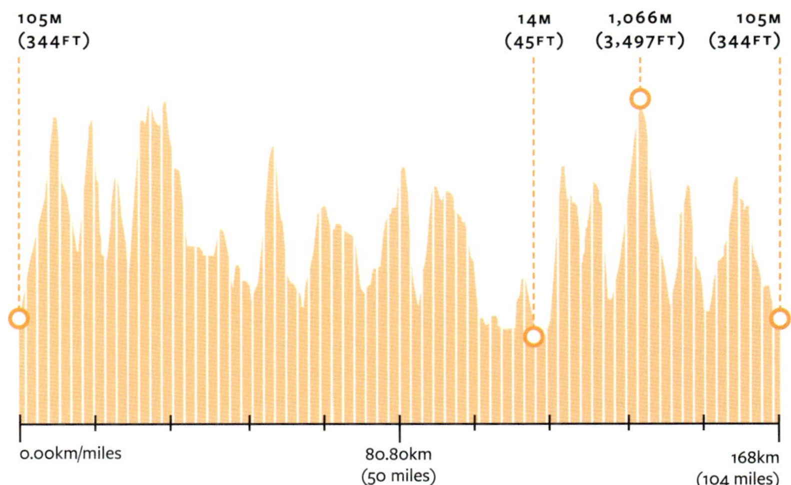

LEFT Climbing Pen yr Ole Wen with Tryfan and the Glyders in the background. The 100-mile and 100-km routes both take on this climb.

TERREX
UTS 100M
8
CORDIS
TERREX

Boggy, featureless terrain eventually gives way to the pretty village of Beddgelert, reached via the spectacular Aberglaslyn Gorge. The final miles of the race are perhaps even more savage than the opening ones, taking in the long slog up Moel Hebog and a scrambly section of the knife-edge Nantlle Ridge before a second ascent up Yr Wyddfa. Only two summits remain – Mynydd Mawr and Moel Eilio – both steep climbs and descents on legs that have already conquered nearly 160km (100 miles) and over 9,000m (29,500ft) of climbing, before the final couple of easy miles back to the National Slate Museum in Llanberis. Combining steep climbs and descents, technical terrain, pathless bog and often wide-ranging conditions, the UTS races are fantastic mountain adventures, well known as one of the toughest 100-milers, if not *the* toughest, on the UTMB race calendar.

The 2024 race took place in beautiful weather, with the heat taking some runners by surprise. From the 260 starters in the 100-mile race, only 99 finished with the final finisher crossing the line just short of 47 hours 30 minutes. Winning man, Mark Darbyshire, put out a stunning performance, finishing in a new course record of 23 hours 41 minutes – only the second person to finish the race in under 24 hours after previous record holder Josh Wade (32:51 in 2023). Having failed to finish the previous year, and having been in the cancelled 2022 race, Darbyshire was keen to conquer the course and did it in style. Second-placed Andy Berry crossed the line more than an hour and a half later. Winning woman in 2024 was Rachel Fawcett,

PREVIOUS PAGES Cordis Hall (USA) descending from Yr Wyddfa (Snowdon) during the 2024 UTS 100M.

ABOVE Challenging weather conditions during one of the many mountain ascents.

OTHER DISTANCES

UTS 100K: 103km (64 miles); 6,400m (20,997ft) ascent

UTS 50K: 55km (34 miles); 3,300m (10,827ft) ascent

Eryri 25K: 25km (15½ miles); 1,300m (4,265ft) ascent

UTS Mini for ages 3–16: approx. 2.5km (1½ miles)

who crossed the line in 34:10:57, claiming first overall finisher in the 50–54 age category. Emma Stuart, winner of the 2023 women's race and current women's record holder, described UTS 100M as 'probably the hardest race I've done'.

The race village, located close to the National Stale Museum in Llanberis, is typical of UTMB races, buzzing with trail running-related excitement, and with a great selection of food, coffee and kit vendors as well as race registration.

While the 100-mile and 100km events offer super-tough mountain challenges, the 50km is the most popular, selling out quickly every year. Perfect for those desiring a less lengthy adventure, the ERYRI 25km race and ERYRI Mini kids' race were both added in 2023.

There's no doubt UTS by UTMB is a special race, capturing the magic of Eryri's mountains and the ultra trail spirit. In the words of UK Event Director, Hayden Arrowsmith:

> 'Hosting Ultra-Trail Snowdonia in the magnificent Eryri National Park is incredibly important to our global trail running community. The mountains and landscapes are stunning and create strong emotions among our participants who travel from all over the world to be here. For many the experience is life-changing, and we want our participants to explore what Eryri has to offer, discover the local communities and enjoy their time within the region. Due to UTS' global profile, we see an increase in our international guests year-on-year, while still retaining the authentic and unique challenge from the very first edition. Our ambition is for UTS to be a world-leading and sustainable trail event, which establishes a positive legacy for the communities we work with in Wales.'

RIGHT Start of UTS 50, Llanberis.

WEST HIGHLAND WAY RACE

MILNGAVIE TO FORT WILLIAM, SCOTLAND, UK

The West Highland Way Race follows the entire route of the West Highland Way, Scotland's most popular long distance trail. Opened in 1980, the trail runs for just under 160km (100 miles) from Milngavie, on the outskirts of Glasgow, northwards to Fort William at the foot of Ben Nevis, the highest mountain in Great Britain.

Early on, local running clubs used the WHW for relays, but in 1985 two men – Duncan Watson and Bobby Shields – undertook the first head-to-head race along the full distance of the trail. Realizing, as they ran neck-and-neck, that self-destruction was the most likely outcome of the endeavour, they eventually agreed to run together, reaching Fort William in a little under 18 hours and setting the scene for the official WHW Race.

In 1987, there were 11 starters and 7 finishers but following the turn of the millennium, under the directorship of Dario Melaragni and Stan Milne, the race grew steadily and by 2010 was routinely attracting over 100 runners each year. Today, the race is capped at 300 runners and fills to capacity every year, although not all will get to the start line.

Other than 10km (6 miles) of road, the event is held entirely on trail. Runners leave Milngavie at 1am and, from 2025, require a crew of at least two in order to take part – some of the checkpoints have large distances between them, including one of over 32km (20 miles).

RACE STATISTICS

MONTH: June
DISTANCE: 153km (95 miles)
TOTAL ASCENT: 4,267m (14,000ft)
HIGHEST POINT: 551m (1,808ft)
STARTERS 2024: 217 (21 female, 196 male)
FINISHERS 2024: 179 (13 female, 166 male)
TIME ALLOWED: 35hr
FEMALE COURSE RECORD: Lucy Colquhoun 17:16:20 (2007)
MALE COURSE RECORD: Rob Sinclair 13:41:08 (2017)
FIRST RUN: 1985
ENTRY FEE: £120

WEBSITE:
www.westhighlandwayrace.org

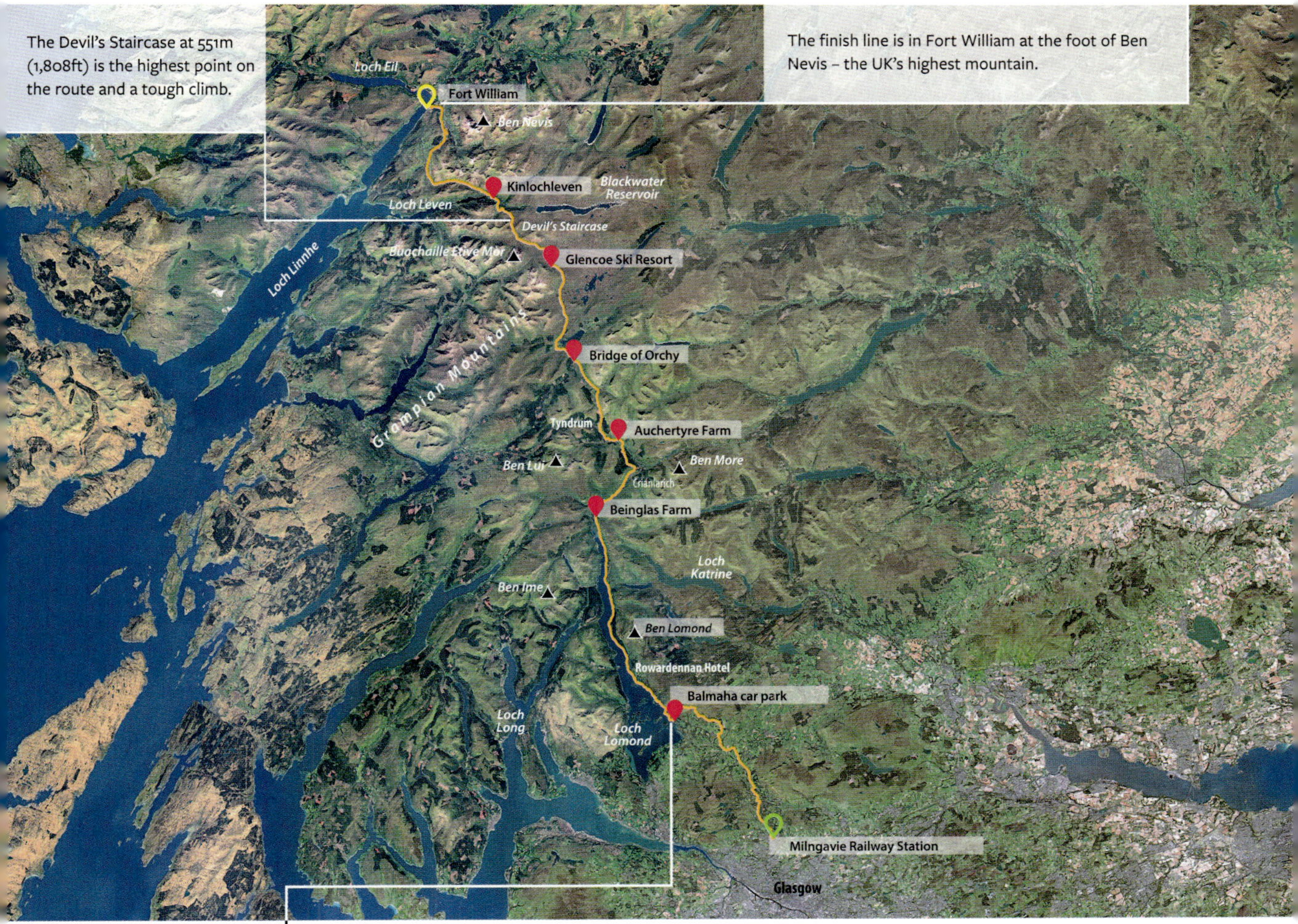

The Devil's Staircase at 551m (1,808ft) is the highest point on the route and a tough climb.
The finish line is in Fort William at the foot of Ben Nevis – the UK's highest mountain.
Loch Eil
Fort William
Ben Nevis
Kinlochleven
Blackwater Reservoir
Loch Leven
Devil's Staircase
Buachaille Etive Mòr
Glencoe Ski Resort
Loch Linnhe
Grampian Mountains
Bridge of Orchy
Tyndrum
Auchertyre Farm
Ben Lui
Ben More
Crianlarich
Beinglas Farm
Loch Katrine
Ben Ime
Ben Lomond
Rowardennan Hotel
Balmaha car park
Loch Long
Loch Lomond
Milngavie Railway Station
Glasgow

Conic Hill is the first notable climb on the trail, offering great views over Loch Lomond.

ELEVATION PROFILE

50M (164FT)
551M (1,808FT)
5M (16FT)
0.00km/miles
76.56km (47½ miles)
153.13km (95 miles)

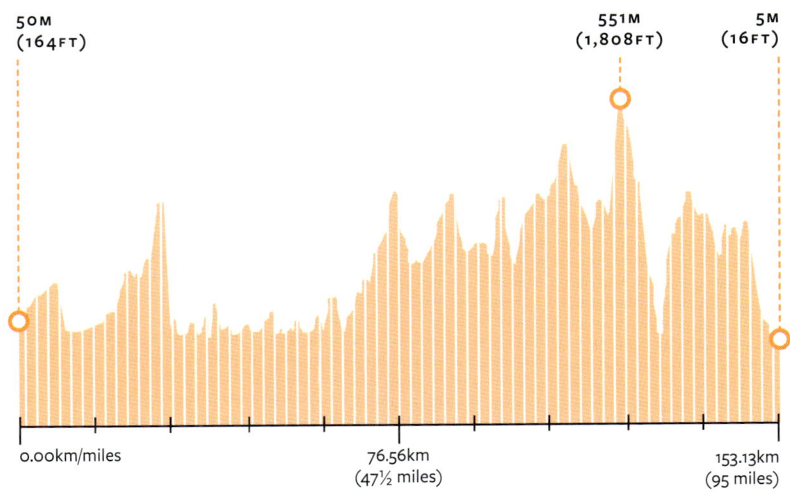

LEFT Duncan Watson and Bobby Shields arriving in Fort William in the first WHW race (1985).

Checkpoints are located at Balmaha (30.5km/19 miles), Beinglas Farm (67.5km/42 miles), Auchtertyre (82km/51 miles), Bridge of Orchy (96.5km/60 miles), Glencoe Ski Centre (114km/71 miles), Kinlochleven (130km/81 miles), and the finish at Fort William (153km/95 miles). From Balmaha, the route runs through Loch Lomond and the Trossachs National Park, climbing Conic Hill before dropping to the water's edge to trace the eastern shores of Loch Lomond. The Old Military Road takes runners through forest at Crianlarich, then along Strath Fillan to Tyndrum. Continuing north, through the Grampian Mountains, the graceful, pyramidal peak of Beinn Dorain – a Munro with a height of 1,076m (3,530ft) – rises above the Bridge of Orchy. Passing Black Mount at the edge of the watery expanses of Rannoch Moor, runners reach Glencoe Ski Centre, travelling down Glen Coe before climbing up the Devil's Staircase to cross to Kinlochleven. The final miles run through forest in Glen Nevis, finishing in the centre of Fort William.

As with a lot of ultras that have been running for many years, several people have clocked up double-digit finishes at the West Highland Way Race. At the time of writing, Neil MacRitchie and Fiona Rennie both have 17 finishes, and Adrian Stott, Jim Drummond and the late Tony Thistlethwaite all have 15 finishes.

The race is currently directed by Ian Beattie, a multi-time WHW race finisher. Race crew is entirely volunteers, and the race has always been run as a non-profit. Runners are guaranteed warm, enthusiastic support throughout the race, and each finisher receives an engraved crystal goblet as a memento of the race.

OTHER DISTANCES

A low-key alternative to the popular and quickly sold-out WHW Race is the West Highland Way Challenge Race, which takes in the full length of the WHW but from north to south, with the option of adding an ascent and descent of Ben Nevis beforehand. The race is directed by Jim Drummond and can be run entirely without support, with food and drink available at nine checkpoints along the way.

FAR LEFT Rob Sinclair at the foot of the Devil's Staircase in 2017, the year he set the course record.

LEFT Dario's post overlooking Loch Lomond. It's a memorial and tribute to former WHW race organizer Dario Melaragni, who died in 2009.

ABOVE Lone runner at the top of the Devil's Staircase looking towards the Mamores.

'The race makes no claims to be the toughest, hardest, or most scenic race on the planet,' says Ian. 'The organizing team simply seeks, while trying to move with the times, to maintain what is a unique and iconic challenge on one of Britain's original and most spectacular long-distance trails. Running the West Highland Way is achievable by anyone with a love of the outdoors who wants to experience Scotland at its finest.'

LAPLAND ARCTIC ULTRA

ÖVERKALIX, SWEDEN

Partner race to the legendary Yukon Arctic Ultra in Canada (see page 160), the Lapland Arctic Ultra is a relatively new addition to the world of winter ultras, with the first edition taking place in 2022. Race director Robert Pollhammer had been organizing the Yukon Arctic Ultra for 20 years and had always been tempted to organize a similar event in Europe. With its established winter sports network and extensive snowmobile and cross-country ski trails, Sweden was a natural choice, and a friend suggested Robert check out the Överkalix and Gällivare municipalities in particular. There he found nature provided everything required for a truly great race: plenty of snow, frozen lakes, rivers, swamps and endless forests. The terrain isn't alpine but it's also not flat, while temperatures are low but not lower than -35°C (-31°F) – much easier to handle than the -50°C (-58°F) sometimes experienced in the Yukon.

The race follows a ten-day, non-stop format through the heart of Swedish Lapland, Europe's last remaining wilderness. Competitors who wish to join the race with no prior experience can take part in a training course just before the race, making it a perfect event for anyone getting into non-stop winter ultras. The race has been embraced by the local community, with locals supportive and quickly becoming part of the race 'family'.

RACE STATISTICS

MONTH: March
DISTANCE: 503km (312½ miles)
TOTAL ASCENT: 4,534m (14,875ft)
HIGHEST POINT: 440m (1,444ft)
STARTERS 2024: 19 (3 female, 16 male)
FINISHERS 2024: 15 (2 female, 13 male)
TIME ALLOWED: 240hr
FEMALE COURSE RECORD: Laura Trentani 158:54:00 (2022)
MALE COURSE RECORD: Thierry Corbarieu 142:47:00 (2024)
FIRST RUN: 2022
ENTRY FEE: €2,650

WEBSITE:
lapland.arcticultra.de

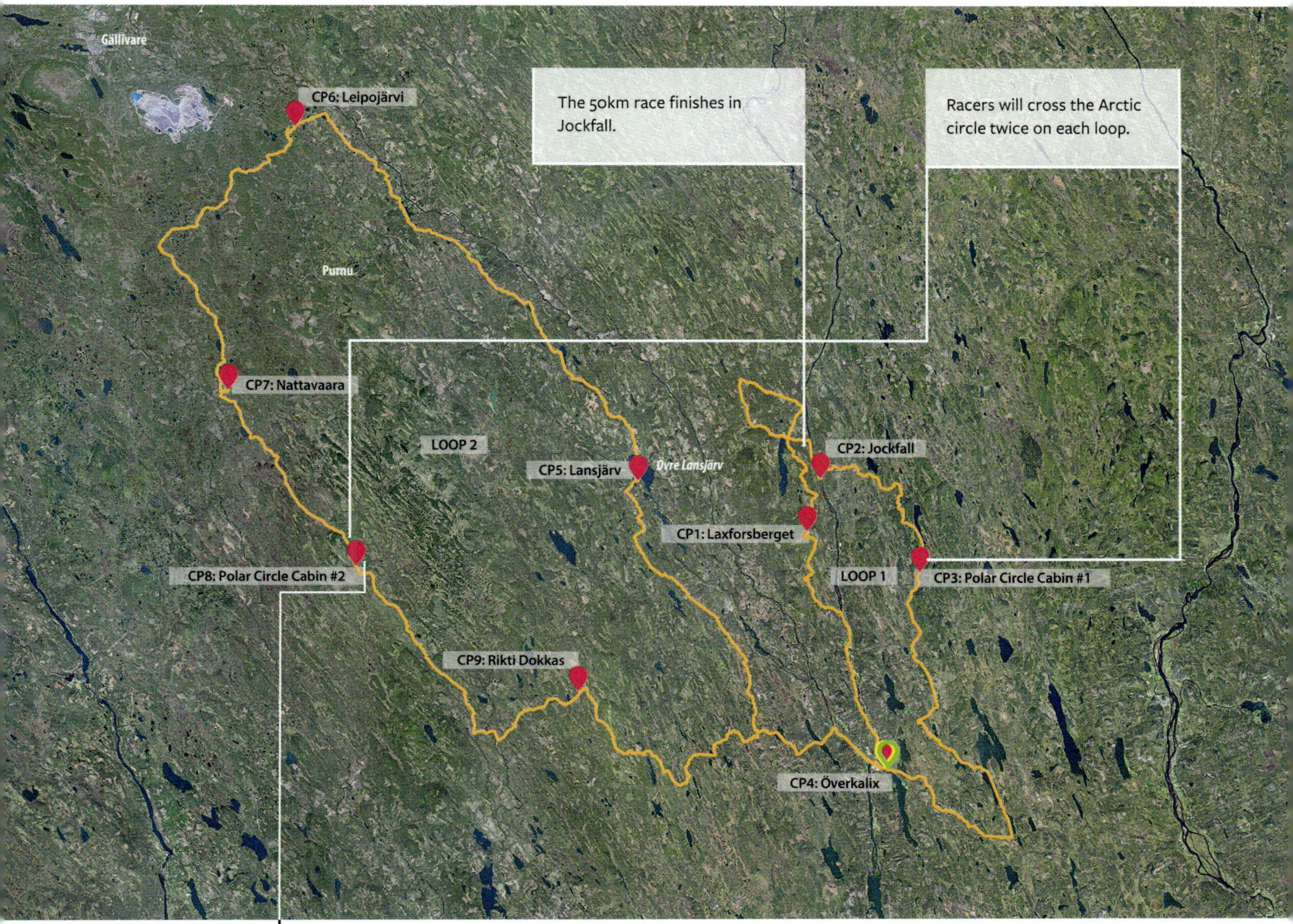

Gällivare
CP6: Leipojärvi
The 50km race finishes in Jockfall.
Racers will cross the Arctic circle twice on each loop.
Purnu
CP7: Nattavaara
LOOP 2
CP5: Lansjärv
Övre Lansjärv
CP2: Jockfall
CP1: Laxforsberget
LOOP 1
CP8: Polar Circle Cabin #2
CP3: Polar Circle Cabin #1
CP9: Rikti Dokkas
CP4: Överkalix

Hot meals await competitors at all checkpoints except for Polar Circle Cabin 2.

ELEVATION PROFILE

36M (118FT)
440M (1,444FT)
36M
36M (118FT)
0.00km/miles
256.79km (159½ miles)
503km (312½ miles)

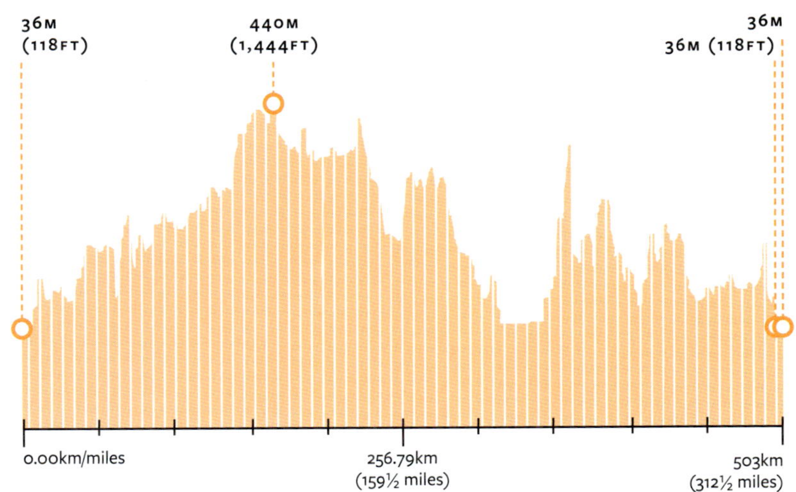

LEFT Frozen forests at Laxforsberget.

HARRIET AND KARL'S RACE FOOD FOR THE LAPLAND ULTRA

- Super-charged coffee-choc mix, mega high-calorie drink (with butter).
- Breakfast of coconut and chia porridge (with butter).
- More coffee-choc, at regular intervals, with accompanying chocolate biscuits.
- Dinner and lunch were both a pepperoni-boosted Huel meal (and butter).
- Pudding, a custard-based dessert with dried fruit (that possibly also had butter in it).
- Two servings of Huel meal replacement powders to be tactically applied as needed.
- Our daily allowance of peppermint teabags, which rapidly became the black-market currency of choice.
- Daily snack bags including chocolate, fruit and nuts, all small enough to allow for easy defrosting in the mouth before chewing, thus avoiding the need for mid-race dentistry.

Competitors say it's that family-like atmosphere of a small race with a highly motivated crew that makes the event special, and which they really enjoy. Add this to the specific joys and challenges of a winter ultra, including the opportunity to race beneath the stunning Northern Lights, and the Lapland Arctic Ultra is a truly special event.

Racers can choose to run, mountain bike or cross-country ski. The first loop sets out from Överkalix, heading north and then back again to Överkalix, crossing the Arctic Circle twice. This is the finish for the 185km (115 miles) race, however the 500km (311 miles) competitors continue onto a second, different loop of 315km (196 miles), again starting out to the north and then coming back to Överkalix. On both race distances the athletes follow snowmobile tracks crossing rivers and lakes and winding through vast forests.

The 20km (12½ miles) and 50km (31 miles) races start in Överkalix, following linear routes to Rödupp (20km) and Jockfall (50km).

All distances follow waymarked trails; however, markers can be covered either by fresh snow or in windy conditions, so GPS devices are recommended in case racers need to navigate.

Intrepid ultrarunning wife and husband team Harriet and Karl Shields are veterans of the sport, having completed the full Winter Spine Race (see page 68) – Harriet has completed the full, Challenger North and Challenger South distances at both the Summer and Winter Spine Races – as well as many other long and very long ultras. Both in their 50s and having worked and played together for a long time, tackling epic, cake-fuelled endurance challenges, usually together, is their retirement hobby.

In his blog on their exploits, Karl says their race plan was to 'get from A to Z with 30 minutes to spare having had a load of sleep on the way.

OTHER DISTANCES

185km (115 miles); 1,700m (5,577ft) ascent
50km (31 miles); 450m (1,476ft) ascent
20km (12½ miles); 20m (66ft) ascent

Anything faster than this was good to have as contingency but our drop dead plan gave us a clear view on where we must get to, and leave, at any stage in the race in order for the train to stay firmly on the tracks.' Training involved running, hiking with heavy packs, strength training and a considerable amount of tyre dragging, simulating the specific demands of hauling a paulk during the race. They took a two-person freestanding Black Diamond mountain tent and Arctic down sleeping bags for the nights.

Arriving ten days before the start of the race, the couple participated in the four-day training course, 'led by Per Johansson, a local ranger and guide who did a great job of alerting us to the hazards of the environment along with teaching good camp craft. We covered cold weather dangers, choosing locations and making camp, stove use (and misuse!), snowshoes, making fires, and even the process and etiquette required when nature calls. Repetition to ensure skills became more second nature worked well and when we went into our first wild camp night we felt a lot more prepared for having done the course than if we had not.'

> 'That was an amazing journey. We loved most of it and hated just a little, and for an ultra endurance event that is a proper result. Never before in a race of this nature and duration had we felt so good, or so content, and yes, that was due in part to our plan and attitude, but mostly due to the amazing place, and the amazing people. Swedish Lapland, Europe's last great wilderness is simply breathtaking in scale and scenery, and I would encourage anyone to get there to experience it for themselves.'

Harriet and Karl finished the Lapland Arctic Ultra a full 12 hours before the race cut-off, crossing the line as the Northern Lights blazed across the sky. 'How Robert arranged that I will never know,' writes Karl.

PREVIOUS PAGES The frozen terrain at Kalixalven.

RIGHT The Rikti-Dokkas check point near the end of the long race.

OTHER EUROPEAN HIGHLIGHTS

OH MEU DEUS ULTRA TRAIL

SEIA MUNICIPAL PARK, SERRA DA ESTRELA, PORTUGAL

RACE STATISTICS

MONTH: June
DISTANCE: 158.3km (98½ miles)
TOTAL ASCENT: 8,987m (29,485ft)
TIME ALLOWED: 34hr

WEBSITE: www.horizontes.pt/oh-meu-deus

'Oh Meu Deus' translates to 'Oh My God'; something you may hear competitors exclaim in response to the stunningly beautiful scenery, or mutter at the base of yet another tough ascent. The route is almost entirely off-road, exploring a big loop of Portugal's largest, oldest and highest National Park. The area has achieved Biogenetic Reservation status for the diversity of plants and animals; you may not see the wolves, boars, otters, foxes and rabbits as they hide away but do look out for golden eagles and black kites in the skies. Expect hot weather, with temperatures up to around 35°C (95°F), but be prepared for cold at the higher altitudes and occasional rainstorms.

It's a tough course, continually climbing or descending, with the largest climb summiting Estrela (1,993m/6,539ft) near the end of the race. The 2024 race was the fastest yet, but only four runners managed a sub 24-hour time. The OMD160 course records, both set in 2024, are held by Goreti Correira (29:14:25 hrs) and Igor Lysyi (21:01:45 hrs).

You can also race 100km (62 miles), 50km (31 miles) or 20km (12½ miles) loops. If the OMD160 feels a bit short, try the Viriatos which adds an extra 40km (25 miles) loop and another 2,000m (6,562ft) of ascent at the end of the OMD160.

SWISS PEAKS

VALAIS, SWITZERLAND

RACE STATISTICS

MONTH: August–September
DISTANCE: 380km (236 miles)
TOTAL ASCENT: 25,900m (84,974ft)
TIME ALLOWED: 159hr

WEBSITE: www.swisspeaks.ch

Since its inception in 2017 Swiss Peaks has offered runners a chance to explore the glaciers, lakes and mountains of the Swiss canton of Valais. There really is something for every runner, with courses ranging from a doable half-marathon to an almost inconceivable 700km (435 miles) trail with 49,000m (160,000ft) of ascent, which claims to be the longest and toughest race in the world. All the routes are single stage; the clock starts at the beginning and stops when you finish. All the trails are waymarked, with amazing aid stations and wonderful views.

The 380km (236 miles) trail is the flagship event, starting in Oberwald and traversing the Valais to Lac Leman, running on technical Alpine trails throughout. The climbs and descents are continuous and unrelenting; you'll have ascended 27,251m (89,406ft) and descended 28,253m (92,694ft) by the end, finishing anywhere from the course record of around 80hrs to the 159hr time limit.

RIGHT Stunning scenery of Lac de Moiry on the Swiss Peaks race.

L'ÉCHAPPÉE BELLE

BELLEDONNE MASSIF, FRANCE

RACE STATISTICS

MONTH: August
DISTANCE: 152km (94½ miles)
TOTAL ASCENT: 11,390m (37,369ft)
TIME ALLOWED: 54hr

WEBSITE: www.lechappeebelledonne.com

L'Échappée Belle offers runners five distances in the Belledonne region of southeast France. The longest, known as the Intégrale, is a complete crossing of the Belledonne massif, running high on technical and inaccessible trails from Vizille (Isère) to Aiguebelle (Savoie). The route climbs 15 passes over 2,000m (6,500ft), runs the shores of 30 high-altitude lakes and traverses 4 panoramic ridges. You'll share this wild Alpine trail with chamois, ibex and 699 other runners. François D'Haene's course record is sub 24 hours, but most runners will be out adventuring for two nights.

Florent Hubert, president of the Association l'Échappée Belle, says, 'Welcome to Belledonne, here we sow with courage and perseverance and we reap wonder!'

GRAND RAID DES PYRÉNÉES

HAUTES-PYRÉNÉES, FRANCE

RACE STATISTICS

MONTH: August
DISTANCE: 163.3km (101½ miles)
TOTAL ASCENT: 9,843m (32,293ft)
TIME ALLOWED: 49hr

WEBSITE: www.grandraidpyrenees.com

Known simply as GRP and described as one of the most legendary and demanding races on the world ultra-trail circuit, the Ultra Tour explores the Hautes-Pyrénées. The little village of Vielle-Aure, which hosts the race, has a population significantly smaller than the number of runners; the locals embrace the event and have contributed to its growth, success and refreshing amateur spirit. There are six distances to test yourself on, from the 160km (100 miles) Ultra Tour to the 43km (26¾ miles) Tour du Néouvielle, all covering technical mountain terrain, high-altitude trails and incredible scenery.

The Grand Raid des Pyrénées is one of the ten World Trail Majors. It features significantly more ascent than any of the other races in the series.

LEFT The first big climb of the 2023 L'Échappée Belle Skyrace du Rocher Blanc.

RIGHT Martin Pfeffer racing through Motovun on the Istria 100 by UTMB.

ULTRA TOUR MONTE ROSA

GRÄCHEN, MATTER VALLEY, SWITZERLAND

RACE STATISTICS

MONTH: September
DISTANCE: 171km (106 miles)
TOTAL ASCENT: 11,600m (38,058ft)
TIME ALLOWED: 60hr

WEBSITE: www.ultratourmonterosa.com

Founded by legendary ultrarunner and five-time UTMB winner Lizzy Hawke, Ultra Tour Monte Rosa (UTMR) circumnavigates the Monte Rosa massif, the second-highest mountain range in the Alps. The main event is a 171km (106 miles) race with 11,600m (38,058ft) of elevation gain – significantly more than other well-known races of a similar distance, including UTMB Mont-Blanc. Runners can opt to complete the distance either non-stop, or over four days, breaking it down into more manageable sections while still covering substantial distances and ascents each day.

The UTMR route follows the Tour de Monte Rosa, a famous hiking circuit that loops around the Monte Rosa massif, crossing the borders between Switzerland and Italy. Key points along the route include Zermatt and Grächen (both Switzerland), and Macugnaga (Italy). Passing through magnificent alpine landscapes as well as delightful *Walser* hamlets and villages, runners are treated to gorgeous views across Alpine meadows to the surrounding mountains. Many of them top 4,000m (13,100ft), including the iconic Matterhorn. Underfoot, the terrain is technical and challenging, taking in high mountain passes, technical ridgelines, rocky trails and even glaciers – spikes for traction on icy and snowy surfaces are often required. It involves steep climbs and descents with sections reaching 3,000m (9,800ft), exposing runners to high-altitude conditions and the possibility of dramatic changes in weather, heightened by the race's timing in early autumn.

ISTRIA 100 BY UTMB

UMAG, ISTRIAN PENINSULA, CROATIA

RACE STATISTICS

MONTH: April
DISTANCE: 169km (105 miles)
TOTAL ASCENT: 6,600m (21,654ft)
TIME ALLOWED: 45hr

WEBSITE: istria.utmb.world

The five different distances offered explore the coast, forest and mountains of the Istrian peninsula, in northwestern Croatia. The point-to-point courses make the most of the terrain, taking you on a journey that will include coasteering, medieval towns, deep forests, muddy valleys, canyons and many beautiful panoramas; it's a stunning place to race! The flagship 169km (105 miles) race runs coast to coast across the peninsula, climbing to the highest point in the area, Učka mountain, before speeding down to finish in Umag. Jim Walmsley ran 17:40:34 in 2023 and Ragna Cathelijne Debats ran 20:14:52 in 2022, but most runners finish between 28 and 32 hours.

Istria 100 is one of the UTMB World Series races, with top-three finishers winning an entry to run at the series finals, UTMB Mont-Blanc.

MOZART 100 BY UTMB

SALZBURGER LAND, AUSTRIA

RACE STATISTICS

MONTH: June
DISTANCE: 119km (74 miles)
TOTAL ASCENT: 5,800m (19,029ft)
TIME ALLOWED: 23hr

WEBSITE: mozart.utmb.world

The UNESCO World Heritage city of Salzburg provides culture, beauty and access to some awesome trails. The Mozart 100 runs the shores of Lake Wolfgang and reaches to 1,471m (4,826ft) on the Zwölferhorn mountain. Participants will run sweeping gravel trails, technical mountain paths, airy ridgelines and lush forest, finishing in the stunning old town. The weekend of running has five races from 23km (14¼ miles) to 119km (74 miles) to choose from.

Mozart 100 is one of the UTMB World Series races; top-three finishers will win an entry to run at the series finals, UTMB Mont-Blanc.

TRANSYLVANIA 100

TRANSYLVANIA, ROMANIA

RACE STATISTICS

MONTH: May
DISTANCE: 103km (64 miles)
TOTAL ASCENT: 6,444m (21,142ft)
TIME ALLOWED: 36hr

WEBSITE: www.transylvania100k.com

Starting in the shadow of Dracula's Castle, in the village of Bran, the Transylvania 100 explores one of the most beautiful and mysterious regions of Eastern Europe. The approximately 100km (62 miles) route traverses the Bucegi Range, following one long loop of twisting singletrack, ancient forest trails, mountain plateaus and windswept ridges. If you'd prefer, there are 80km (49¾ miles), 50km (31 miles), 30km (18½ miles) and 20km (12½ miles) routes to race.

2025 marked the tenth anniversary of the event. During that time more than 10,000 competitors from around 60 countries worldwide took part.

TRANSVULCANIA

LA PALMA, CANARY ISLANDS

RACE STATISTICS

MONTH: May
DISTANCE: 73km (45 miles)
TOTAL ASCENT: 4,350m (14,272ft)
TIME ALLOWED: 16hr

WEBSITE: www.transvulcania.com

The volcanic island of La Palma is covered with prehistoric forest, and light pollution is controlled, so it's an amazing place for star-gazing. In 2002 UNESCO declared the whole island a World Biosphere Reserve, a learning place for sustainable development.

The trail crosses the island from Fuencaliente Lighthouse on the southernmost tip, running north along the Ruta del Bastón (GR 131), to the western coast at Puerto de Tazacorte. The final section takes you up and inland on the GR 130, Camino Real de la Costa, to the finish at Los Llanos de Aridane.

This is one of the hardest trail races around. The first 17km (10½ miles) takes you from sea level to 1,827m (5,994ft), a small descent creates another big climb to Roque de los Muchachos at 2,421m (7,943ft), the highest point of the island, then it's a quad-busting descent to the sea. The gravel trails are hard and technical, but the scenery is beautiful; you'll often climb through the clouds on the highest points of the route which is spectacular.

It's a super-competitive race and, although the majority of runners finish in between 12 and 14 hours, the records are held by Luis Alberto Hernando who ran 6:52:39 in 2015 and Ruth Croft who ran 8:02:49 in 2024.

There is also a marathon or half-marathon on the same day and a Vertical KM a couple of days before if you fancy a warm-up.

LEFT Manuel Schönhuber at Nockstein during the Mozart 100.

THE KERRY WAY ULTRA

IVERAGH PENINSULA, COUNTY KERRY, IRELAND

RACE STATISTICS

MONTH: September
DISTANCE: 200km (124 miles)
TOTAL ASCENT: 5,100m (16,732ft)
TIME ALLOWED: 36hr competitive (40hr non-competitive)

WEBSITE: www.kerrywayultra.com

The Kerry Way is one of Ireland's longest waymarked trails, looping the Iveragh Peninsula in southwestern Ireland. You'll run through the Old Red Sandstone mountains of Kerry; which are the highest points in the country, touching Irish history, archaeology and folklore along the way. This friendly race limits entrant numbers to protect the trails; it offers an early non-competitive start option and finishes with an UltraBrunch and prizegiving.

Justin Hamill was a participant in the 2024 event and was full of praise for the crew, other runners and random strangers he met en route. 'I've had such a brilliant time in Killarney and really enjoyed the whole experience', although he did want to point out 'that this is a super tough event and that it tests you (as it did me), physically and mentally'. Justin signed up again for the following year.

If you fancy a shorter challenge, the Ultra Lite is a 58km (36 miles) point-to-point. Other options are the Ultra Nite, which runs 101km (62¾ miles) overnight, and the Ultra Relay in which you take on the full distance as a team in a relay race.

ARC OF ATTRITION BY UTMB

CORNWALL, UK

RACE STATISTICS

MONTH: January
DISTANCE: 160km (100 miles)
TOTAL ASCENT: 4,250m (13,944ft)
TIME ALLOWED: 36hr

WEBSITE: arcofattrition.utmb.world

A winter traverse of the coast path around Cornwall in the far southwest of England promises to be both beautiful and brutal. In good weather it's stunning, but bad weather places runners in the full force of the wind and rain lashing in from the Atlantic. The Arc offers races of three distances: 100 miles, 50 miles and – in a new addition since being taken over by UTMB for the 2024 race: 25 miles. Underfoot, the South West Coast Path mixes technical, muddy, boggy, bouldery and sandy terrain, with relentless short but steep climbs, and descents accumulating a surprising amount of elevation. Watch out for the wild and remote Penwith coast and the infamous Dunes of Doom! Runners are guaranteed fantastic support from the army of Arc Angel volunteers, along with great local support and hospitality throughout the race.

The Arc is one of the UTMB World Series races, with top 3 finishers gaining guaranteed entry to the series finals at UTMB Mont-Blanc.

RIGHT Dramatic granite cliffs edge the South West Coast Path, followed by the Arc of Attrition.

DRAGON'S BACK RACE

WALES, UK

RACE STATISTICS

MONTH: September

STAGE RACE: Six stages in six days

DISTANCE: 380km (236 miles)

TOTAL ASCENT: 16,400m (53,800ft)

TIME ALLOWED: 96hr

WEBSITE: www.dragonsbackrace.com

A legendary six-day stage race crossing the length of Wales from Conwy Castle on the north coast to Cardiff Castle in the south. The route was inspired by the original 1992 race, taking in the highest mountains, with summit checkpoints and extreme terrain. You'll cross the mountains of Eryri (Snowdonia) National Park, the Cambrian Mountains of Mid-Wales and the Bannau Brycheiniog (Brecon Beacons) National Park. Participants have from 06:00–22:00 to compete each day, finishing at a fully stocked pre-erected camp. The average daily distance is 63km (39 miles) with around 2,900m (9,500ft) of ascent; the longest (third) day is 71km (44 miles) with 3,500m (11,500ft) of ascent!

The Hatchling was introduced in 2023; participants run part of the route – typically the first and second half – on the same course as the full Dragon's Back race and it's a great way to recce or prepare for the full distance.

SOUTH DOWNS WAY 100

SOUTH DOWNS NATIONAL PARK, UK

RACE STATISTICS

MONTH: June

DISTANCE: 161km (100 miles)

TOTAL ASCENT: 3,800m (12,700ft)

TIME ALLOWED: 30hr

WEBSITE: www.centurionrunning.com

Running from Winchester, the historic capital of Saxon England and finishing at the coast in Eastbourne, this race takes in the entire South Downs Way National Trail. The South Downs are the chalky hills of southeastern England, and runners are afforded glorious views across the lower lying countryside and south over the coast and out to sea. This is an ancient trail following old military, trade and drovers' routes, passing ancient hill forts, castles and picturesque villages.

This is a popular and well-managed race. Runners are well looked after with 12 fully stocked aid stations and a fully marked trail. The South Downs Way 50km (31 miles) race is on the same weekend.

The South Downs Way 100 is one of the ten World Trail Majors.

LEFT Runners cross the knife-edge scramble of Crib Goch on day 1 of the Dragon's Back Race.

FIRE AND ICE ULTRA

REYKJANES AREA OF ICELAND

RACE STATISTICS

MONTH: August–September
STAGE RACE: Six stages, six days
DISTANCE: 250km (155 miles)
TOTAL ASCENT: 2,675m (8,776ft)
TIME ALLOWED: Varies according to conditions

WEBSITE: www.fireandiceultra.com

This six-day stage race crosses the rugged volcanic interior of Iceland, running on cooled lava fields, over dunes of volcanic ash and across glacial rivers. The remote base camp start point, on the edge of the Vatnajokull glacier, is over 100km (62 miles) from the closest road. Runners must be self-reliant in terms of food and kit for the whole event, but you don't have to carry tents or stoves. The course is marked and there are normally a couple of water stations per day as well as assistance on the deeper river crossings.

Stage 4 is the longest day, running 70.5km (43¾ miles) across lava fields and volcanic sand. The 19km (11¾ miles) last stage is the shortest, bringing all the competitors together to the finish line. The other stages are between 36.6km (22¾ miles) and 42.8km (26½ miles).

The race package includes accommodation before and after the race and a celebration meal at the end. There are options to extend your stay to visit if you wish.

ÖTILLÖ, THE SWIMRUN WORLD CHAMPIONSHIP

STOCKHOLM ARCHIPELAGO, SWEDEN

RACE STATISTICS

MONTH: September
DISTANCE: 9km (5½ miles) swimming, 61km (38 miles) running
TOTAL ASCENT: 480m (1,575ft)
TIME ALLOWED: 14hr

WEBSITE: www.otilloswimrun.com/races/otillo-swim-run-world-championship-sweden

Back in 2022 four friends challenged each other in a late-night bet to see who could cross the Stockholm Archipelago fastest, by only swimming and running. The first official race happened in 2006, named ÖTILLÖ from the Swedish words 'ö' (island) and 'till' (to), meaning 'island to island'. Teams of two race together across the 70km (43½ miles) course, swimming about 9km (5½ miles) and running 61km (38 miles) over 24 islands with a challenging mix of rocky trails, dense forest and open water sea swimming – and finishing on the island of Sandhamn. The whole race incorporates 46 transitions between land and water.

ÖTILLÖ has evolved into a global series of races, with this race set as the world championship of swimrun. In the early days the winning time was around 26 hours; the current records have smashed that – men's 7:00:59 by Hugo Tormento and Max Andersson, women's 8:35:55 by Helena Sivertsson and Ulrika Eriksson and mixed 7:49:54 by Alexander Berggren and Desiree Andersson.

LEFT Fire and Ice Ultra endurance race, 2017.

RIGHT A-run-to-swim transition at the ÖTILLÖ Swimrun World Championship.

UNITED STATES AND CANADA

UNITED STATES AND CANADA INTRODUCTION

North America has a long and rich tradition of ultrarunning, from the era of pedestrianism in the 1800s, when men and women alike would race over distances for up to six days in front of large crowds of spectators, to trail races following ancient routes used over millennia by humans for transport, trading and communication. Post-pedestrianism, Canadian ultra-endurance athletes competed over distances of up to 500 miles (800km) on snowshoes. Road and track ultras attracted strong elite fields in Canada throughout the 20th century, with French-Canadian athlete Gerard Cote setting fast times over both 50 miles (80.5km) and the marathon before achieving similar success in England.

The oldest official ultramarathon in the US is the JFK 50 Mile (see page 156), which began in 1963 as part of a campaign by President John F. Kennedy to improve the country's physical fitness. However, a now-extinct mountain trail ultramarathon was held way back in 1911: the Mount Baker 50K in Bellingham, Washington, required runners to race by car or train to the trailheads and run up and down Mount Baker (10,000ft /3,000m) before returning to the city.

The US also has a history of putting on the longest ultras and hosts six- and ten-day events overseen by GOMU – the Global Organization of Multi-Day Ultramarathoning. In 1928, sports agent C. C. Pyle organized the first edition of the short-lived 3,455-mile (5,560km) Bunion Derby along Route 66 from Los Angeles to Chicago before heading towards New York. New York still hosts the world's longest ultramarathon: the Self-Transcendence 3,100 Mile Race (4,989km) (see page 156), established as a 'mere' 2,700-mile (4,345km) race in 1996 by US-based Indian spiritual leader Sri Chimnoy, who increased the distance to its current length in 1997. The race, held each summer, involves completing 5,649 laps of a city block in Jamaica, Queens, bounded by 164th Place, Abigail Adams (84th) Avenue, 168th Street, and the Grand Central Parkway, a distance of .5488 miles (883m). For those who prefer to escape race day crowds and create their own challenges, Fastest Known Times (FKT) are growing rapidly in popularity across the globe, with some notable North American routes including the Pacific Crest Trail, Appalachian Trail and Colorado Trail.

A particularly strong 100-mile (162km) tradition sees some of the world's most iconic ultraruns held in the US and Canada, including the Western States Endurance Run (see page 112) which, founded in 1977, is the oldest 100-mile trail run in North America; Leadville 100; Quebec Megatrail; and the Hardrock 100 (see page 134). First run in the early 1990s by a field of 18 in Colorado's San Juan Mountains, Hardrock is now a celebrated fixture on

PREVIOUS PAGE On the Sedona Climb during the 2024 Cocodona 250.

BELOW The switchback down the Panamint Valley, part of the Badwater 135 route.

the ultramarathon calendar and a must-do for elites and adventurers alike. The largest 100-mile trail run is the utterly fabulous Javelina Jundred (see page 122), also known as the original costumed 100-mile trail run party, held on Jalloween weekend in beautiful McDowell Mountain Regional Park near Fountain Hills, Arizona. Another iconic ultra, made famous by Dean Karnazes in his book *Ultramarathon Man*, is the infamous Badwater 135 (see page 118), which takes runners 135 miles (217km) from Death Valley to Mount Whitney, California. The inaugural race in 1987 was won overall by British woman, Eleanor Robinson, while Pam Reed also finished first overall in the 2002 edition.

In 1986 Gary 'Lazarus Lake' Cantrell and Karl 'Raw Dog' Henn organized the first Barkley Marathons (see page 138), an annual trail race held in March or April in Frozen Head State Park, Tennessee. Runners have 60 hours to complete five 20+mile loops of unmarked steep, backcountry terrain with approximately 11,000ft (3,350m) of vertical climb per lap. But very few do. Getting to the start line is an ordeal in its own right, and at most only a few runners complete the full five loops each year – often there are no finishers. 'Laz' Cantrell is also famous as the brains behind the increasingly popular backyard ultra concept, in which runners complete a loop of 4.167 miles (6.706km) on the hour, every hour, until only one runner is left – the winner – with everyone else receiving a DNF (did not finish). Originally a single event – Big Day's Backyard Ultra (see page 159) – backyard ultras have now spread across the globe.

WESTERN STATES ENDURANCE RUN

OLYMPIC VALLEY TO AUBURN, CALIFORNIA, USA

Every December, the eagerly awaited lottery for entry into the Western States Endurance Run (WSER) selects just 350 or so lucky runners from around 10,000 applicants to head to California's Sierra Nevada and experience one of the most famous 100-milers in the world.

WSER follows the middle portion of the Western States Trail, a national recreational trail that runs between Salt Lake City, Utah, and Sacramento, California. It traces the route taken by gold and silver miners in the 1850s through the lands lived in by the Washoe and Nisenan Indigenous People for thousands of years.

Starting out from Olympic Valley, venue for the 1960 Winter Olympic Games, at 5am, runners have until 10:59:59am on the following day to cross the finish line. They'll climb nearly 2,600ft (800m) in the first 4½ miles (7.25km), as the sun rises over the mountains, to reach Emigrant Pass at an altitude of 8,750ft (2,667m). From the pass runners travel west through remote and rugged country, finishing with a lap of Placer High School athletics track in Auburn. The route has a net downhill trajectory, climbing around 18,000ft (5,500m) and descending 22,000ft (6,700m). Conditions vary significantly from year to year, and also over the course of the race, with snow and sub-zero temperatures common in the high country and, on warmer years, 104°F (40°C) in the canyons.

RACE STATISTICS

MONTH: June
DISTANCE: 100¼ miles (161.2km)
TOTAL ASCENT: 16,959ft (5,169m)
HIGHEST POINT: 8,750ft (2,667m)
STARTERS 2024: 375 (98 female, 277 male)
FINISHERS 2024: 286 (62 female, 224 male)
TIME ALLOWED: 30hr
FEMALE COURSE RECORD: Courtney Dauwalter 15:29:33 (2023)
MALE COURSE RECORD: Jim Walmsley 14:09:28 (2019)
FIRST RUN: 1977
ENTRY FEE: $475

WEBSITE:
www.wser.org

The Rucky Chucky river crossing is undertaken on foot when the water is low and by boat when it's high.

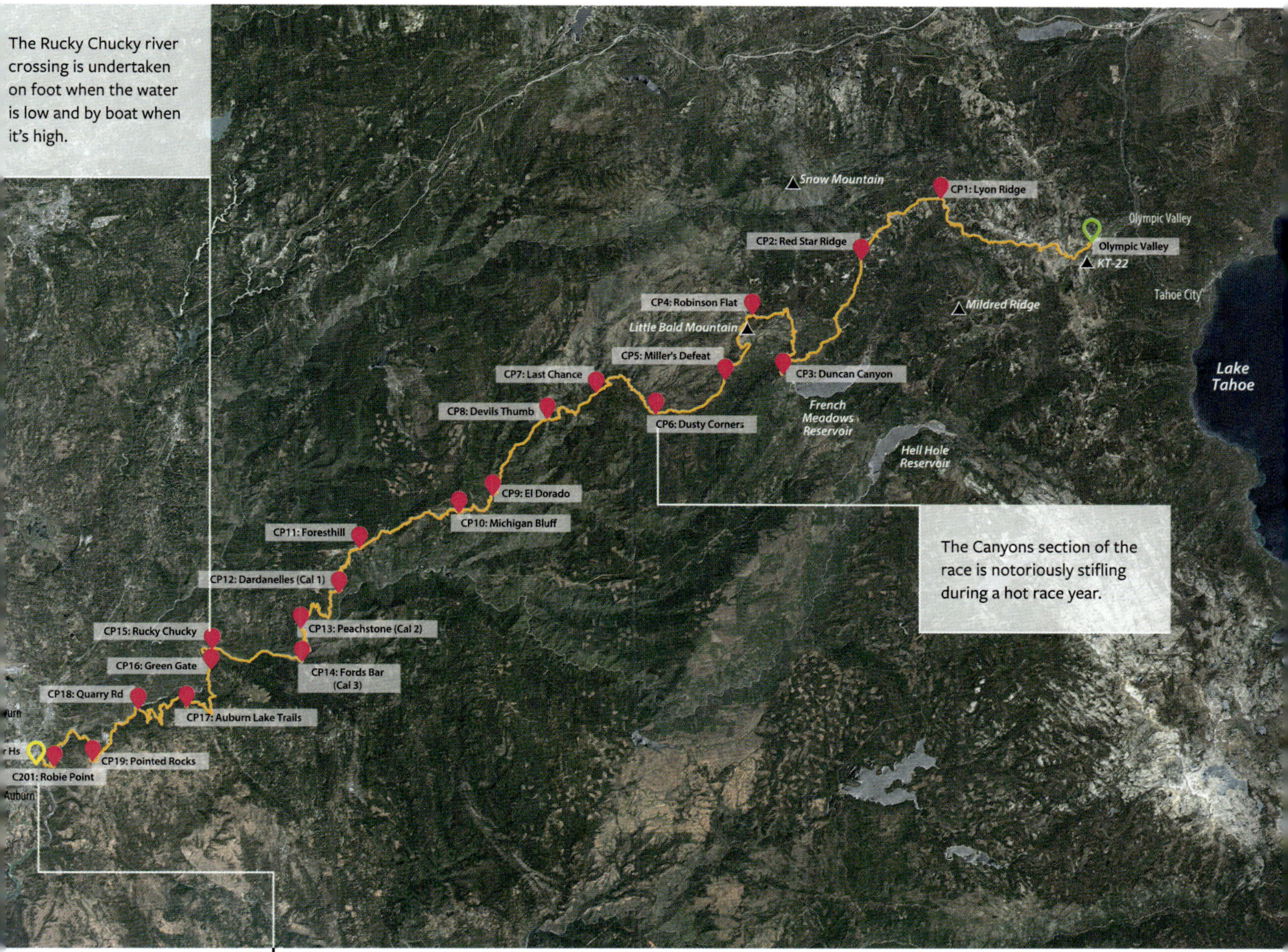

The Canyons section of the race is notoriously stifling during a hot race year.

Runners finish with a lap of Placer High School athletics track – always to a rapturous welcome from crowds of supporters.

ELEVATION PROFILE

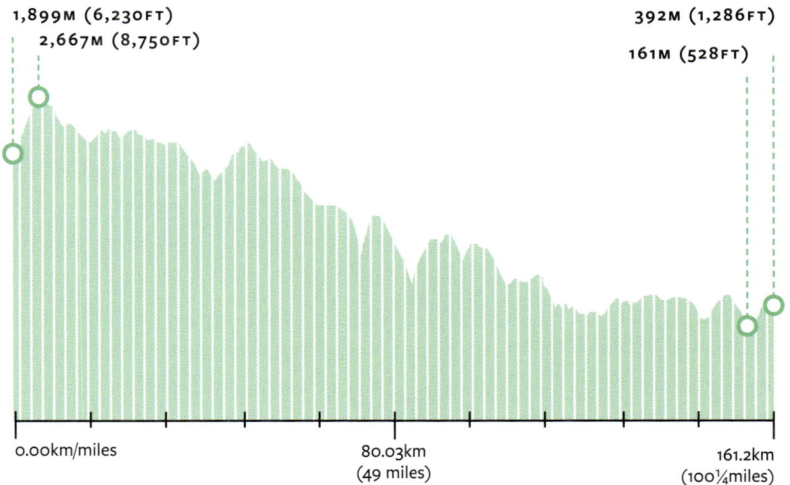

LEFT Runners on Red Star Ridge during the 2024 race.

LEFT Flowing trails near Cougar Rock in the first half of the 2024 race.

ABOVE The Rucky Chucky river crossing at Western States. Runners wade across when the water level is low and catch a boat ride when it's high.

At mile 78, runners are ferried across the American River by boat on years when water levels are high, and cross on foot with the assistance of a guide rope when water levels are lower. In 2016 Jim Walmsley, leading the men's race in record time, lost his footing while crossing the river and ended up swimming. A subsequent navigational error cost him his lead, and he finished 19th. Walmsley eventually set a smoking fast course record in 2019 that even he hasn't beaten since. In the women's race, British Canadian runner Ellie Greenwood's 2012 record of 16:47:19 stood for over 11 years until Courtney Dauwalter broke it by over an hour in 2023, finishing in 15:29:33. The race is known for drawing a particularly strong women's field and, in 2021, 15 of the top 30 finishers were women.

While most runners wanting to enter the race must first run a qualifier, of which there are many across the globe, and then enter the lottery, with their chances of being picked increasing with every consecutive year's entry, there are other ways to guarantee a place on the hallowed start line. Elite runners can gain a place by finishing in the top two or three of a Golden Ticket Race, or placing in the top ten in the men's or women's race the previous year.

WSER grew from the Tevis Cup, a 100-mile horse ride created by Wendell Robie, a successful Auburn businessman and mountain enthusiast, in 1955.

Several runners and walkers completed the route on foot and, in 1974, 27-year-old Gordy Ainsleigh, whose horse had gone lame, ran with the horses of the Tevis Cup and successfully completed the course in under 24 hours. In 1977, the first official race for runners was held, with 14 runners from four states starting the Western States National One Day Run and three finishing.

In the decades since, WSER has seen epic battles unfold along its 100 miles, right through the field from those fighting for a podium place to those racing the cut-offs. In 2024, 76.3 per cent of the 369 starters finished, with the women's race featuring the second-, third-, fourth-, seventh-, eighth- and ninth-fastest female finishing times in the event's history.

With more than 1,500 dedicated volunteers, including local running clubs making sure the aid stations offer the best support and entertainment en route, finishers receive a coveted sub-30-hour bronze belt buckle or a sub-24-hour finisher's silver belt buckle.

The Western States Endurance Run Foundation is a non-profit corporation. The 15-member board of trustees is responsible for ensuring the mission of the foundation is achieved in three key areas, each of equal importance: The Run, Trail Stewardship and Research. It is a world-leading race in pushing the sport of ultrarunning forward in many areas, including:

- In 2017, successfully implementing drug testing to ensure the integrity of the competition, and creating a wait list so that the maximum number of runners could participate in the event.
- In 2018, implementing an inclusive transgender policy.
- In 2019, implementing a trail Stewardship programme to maintain the Western States trail year-round.
- In 2021, after a year off due to the COVID pandemic, the race implemented its first-ever live broadcast, bringing the unfolding drama and unique course into homes.
- In 2024, after working collaboratively with the Indigenous People of Nevada and California, Western States produced a 'Land Acknowledgment' which acknowledges the history of the land upon which the race is held every year.

WSER is also committed to advancing knowledge of the sport of ultrarunning by supporting applied, clinical and behavioural research associated with the race, awarding several thousand dollars each year to researchers conducting studies at the race. Each year, WSER hosts a medical conference the week of the Run at Palisades Tahoe to further insights and share translational research to benefit sports science and ultrarunning performance.

RIGHT Chris Myers crossing the finish line of the 2024 Western States in 10th place.

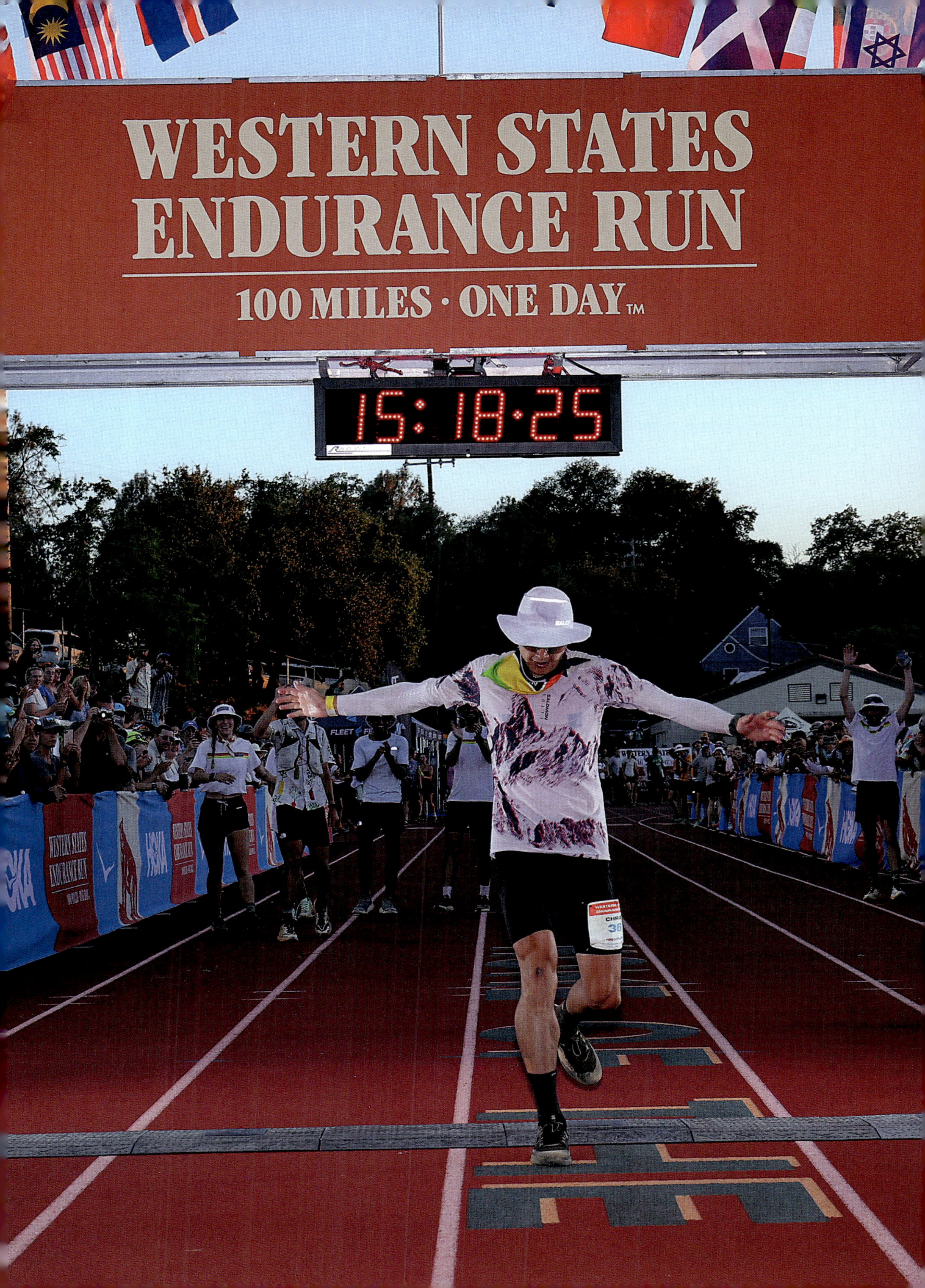
WESTERN STATES
ENDURANCE RUN
100 MILES · ONE DAY™
15:18·25

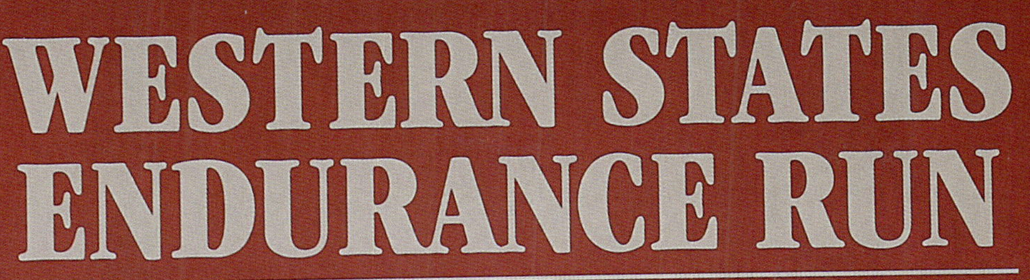

BADWATER 135

DEATH VALLEY TO MOUNT WHITNEY, CALIFORNIA, USA

In the summer of 1986, two Californians, Tom Crawford and Mike Witwer, decided to organize an ultramarathon from Badwater Basin to the summit of Mount Whitney (the highest point in the contiguous United States) through the infamous Death Valley. Twenty-two runners signed up, but the race had to be cancelled before it began as the organizers had failed to secure liability insurance for the all-important support crews. Crawford and Witwer headed out to tackle the route anyway, finishing in 70 hours 27 minutes.

A year later, on the morning of 31 July 1987, five runners started the first official Badwater ultramarathon. This intrepid field comprised two women: 39-year-old British runner Eleanor Robinson and US runner Jean Ennis, and three men: Tom Crawford, British adventurer and ultrarunner Ken Crutchlow along with journalist David Bolling, who would accompany the runners and report on the race. Crutchlow had originally challenged Crawford and Witwer – the completers of the previous year's run – to the race. It's said that when Witwer heard he would be competing against Eleanor Robinson – then possibly the best ultrarunner in the world – he backed out, perhaps fearing being beaten by a woman. In the event, Robinson led from the start, finishing in 52:45:00 while Crawford and his new partner, Jean Ennis, finished in 58:57:00.

RACE STATISTICS

MONTH: July
DISTANCE: 135 miles (217km)
TOTAL ASCENT: 14,600ft (4,450m)
HIGHEST POINT: 8,343ft (2,543m)
STARTERS 2024: 97 (33 female, 64 male)
FINISHERS 2024: 74 (25 female, 49 male)
TIME ALLOWED: 48hr
FEMALE COURSE RECORD: Ashley Paulson 21:44:35 (2023)
MALE COURSE RECORD: Yoshihiko Ishikawa 21:33:01 (2019)
FIRST RUN: 1987
ENTRY FEE: $1,595

WEBSITE:
badwater.com

The final mile is the steepest. The finish line stands at Mount Whitney Portal at 8,343ft (2,543m).

The race starts along Death Valley, where temperatures can reach 122°F (54°C). This is the lowest place in the USA, at 282ft (86m) below sea level.

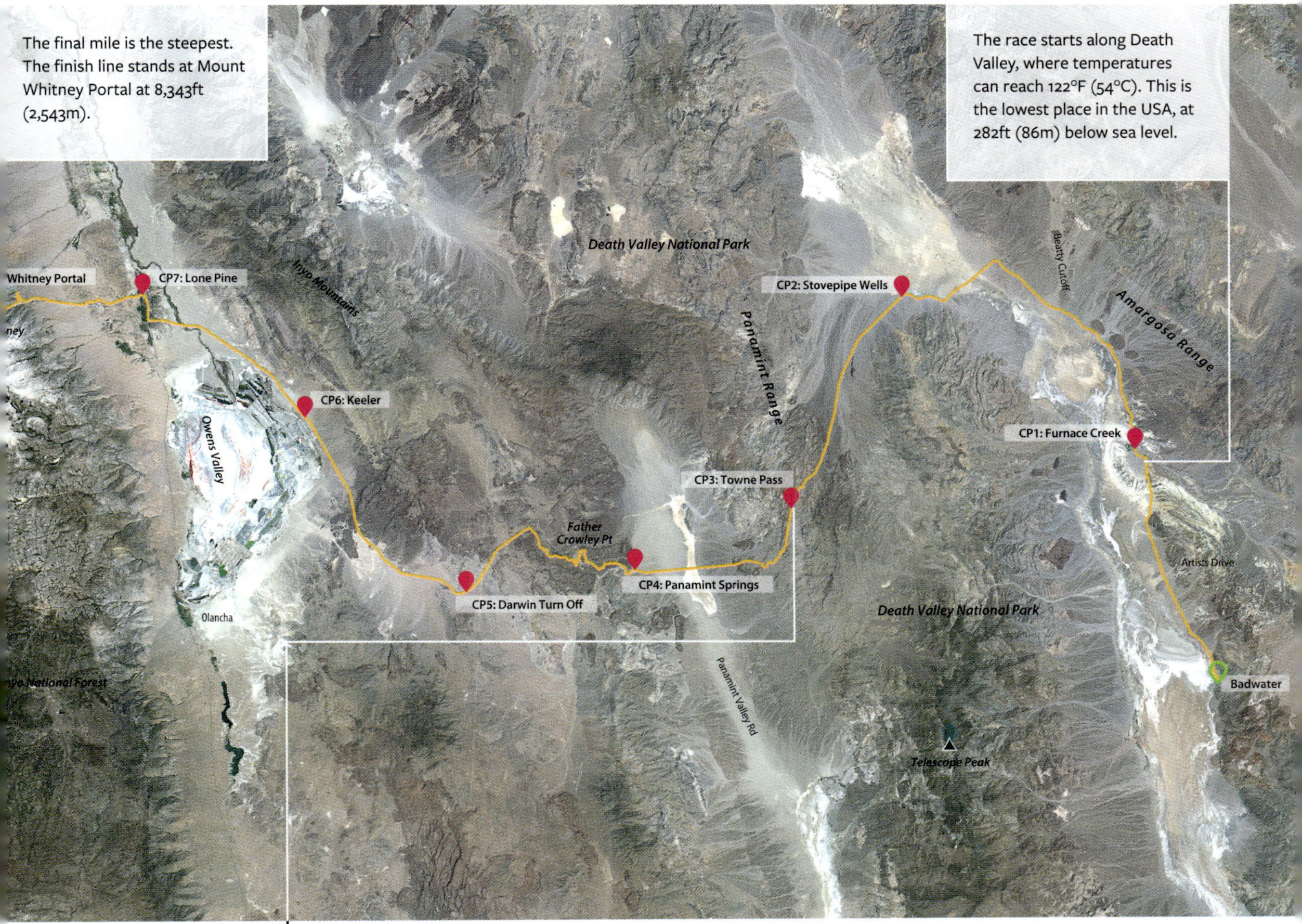

At 42 miles (67.5km) into the race, runners tackle their first climb, gaining 4,921ft (1,500m) of elevation in 16¾ miles.

ELEVATION PROFILE

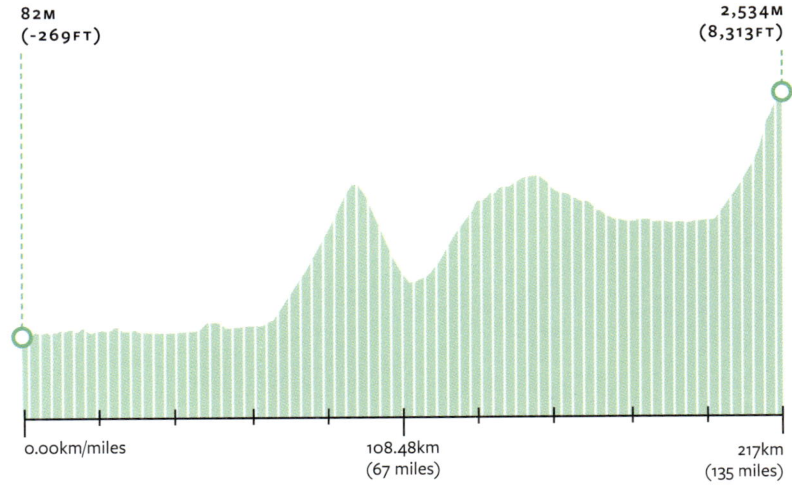

FAR LEFT Chris Rice and pacer starting up Towne Pass during the 2022 race.

LEFT Amy Costa and her pacer during the 2022 race.

The original route was an absolutely epic undertaking, covering 146 miles (235km) to the finish on the summit of Mount Whitney which, at over 14,400ft (4,400m), required runners to be accompanied by a mountain guide. Today's route is 135 miles (217km) long and finishes at Whitney Portal at just over 8,200ft (2,500m). But it still tops the charts in *National Geographic*'s top ten toughest races. Dean Karnazes' bestselling book, *Ultramarathon Man*, which brought the world of ultrarunning to many on its publication in 2005, describes the author's experiences out on the Badwater course.

Now hosted by AdventureCORPS, Badwater 135 has been completed by runners of between 18 and 71 years of age, and continues to fascinate and inspire those keen to take on the unique challenge of crossing Death Valley. Starting in Badwater Basin, which is below sea level, runners must cross three mountain ranges on a net uphill course, totalling 14,600 ft (4,450m) of cumulative ascent and 6,100ft (1,859m) of cumulative descent. Along the way, they'll pass through Furnace Creek, and cross the Alabama Hills and the Sierra Nevada. Temperatures can reach 129°F (54°C), and regular crew stops (runners must have a crew, with one support car and a maximum of four crew, whom they meet every 1–2 miles) are essential for keeping runners cool. Famously, competitors run on the slightly cooler reflective white line on the road to stop their shoes melting. Despite the heat, and the fact that the race is run entirely on road, the landscapes are breath-takingly beautiful. The small size of the field – around 100 each year – along with the support of crew teams means the experience is very much focused on community and camaraderie rather than competition.

BELOW The race starts in the Badwater Basin, at 282ft (85.5m) below sea level – this is the lowest point in North America and the United States.

ABOVE Running along the edge of the salt flats.

Scottish runner Debbie Martin-Consani finished Badwater in 2023 in temperatures that hit 50°C (122°F). 'I had to get quite creative in my training,' she says in an interview with *Ultrarunner* magazine. 'In Glasgow where I live we hit the dizzy heights of 19 degrees [66°F] before I left for Badwater. So I used a heat chamber at a local university and spent a lot of time sitting in saunas. I also built a DIY heat chamber in my garage, with fan heaters and my treadmill which I could get up to about 38 degrees [100°F]. I spent quite a lot of time sweating in my garage!'

JAVELINA JUNDRED

MCDOWELL MOUNTAIN REGIONAL PARK NEAR FOUNTAIN HILLS, ARIZONA, USA

Javelina Jundred (pronounced Havelina Hundred) is billed as 'the ultimate 100-mile social run' and 'the original costumed 100-mile trail run party'. Taking place on the weekend closest to Hallowe'en (Jalloween, obviously), the race is held on a looped 20-mile (32km) trail through the desert in the beautiful McDowell Mountain Regional Park near Fountain Hills, Arizona, on the ancestral homelands of the Hohokam Indigenous People. Four aid stations on each loop are located at Javelina Jeadquarters, Coyote Camp, Jackass Junction and Rattlesnake Ranch, with runners permitted to meet crew only at Javelina Jeadquarters.

Attracting both the party runners who dress up in wacky costumes for the occasion, and serious elite runners (finishing in the top two in the men's or women's race gets runners a coveted Golden Ticket entry for the Western States Endurance Race), and with films, fashion shows and a night race on offer, it's a joyful celebration of all things ultrarunning. But it may not be the most family-friendly event – according to its website, the Javelina Jundred has self-identified as R-rated, so expect music with explicit lyrics, risqué costumes and a 'bare-ass' award. There are Misfit awards, too, including best costume, first virgin (fastest time of a first-time Javelina finisher) and best crew camp decorations among others. In the words of race founder and

RACE STATISTICS

MONTH: October
DISTANCE: 100 miles (161km)
TOTAL ASCENT: 7,900ft (2,408m)
HIGHEST POINT: 2,484ft (757m)
STARTERS 2024: 747 (302 female, 442 male, 3 transgender & non-binary)
FINISHERS 2024: 421 (164 female, 255 male, 2 transgender & non-binary)
TIME ALLOWED: 30hr
FEMALE COURSE RECORD: Camille Herron 14:03:23 (2021)
MALE COURSE RECORD: Jonathan Rea 12:43:10 (2023)
FIRST RUN: 2003
ENTRY FEE: $510

WEBSITE: aravaiparunning.com/network/javelinajundred

Rio Mountain Estates
kass Junction
Rattlesnake Ranch
1st Loop Split
Sonoran Desert
Verde Village
McDowell Mountain Regional Park
McDowell Mountain Range
Start/Finish
Coyote Camp
Fort McDowell Yavapai Nation Reservation

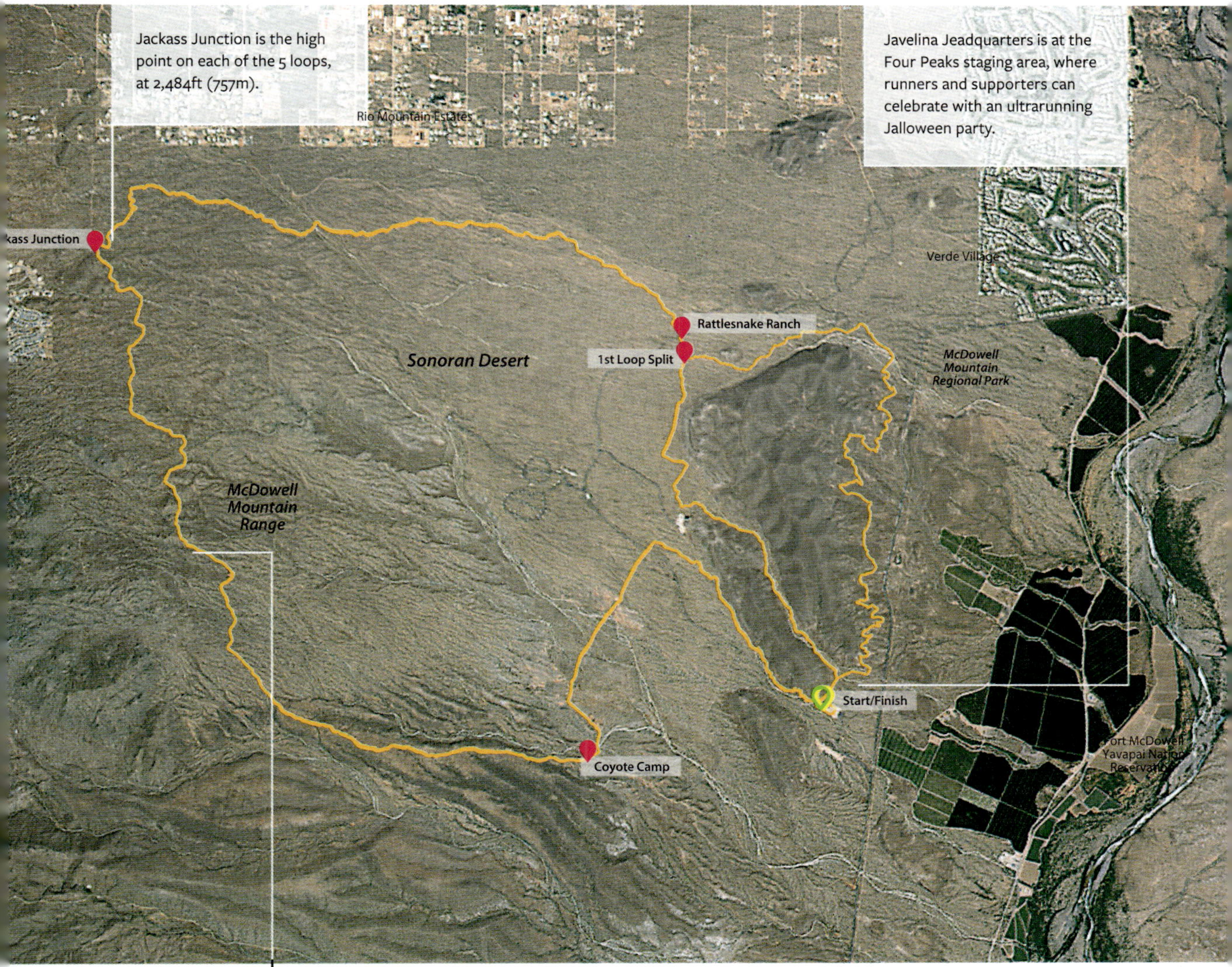

Jackass Junction is the high point on each of the 5 loops, at 2,484ft (757m).

Javelina Jeadquarters is at the Four Peaks staging area, where runners and supporters can celebrate with an ultrarunning Jalloween party.

The trail passes through the foothills of the McDowell Mountains, and many unusual boulder formations.

ELEVATION PROFILE

515M (1,689FT)
494M (1,620FT)
757M (2,483FT)
515M (1,689FT)
0.00km/miles
79.52km (49 miles)
161km (100 miles)

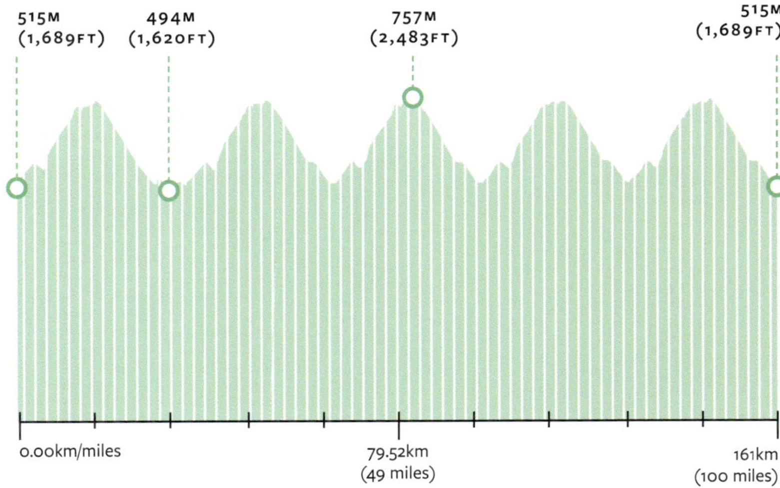

LEFT Javelina Jundred is known as the original costumed trail run party, with runners embracing the Jalloween spirit.

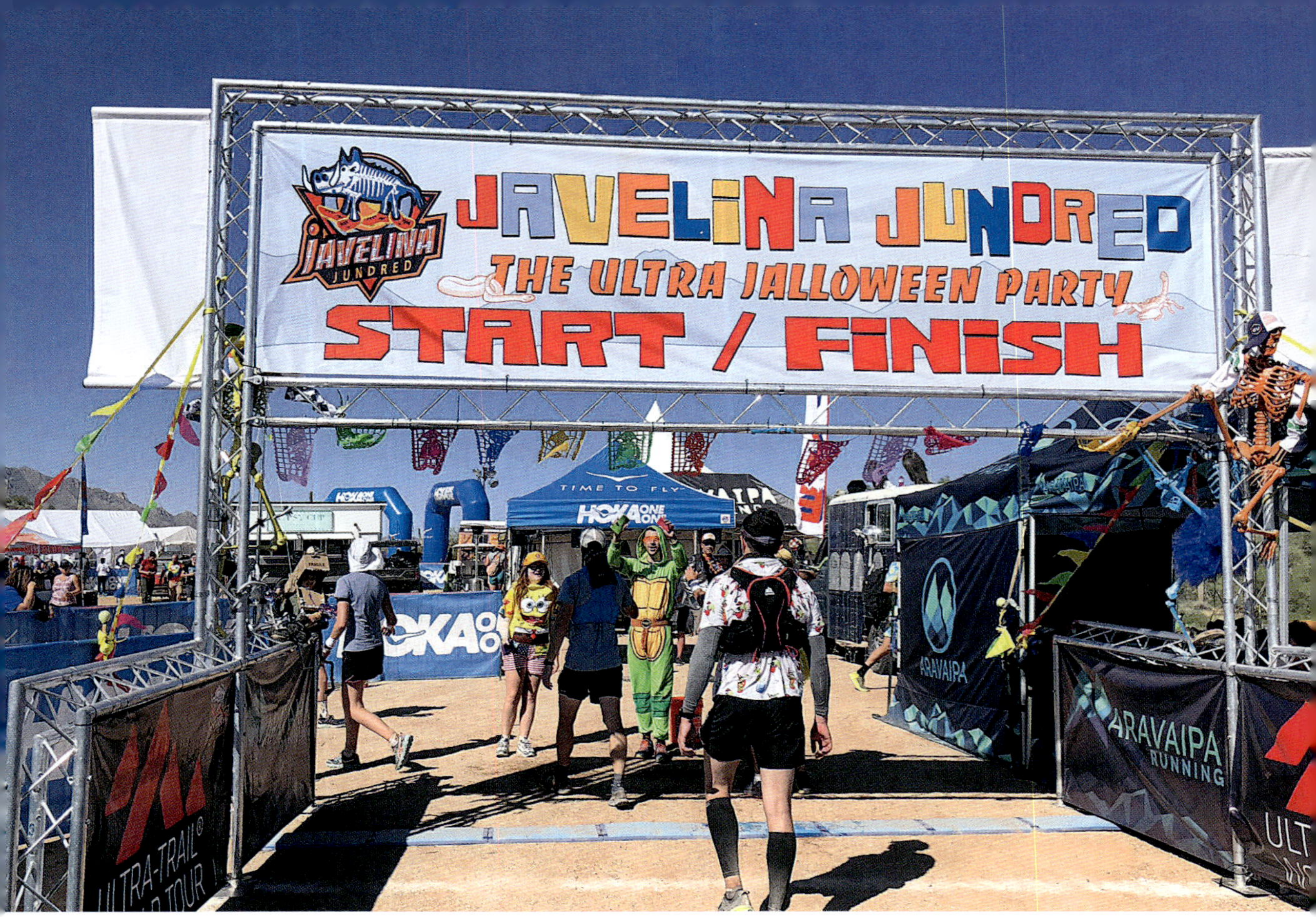

OTHER DISTANCES

62 miles (100km);
4,741ft (1,445m) ascent

19¼ miles (31km);
1,580ft (481½m) ascent

first race director, Geri Kilgariff, 'Javelina was born out of the spirit of fun. So have fun! Make your run one to remember always with a smile.'

Organized by Aravaipa Running and first held in 2003, Javelina has gone from strength to strength and is now an established classic on the ultra calendar.

The 100-mile (161km) route encompasses five loops on the Shallmo, Pemberton and Cinch trails, including a segment of the Escondido Trail in the first loop. The trails follow rolling singletrack, winding through the Sonoran Desert, a landscape dotted with giant Saguaro cacti and granite boulders. Runners in the 62-mile (100km) race complete three loops, while the Jackass 19¼-mile (31km) takes in one loop.

Each loop begins with a gentle climb to the route's high point near the foothills of the McDowell Mountain range. The trail then meanders through dry washbeds before descending to complete the loop. Diverse underfoot terrain ranges from hard-packed granite to rocks and soft sand.

Javelina Jeadquarters is at the Four Peaks Staging Area, from where runners head down the Shallmo wash, crossing McDowell Mountain Park Drive before venturing into an area of undulating hills and sandy areas, including Pemberton Wash. A gradual climb reaches Coyote Camp aid station, from where the trail transitions into a steady climb on a rocky path, eventually evening out as the route heads north towards the McDowell Mountains. The next, undulating section passes fascinating boulder formations before descending near Granite Tank, home to the Jackass Junction Aid Station, to join the Pemberton Trail. A gradual downhill stretch of singletrack parallel to the old jeep road meets the next aid station at the North Road crossing. Continuing south, the Rattlesnake Ranch aid station marks the point of difference between the first and subsequent loops. On the first loop, the trail follows the Escondido trail back to Javelina Jeadquarters; after that, it follows the Pemberton trail to the Cinch trail, eventually returning to Javelina Jeadquarters.

ABOVE Approaching the finish line and post-race party.

FAR LEFT Anna and Milly Troup running the 2019 Javelina Jundred. Milly finished the race aged just 16.

LEFT The race takes its toll on many runners!

BLACK CANYON ULTRAS

ARIZONA, USA

Taking place in February each year, the Black Canyon Ultras follow point-to-point 62-mile (100km) and 31-mile (50km) routes along the stunning Black Canyon National Recreation Trail in Arizona, with runners heading out into the desert at sunrise. Like Javelina Jundred, Black Canyon is organized by Aravaipa Running and the 100km race is a Western States qualifier, with the top three men and women receiving a Golden Ticket entry to the famous race. It's also one of the World Trail Majors series. As a result, despite being early in the racing season, it's an event that draws some of ultrarunning's biggest names and is widely regarded as one of the USA's most competitive 100km races.

The Black Canyon Trail winds through the Arizona mountains and desert, featuring a mixture of singletrack trail, 4x4 track and stretches of an old stagecoach route. The Trail in its entirety is approximately 80 miles (130km) long, and permits hiking/running, mountain biking and horse riding. With roots tracing back to use by Indigenous People and early traders, this historic route holds national significance. It was established by the Department of the Interior in 1919 as a livestock driveway, serving woolgrowers herding sheep between Phoenix and the Bradshaw and Mingus Mountains. Still utilized as a cattle driveway north of highway 69, the trail ends at the Prescott National Forest boundary.

RACE STATISTICS

MONTH: February
DISTANCE: 62¾ miles (101km)
TOTAL ASCENT: 5,254ft (1,601m)
HIGHEST POINT: 4,190ft (1,277m)
STARTERS 2024: 929 (277 female, 652 male)
FINISHERS 2024: 740 (222 female, 518 male)
TIME ALLOWED: 20hr
FEMALE COURSE RECORD: Riley Brady 8:16:18 (2025)
MALE COURSE RECORD: Seth Ruhling 7:24:55 (2025)
FIRST RUN: 2014
ENTRY FEE: $340

WEBSITE: aravaiparunning.com/network/blackcanyon

The Bradshaw Mountains create a stunning backdrop to the race.

The first half of the route is predominantly downhill – the challenge is leaving enough in the legs for the climbs later on.

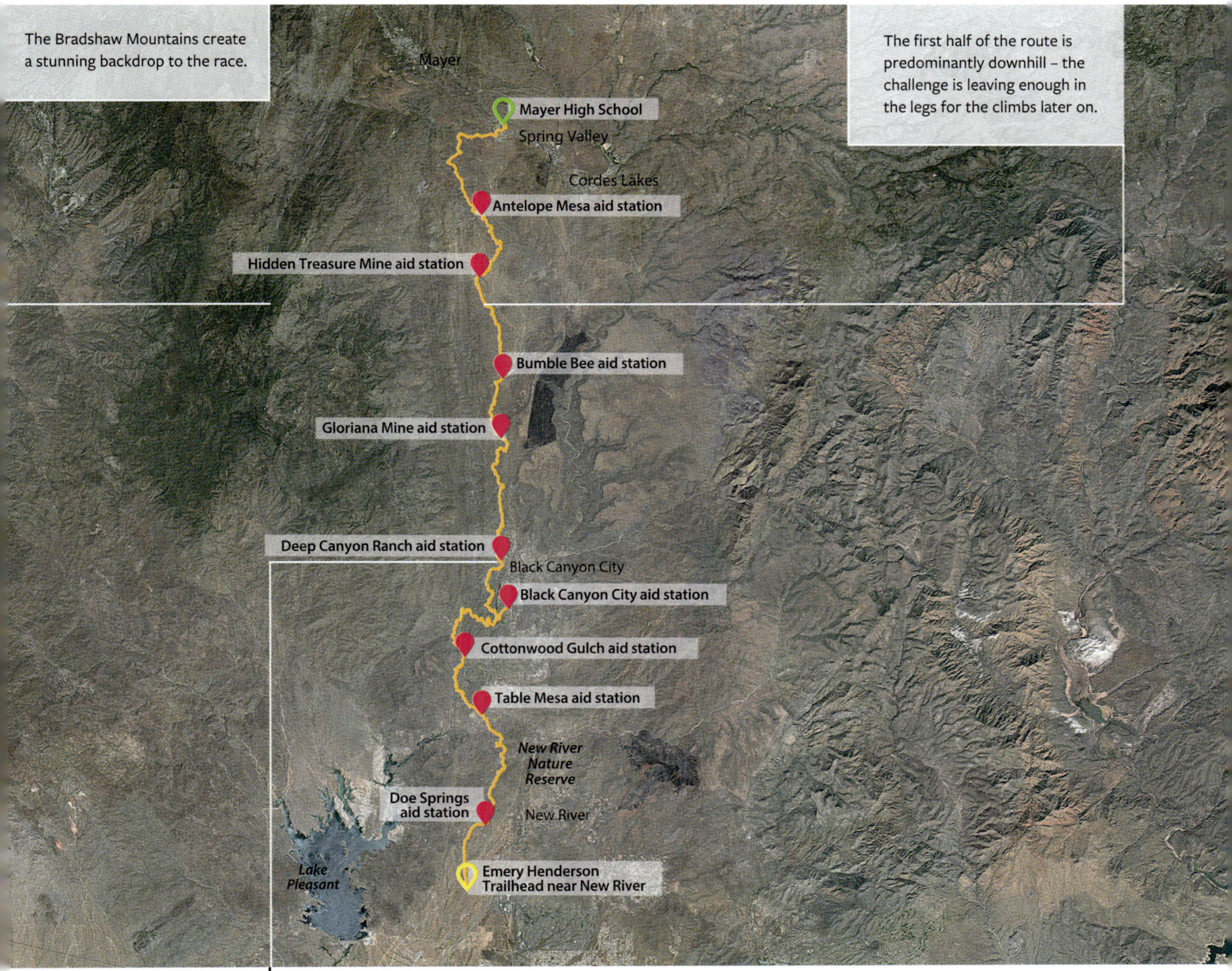

Mayer
Mayer High School
Spring Valley
Cordes Lakes
Antelope Mesa aid station
Hidden Treasure Mine aid station
Bumble Bee aid station
Gloriana Mine aid station
Deep Canyon Ranch aid station
Black Canyon City
Black Canyon City aid station
Cottonwood Gulch aid station
Table Mesa aid station
New River Nature Reserve
Doe Springs aid station
New River
Lake Pleasant
Emery Henderson Trailhead near New River

The 31 mile (50km) race finish is at Deep Canyon Ranch aid station.

ELEVATION PROFILE

1,218M (3,996FT)
1,277M (4,190FT)
533M (1,748FT)
573M (1,879FT)
0.00km/miles
50.45km (31 miles)
101km (62¾ miles)

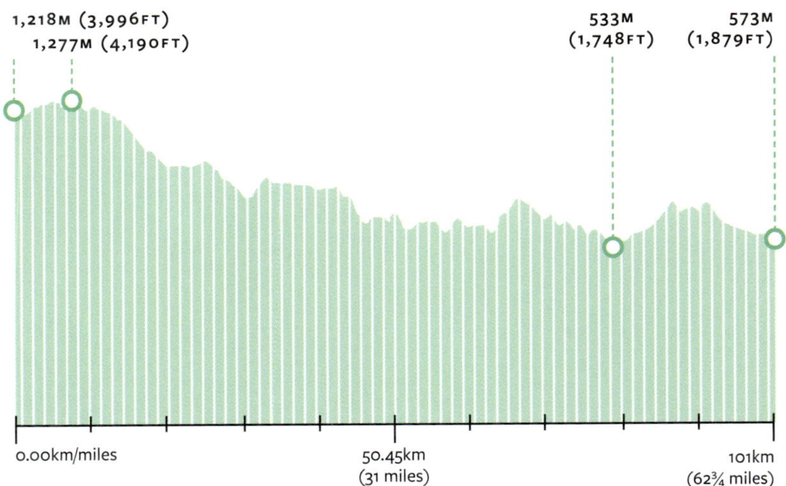

LEFT The Bradshaw Mountains offer a stunning backdrop for runners in the Black Canyon Ultras.

OTHER DISTANCES

Black Canyon offers two race distances, both starting at Mayer High School. The 50k covers the first half of the 100k route, finishing at Deep Canyon Ranch

31 miles (50km);
1,995ft (608m) ascent

Now primarily a National Recreation Trail, it also parallels segments of the old Black Canyon stagecoach road between Phoenix and Prescott. Entrants can attend three free-of-charge pre-race training runs between November and January prior to the race to familiarize themselves with the course. Runners are also encouraged to get involved in trail work, helping to maintain the trail for all who use it.

The Black Canyon Ultra route takes in a 55-mile (88.5km) section of this trail, commencing at Mayer High School in Spring Valley and finishing at the Emery Henderson Trailhead near New River. Runners traverse the dramatic Black Canyon, edged by Arizona's rugged Bradshaw Mountains, and cross the Agua Fria river multiple times. The course is fast and runnable, with a profile that gradually descends throughout its length, from around 4,000ft (1,220m) at the start to 1,870ft (570m) at the finish, with only a few short inclines along the way. Nine well-stocked checkpoints mean runners need to carry very little with them – a far cry from the kit-heavy mountain ultras.

Conditions can, however, change markedly throughout the race: in 2024, the 6am start was delayed by two hours as there was snow on the ground, yet later in the day conditions were far more desert-like, with runners weaving through sandy scrubland and arroyos (dry watercourses) on beautiful singletrack, forests of saguaro cactuses towering overhead.

Despite the start line conditions in 2024, a highly competitive race unfolded, with US wins in both the men's and women's races. Hayden Hawks, returning to form after a DNF at the previous year's Western States and knee surgery just six months before Black Canyon, set a new men's course record by just over two minutes. Rachel Drake took the win in the women's race, and the top three from each race took home Western States 100 Golden Ticket entries.

LEFT The route winds through forests of giant saguaro cactuses.

LEADVILLE TRAIL 100

LEADVILLE, COLORADO ROCKIES, USA

Known as the 'Race Across the Sky' because of its high-altitude course, Leadville was first run back in 1983, created to bring attention to the town after the closure of the Climax Mine. It's been a huge success and Leadville is now a destination town for outdoor recreation with a whole series of races happening through the year. Being located at an altitude of just over 9,850ft (3,000m), it's also home to some of the world's greatest ultrarunners, including Courtney Dauwalter who, with husband Kevin Schmidt, relocated to the town from Golden, Colorado in 2020.

The 100-miler (161km) is a brutal out-and-back, high-altitude course; throughout the entirety of the race the route never drops below 9,200ft (2,804m). Starting in Leadville, runners follow forest trails and mountain roads over high mountain passes, with some technical terrain on the Colorado Trail. The (in)famous climb to Hope Pass reaches the highest point on the course at 12,600ft (3,840m), twice, the first time steeply from the lowest point on the course.

Finishing Leadville earns runners one of the most coveted belt buckles in ultrarunning. To earn a Big Buckle you must finish in under 25 hours; the Small Buckle is awarded for times under 30 hours. The last finisher wins the Last Ass Over the Pass award.

RACE STATISTICS

MONTH: August
DISTANCE: 100 miles (161km)
TOTAL ASCENT: 15,492ft (4,722m)
HIGHEST POINT: 12,600ft (3,840m)
STARTERS 2024: 707 (146 female, 561 male)
FINISHERS 2024: 404 (72 female, 332 male)
TIME ALLOWED: 30hr
FEMALE COURSE RECORD: Ann Trason 18:06:24 (1994)
MALE COURSE RECORD: David Roche 15:26:34 (2024)
FIRST RUN: 1983
ENTRY FEE: $450

WEBSITE: leadvilleraceseries.com/run/leadvilletrail100run-2

Leadville is run entirely at high altitude: the lowest point on the course is Twin Lakes at 9,215ft (2,809m) above sea level.

The town of Leadville, at 9,842ft (3000m), is home to several well-known ultrarunners, including the G.O.A.T (greatest of all time) Courtney Dauwalter.

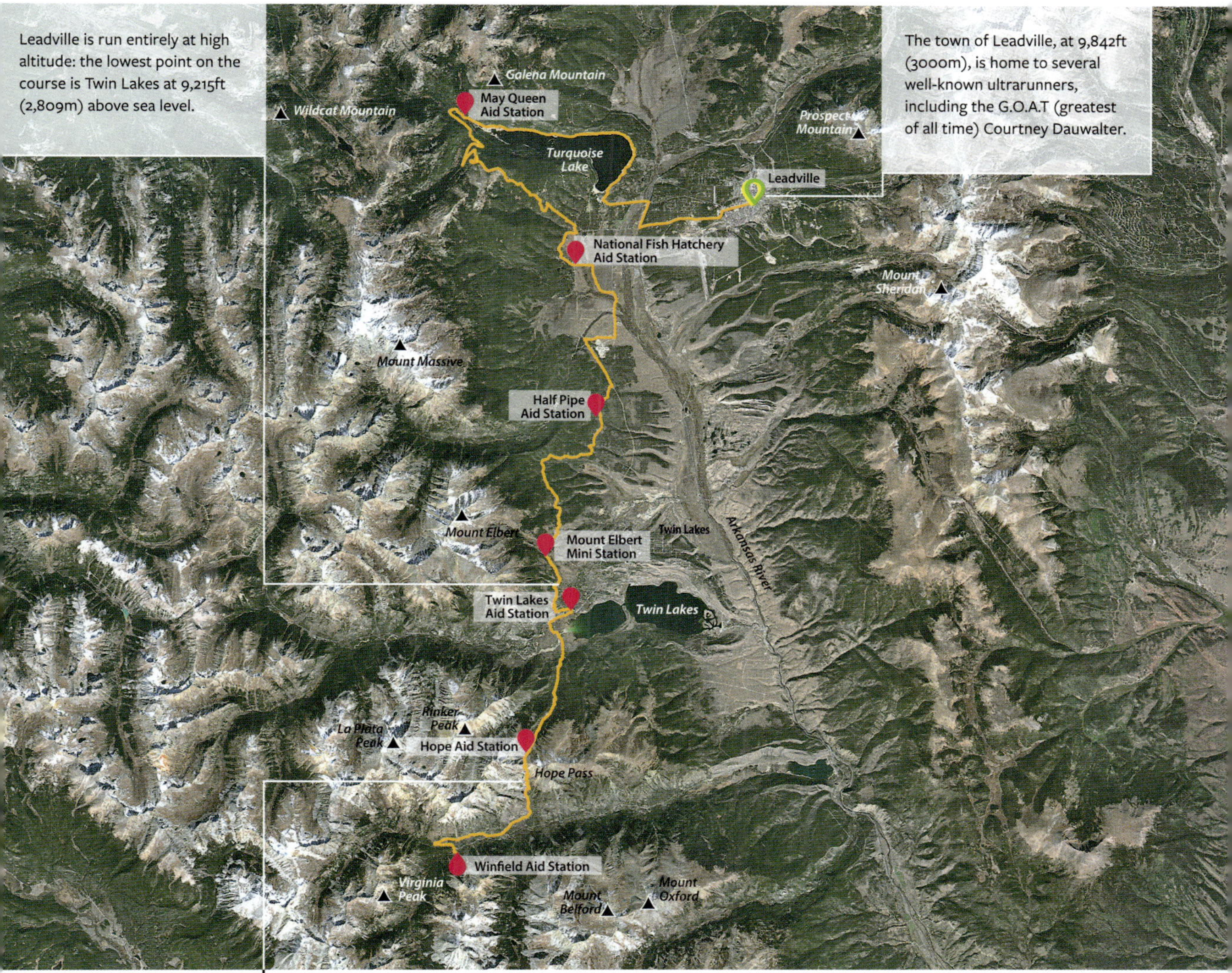

Hope Pass is the infamous high point of the route at 12,600ft (3,840m), and is tackled twice.

ELEVATION PROFILE

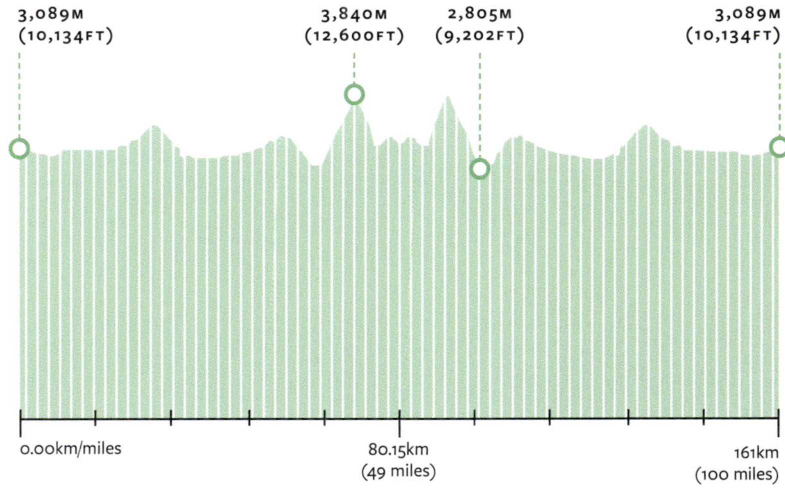

LEFT Ian Sharman (right) and his pacer run towards the Outward Bound/Fish Hatchery aid station at mile 74.5 during the 2017 Leadville 100.

Ann Trason's historic, course record-setting win at Leadville in 1994 came during the peak of the US ultrarunning legend's career. Setting an incredible 20 world records, some of which remained unbeaten for decades, Trason took the Leadville 100 win four times. The year of her Leadville record, she had outsprinted winning man Joe Schlereth in the final moments of the Silver State 50 Mile in a time of 7:29, which remains the women's course record. A month later she took her sixth consecutive Western States win, finishing second overall and setting a course record that stood until 2012, when it was broken by Ellie Greenwood.

In 1994, Ann was the clear women's favourite, and possibly the overall favourite too, but a team of Tarahumara runners – a tribe made famous by Chris McDougall's bestseller *Born to Run* – had been brought in from Mexico to challenge for the win. The race received significant media attention, with film crews on hand to document the Tarahumara and Ann Trason in their 'race across the sky'. After a neck-and-neck battle, Tarahumara runner Juan Herrera took the win, with Trason crossing the line as first-placed woman and second overall. Her time of 18:06 still stands at the time of writing, but surely it's a record that must be in the sights of Leadville local Courtney Dauwalter – who to date hasn't taken part in the race.

2024 saw Matt Carpenter's 19-year-old men's record – one which many had considered unbeatable – broken by Boulder-based David Roche. Roche who, alongside his wife Megan, coaches many of the biggest names in ultrarunning, chose Leadville as his first 100-miler. He prepared meticulously using the latest scientific evidence, experience from coaching high-level ultrarunners, research on other elite endurance sports such as cycling, and many years of hard training and self-experimentation. It all came together on race day, and Roche crossed the line 16 minutes faster than the previous record.

ABOVE Iso Yukra descending Hope Pass during the 2017 Leadville 100.

BELOW Ian Sharman climbing Hope Pass from the Winfield aid station during the 2017 Leadville 100.

HARDROCK 100

SILVERTON, COLORADO, USA

'Each July, the San Juan Mountains in Colorado play host to a gathering of runners, families and friends at the Hardrock Hundred Endurance Run. This gathering brings people together from around the world to test their abilities against Mother Nature, celebrate the community of ultrarunning and bear witness to ordinary people doing an extraordinary thing. Running the equivalent of sea level to the top of Mount Everest and back at an average elevation of 2 miles (3.2km) above sea level, Hardrock challenges runners in ways very few other events can. In the words of ultrarunner and photographer Kunal Patel, "The Hardrock 100 is not just a race but a transformative experience."'

DALE GARLAND, RACE DIRECTOR

Setting out from Silverton, Colorado, Hardrock runners pass through the towns of Telluride, Ouray and the ghost town of Sherman, crossing 13 major passes at altitudes between 12,000 and 13,000ft (3,660–3,960m) and the 14,048-ft (4,282m) summit of Handies Peak. Each year, the route switches between a clockwise and anticlockwise direction, with many debates over which is the tougher. At the end of the race, instead of crossing a finish line, tradition dictates that runners kiss the Hardrock – a picture of a ram's head painted on a large block of stone mining debris.

RACE STATISTICS

MONTH: July
DISTANCE: 102½ miles (165km)
TOTAL ASCENT: 33,197ft (10,118m)
HIGHEST POINT: 14,048ft (4,282m)
STARTERS 2024: 146 (31 female, 115 male)
FINISHERS 2024: 119 (26 female, 93 male)
TIME ALLOWED: 48hr
FEMALE COURSE RECORD: Courtney Dauwalter 26:11:49 (2024)
MALE COURSE RECORD: Ludovic Pommeret 21:33:06 (2024)
FIRST RUN: 1992
ENTRY FEE: $435

WEBSITE:
hardrock100.com

The Hardrock route was designed to link the four former mining towns of Telluride, Silverton, Ouray and Lake City.

The highest point on the route is at Handies Peak, at 14,048ft (4,282m).

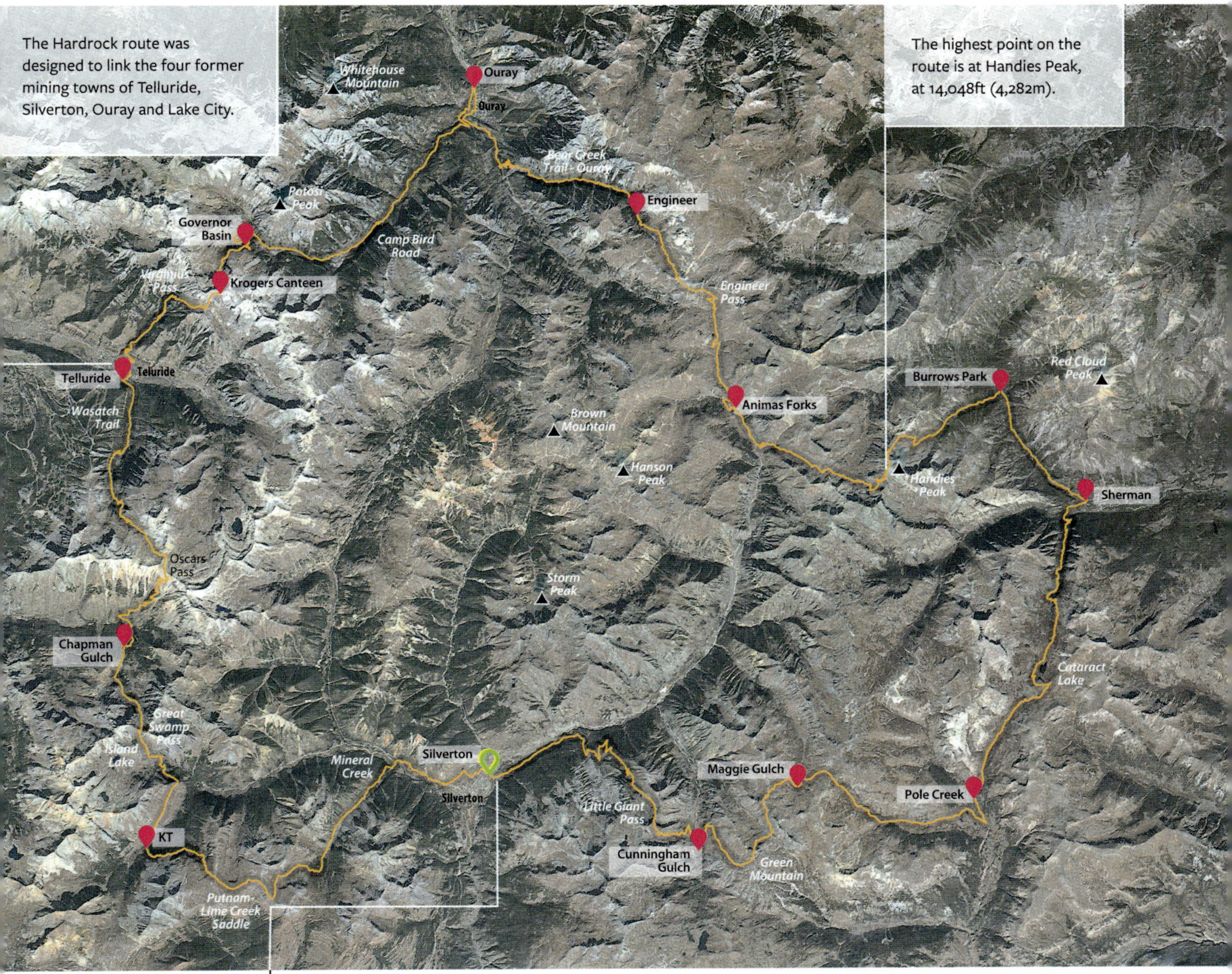

Whitehouse Mountain
Ouray
Ouray
Bear Creek Trail - Ouray
Engineer
Potosi Peak
Governor Basin
Camp Bird Road
Virginius Pass
Krogers Canteen
Engineer Pass
Telluride
Telluride
Wasatch Trail
Animas Forks
Brown Mountain
Hanson Peak
Burrows Park
Red Cloud Peak
Handies Peak
Sherman
Oscars Pass
Storm Peak
Chapman Gulch
Cataract Lake
Great Swamp Pass
Island Lake
Mineral Creek
Silverton
Silverton
Maggie Gulch
Pole Creek
Little Giant Pass
KT
Cunningham Gulch
Green Mountain
Putnam-Lime Creek Saddle

The famous Hardrock awaits runners at the finish – a kiss is traditional!

ELEVATION PROFILE

2,839M (9,314FT)
2,343M (7,687FT)
4,282M (14,048FT)
2,839M (9,314FT)
0.00km/miles
79.61km (49 miles)
165km (102½ miles)

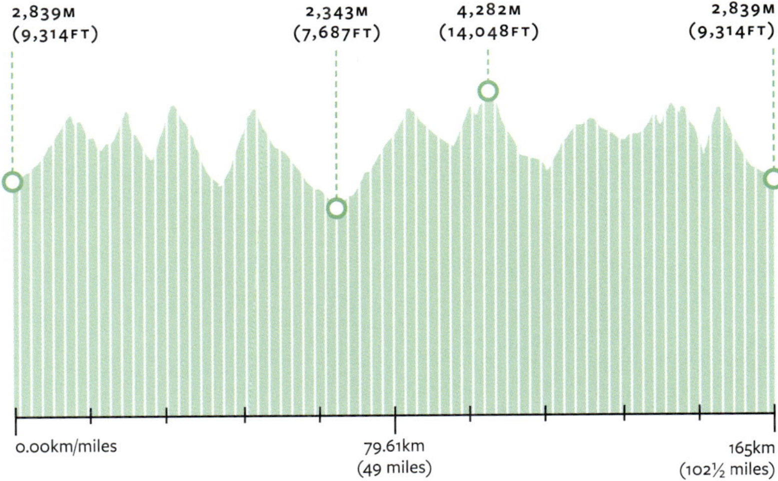

FAR LEFT Big mountain views on the Hardrock 100 course.

LEFT Awesome forest trails through aspen, pine and spruce on the lower slopes.

Hardrock was established in the early 1990s by local runners Gordon Hardman, Charlie Thorn, John Cappis, Rick Trujillo and current Race Director Dale Garland as a route connecting the four former mining towns of Silverton, Telluride, Ouray and Lake City using historic mining trails and paths. The first Hardrock Endurance Run had 18 entrants, which rapidly increased over the years that followed to 30, then 40. Today's Hardrock 100 sees 140 registered runners picked from a lottery of over 2,400 entrants.

Hardrock is not for the faint-hearted. Described by its organizers as a 'graduate level challenge', runners are warned to expect extreme conditions out on the course, including crossing freezing and knee-deep rivers, snow fields and cliff-edge trails; tackling remote wilderness, altitude, technical terrain and sections of hands-on scrambling; and a high risk of thunderstorms while running above the treeline. To be successful here, mountaineering, wilderness survival and wilderness navigation skills are as important as endurance.

Despite its challenges, dangers and unpredictable conditions, Hardrock is a race many runners return to, year after year. Courtney Dauwalter has run, and won, three times. Kirk Apt, a 62-year-old from Fruita, Colorado, is a 26-time finisher, with times ranging from 29:35:00, in 2000, to 46:53:28 in 2021. Betsy Kalmeyer, 63, from Leadville, Colorado, has 21 finishes, clocking her fastest time of 29:58:00 in 2001 and her slowest, 47:34:50, in 2023. Ludovic Pommeret's victory in 2024 was particularly notable, both for breaking Kilian Jornet's longstanding course record and for doing it a few days short of his 49th birthday.

Despite attracting an elite field, the enthusiastic community surrounding the Hardrock Endurance Run insists it is a run, not a race. In a 2023 interview with *Outside* magazine, Courtney Dauwalter explains, 'It doesn't matter where you finish in the race, sharing stories afterward with the other runners, the volunteers, and the entire community is what it's all about.'

The Hardrock 100 is the main event in the Rocky Mountain Slam, which runners can complete in by finishing Hardrock plus three of four other races in the Rocky Mountains: Leadville Trail 100 (see page 100), the Bear 100 Mile Endurance Run, the Bighorn 100, or the Wasatch Front 100 Mile Endurance Run (see page 157). The award is presented at and hosted by the Bear 100 Mile Endurance Run, the final run in the series.

ABOVE Courtney Dauwalter on Engineer Pass Road, on her way to winning the 2024 Hardrock 100.

BELOW Jason Schlarb (Durango, CO) kissing the rock at the finish. Jason finished 3rd in 2024, and finished joint 1st (with Kilian Jornet) in 2016.

THE BARKLEY MARATHONS

FROZEN HEAD STATE PARK, TENNESSEE, USA

Each year, on a weekend in March close to April Fools' Day, 40 runners and their crew wait nervously in a small campground in Frozen Head State Park, Tennessee. At a time unknown in advance by the runners, the low note of someone blowing into a conch shell echoes through the trees. It is the signal the runners have been waiting for: they have precisely 1 hour to get ready. An hour later, the runners stand at the famous (in ultrarunning circles, at least) yellow gate, waiting for Race Director Gary 'Lazarus Lake' Cantrell to light a cigarette: the signal that the Barkley Marathons has started.

Runners have 60 hours to make their way around a self-navigated, unmarked, five-loop course, finding books hidden within the woods as they go. Once they've located a book, they must tear out the page corresponding to their race number and stow it carefully away, ready to hand over at the end of each loop as proof. The books have names that echo the sentiments many runners are feeling as they stumble through briars, climb and descend precipitously steep hills, and try to make as few navigational errors as possible. Barkley first-timers are advised to team up with more experienced runners, learning the complexities of what is perhaps the world's hardest race from those who have endured it before.

The race was the brainchild of Laz and his friend, Karl Henn. It was inspired by the 1977 escape of James Earl Ray, convicted for the assassination of Martin Luther King Jr., from nearby Brushy Mountain State Penitentiary. Ray covered only about 8 miles (13km) during the 54 hours of his escape, but Laz

RACE STATISTICS

MONTH: March or early April
DISTANCE: 100 miles (161km)
TOTAL ASCENT: At least 55,000ft (16,500m)
HIGHEST POINT: 3,324ft (1,013m)
STARTERS 2024: 40 (female/male not published)
FINISHERS 2024: 5 (1 female, 4 male)
TIME ALLOWED: 60hr (12hr per lap), 40hr for the fun run
FEMALE COURSE RECORD: Jasmin Paris 59:58:21 (2024 – first female finisher)
MALE COURSE RECORD: Brett Maune 52:03:08 (2012)
FIRST RUN: 1986
ENTRY FEE: $1.60. New runners must bring a licence plate and previous attempters a themed gift. Prior finishers must bring a packet of Camel cigarettes.

WEBSITE: n/a

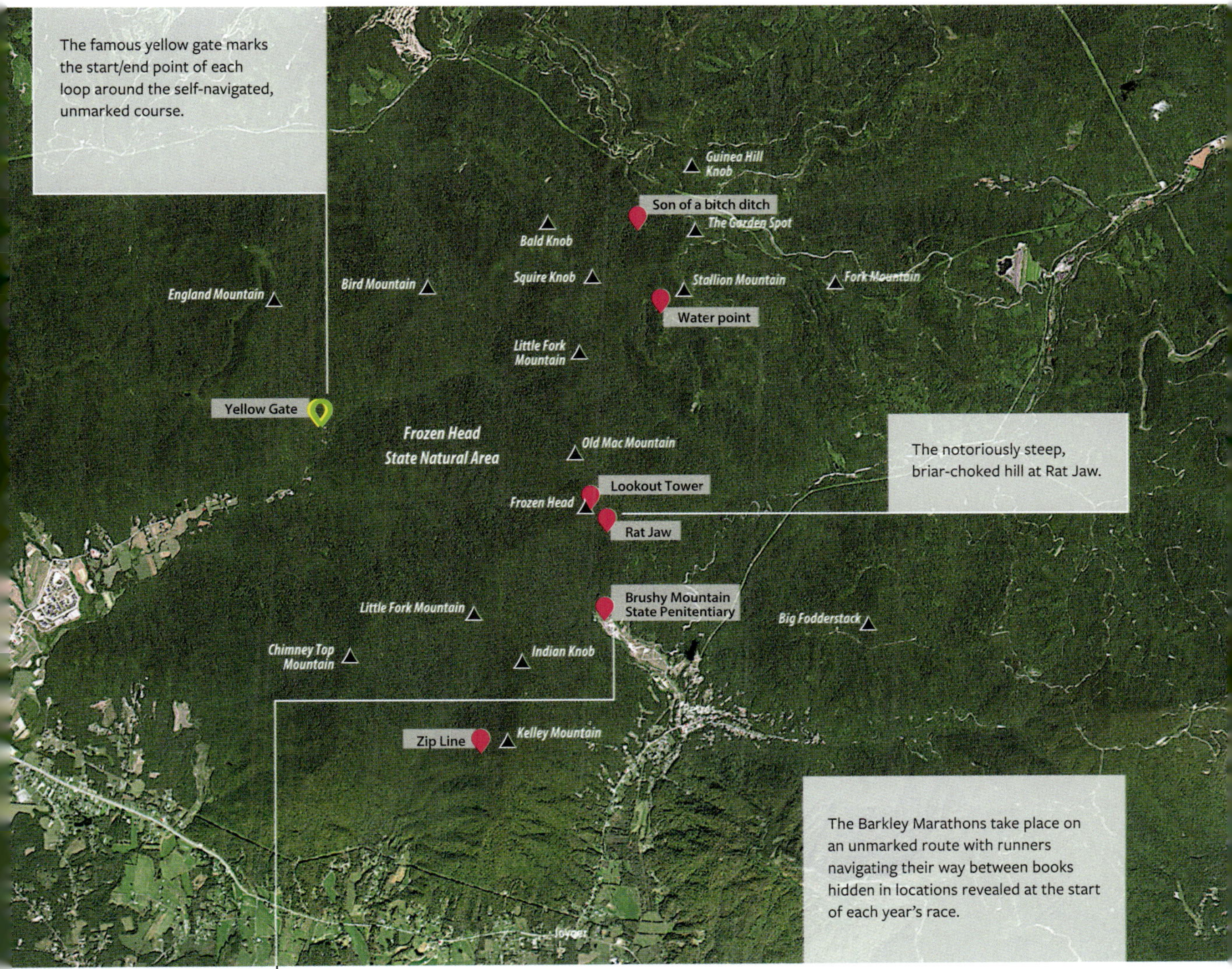

The famous yellow gate marks the start/end point of each loop around the self-navigated, unmarked course.

Guinea Hill Knob

Son of a bitch ditch

The Garden Spot

Bald Knob

England Mountain

Bird Mountain

Squire Knob

Stallion Mountain

Fork Mountain

Water point

Little Fork Mountain

Yellow Gate

Frozen Head State Natural Area

Old Mac Mountain

The notoriously steep, briar-choked hill at Rat Jaw.

Lookout Tower

Frozen Head

Rat Jaw

Brushy Mountain State Penitentiary

Little Fork Mountain

Big Fodderstack

Chimney Top Mountain

Indian Knob

Zip Line

Kelley Mountain

The Barkley Marathons take place on an unmarked route with runners navigating their way between books hidden in locations revealed at the start of each year's race.

Runners pass through a tunnel under Brushy Mountain State Penitentiary – inmate James Earl Ray's failed escape from here inspired the Barkley Marathons.

FAR LEFT Runners navigate around a series of books in hidden locations around Frozen Head State Park.

LEFT Barkley Marathons co-founder Gary Cantrell, aka Laz, lights a cigarette, signifying the start of the race.

RIGHT The blowing of the conch marks 1 hour until the race is due to start.

DO NOT
BLOCK GATE

LEFT, ABOVE The famous sign posted on the yellow gate marking the start/finish of each loop.

LEFT Jasmin Paris climbs Rat Jaw on her way to becoming the first female finisher of the Barkley Marathons in 2024.

ABOVE First-timers must bring a number plate from their country as part of their entry to the race.

reckoned he could do at least 100, and the Barkley Marathons were born. The race was named after Laz's longtime neighbour and running companion, Barry Barkley, who died in 2019 at age 70.

Since it was first held in 1986 more than 1,000 runners have attempted the Barkley Marathons. But, as of 2024, only 20 have ever finished all 5 loops of the approximately 100-mile (161km) course, with 55,000ft (16,500m) of climbing within the 60-hour time limit. Until 2024, no women had finished the Barkley, but Jasmin Paris, a 40-year-old mum of two and senior veterinary lecturer, changed everything, crossing the line with just 99 seconds to spare – and promptly collapsing. Not for the first time (see page 75), Jasmin found herself at the centre of a media storm surrounding her incredible achievement, and later that year was awarded an MBE. Jasmin was one of a record five finishers in 2024, with Ihor Verys, John Kelly, Jared Campbell and Greig Hamilton also completing the full five loops. UK-based Damian Hall narrowly missed out on his five-loop finish.

It's hard to believe that the Barkley Marathons, one of the most eagerly anticipated events on the ultrarunning calendar, offers just 40 runners the opportunity to run each year. While the race is, in some ways, shrouded in myth and secrecy, the reasons for many of its eccentricities are surprisingly logical.

Taking place in Frozen Head State Park, Tennessee, much of which covers ecologically sensitive areas where the public is not permitted, the race may only continue with a small field to minimize damage. For similar reasons, plus the lack of space in the campground, the route and event date are kept secret. Selection criteria are as fair as it's possible to be with hundreds of applications for so few places. Applicants must request an entry form by writing an essay on 'Why I Should Be Allowed to Run the Barkley', which helps with the selection process, but even the best essay doesn't guarantee selection. Some groups are guaranteed entry, however, including those who had a place but deferred for any reason the previous year; winners of the previous year's Barkley Fall Classic or Big Dog's Backyard Ultra (see page 159) Laz's other races; and previous finishers of the Barkley.

All other applicants are weighted, according to various criteria. No one who is considered to have no chance at all of finishing is selected, so applicants need to be able to prove their pedigree, both in ultrarunning and mountaincraft, wilderness survival, navigation and generally a combination of extreme gnarliness and outstanding problem-solving skills. Those from groups under- (or un-) represented at Barkley have a better chance of selection, along with those who have shown finisher potential on previous attempts. It's said that persistence in applying gives applicants a better chance of getting in each year. Individuals who have made a significant contribution to the race also receive slots each year, decided by the race management.

After the field is drawn, those selected are notified individually via a letter of 'consolation', and given the opportunity to back out with honour. All remaining applicants go through one final drawing to determine a 'weight list' of 50 runners, who will then move into any places vacated by selected runners. Anyone who secures a place and doesn't show up will never be invited back. All pretty simple, right? Next, on to the entry fee . . .

The application fee is $1.60 and is non-refundable. Barkley virgins (those making their first attempt) must bring a car licence plate from their home state or country. For veterans (those who have failed at the Barkley before) the entry fee is an item of Laz's request – most recently a pair of gold-toe dress socks in dark blue or black. For alumni (previous completers) the entry fee is a pack of regular Camel filter cigarettes.

For those who are lucky enough to secure a place, completing three loops earns runners a 'fun run', which they concede if they continue and then go on to fail. Finishing the full five loops earns them a coveted place in ultrarunning history.

In 2025, Carl Laniak took over the role of Race Director from Laz. With the addition of a tough new section to the route, there were no finishers of the Barkley Marathons in 2025.

PREVIOUS PAGES Christophe Nonorgue ascending Rat Jaw during the 2023 Barkley Marathons.

RIGHT Karel Sabbe, one of three finishers at the 2023 Barkley Marathons.

QUEBEC MEGA TRAIL

CHARLEVOIX AND THE CÔTE DE BEAUPRÉ, QUEBEC, CANADA

First held in 2012, and having since grown to become Canada's biggest trail-running event, the Quebec Mega Trail (QMT) connects the largest two mountains in Quebec's Laurentian range to the event base at Mont-Sainte-Anne ski resort. The races are known for being challenging, with high altitude, technical trails, mud, climbing and exposure tempered by the breathtaking beauty of the Laurentian mountains.

This annual Canadian festival of trail and ultrarunning includes eight races across distances from 3¾ miles (6km) to 84 miles (135km), plus a 1km kids' run, with the main event attracting around 3,000 participants from 12 countries, including some of the biggest names in the sport. As of 2025, the previously separate 100-mile and 110km races have been merged into a 135km event. The new route packs in more climbing for the distance, with 19,700ft (6,000m) of cumulative altitude gain. The additional climbing will take runners from the starting point in the pretty town of Baie-Saint-Paul, on the northern shore of the St. Lawrence River, to Mont-Sainte-Anne in the Laurentian Mountains.

Following wild and spectacular trails along the banks of the river, the terrain is technical and demanding underfoot, with rocks, mud and savagely steep climbs and descents. Race day weather is notoriously variable, with conditions ranging from hot sun to mist and rain.

RACE STATISTICS

MONTH: July

DISTANCE: 84 miles (135km)

TOTAL ELEVATION: 20,000ft (6,096m)

HIGHEST POINT: 803m (2,634ft)

STARTERS 2024 (100-MILE): 176 (23 female, 153 male)

FINISHERS 2024 (100-MILE): 99 (15 female, 84 male)

TIME ALLOWED: 30hr

FEMALE COURSE RECORD: (100-mile): Anne Champagne 24:28:27 (2024)

MALE COURSE RECORD: (100-mile): Jean-François Cauchon 19:01:28 (2024)

FIRST RUN: 2012

ENTRY FEE: CAD $375

WEBSITE:
www.ultratrailcanada.com

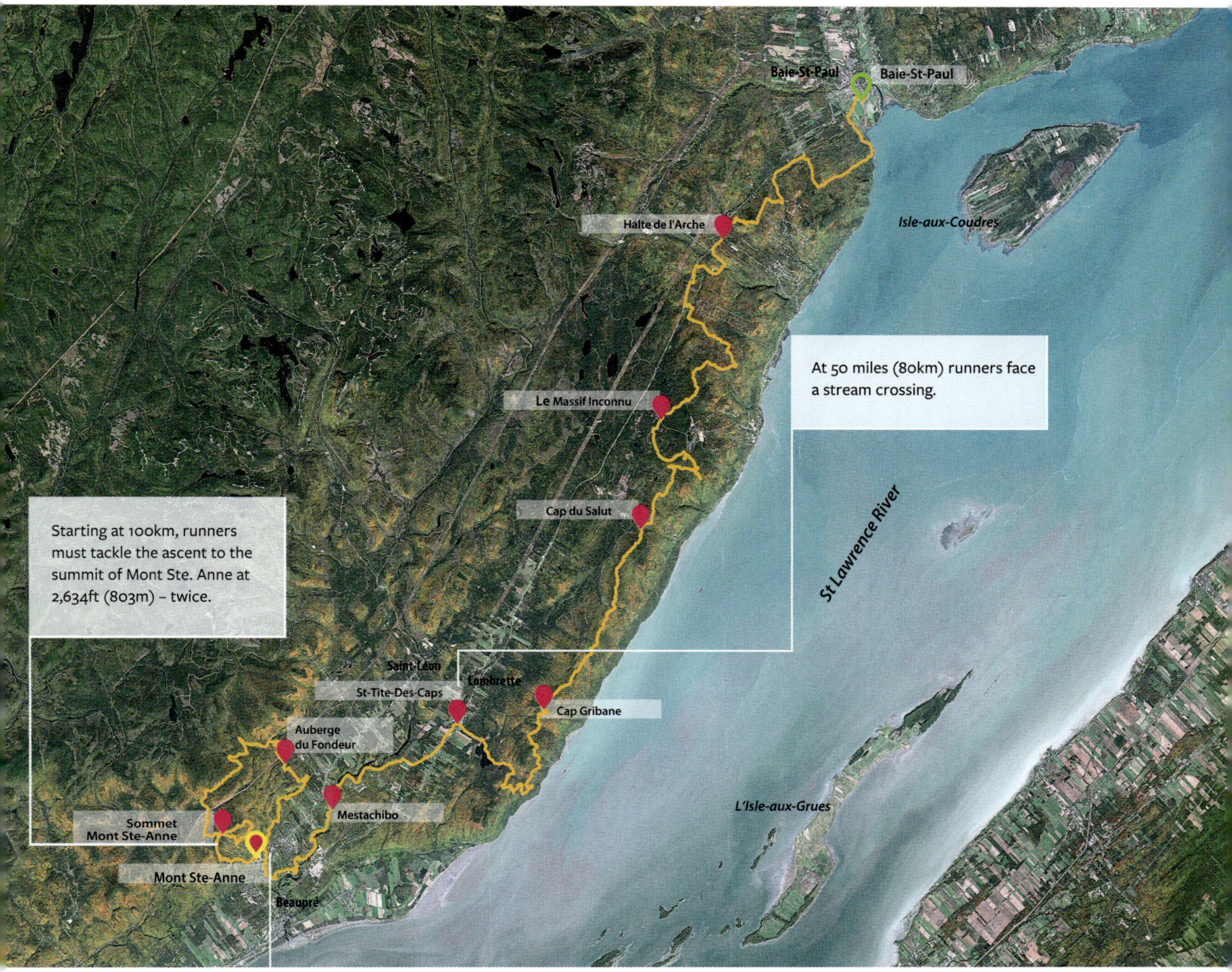

At 50 miles (80km) runners face a stream crossing.

Starting at 100km, runners must tackle the ascent to the summit of Mont Ste. Anne at 2,634ft (803m) – twice.

Runners can expect a grand feast offered at aid stations along the route, including ginger cookies, banana bread, praline pancakes and fudge. A veggie chilli also awaits all finishers at Mont Sainte Anne.

ELEVATION PROFILE

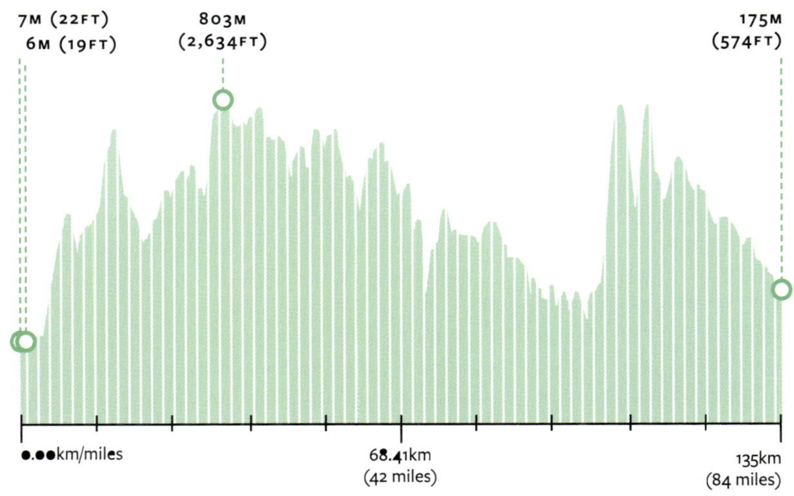

FAR LEFT Participants of the 2023 QMT-50 cross the Jean-Larose river a few hundred metres from the finish line at Mont-Sainte-Anne.

LEFT A runner on the 2024 QMT-80 runs in Saint-Tite-des-Caps towards the rugged Mestachibo Traill.

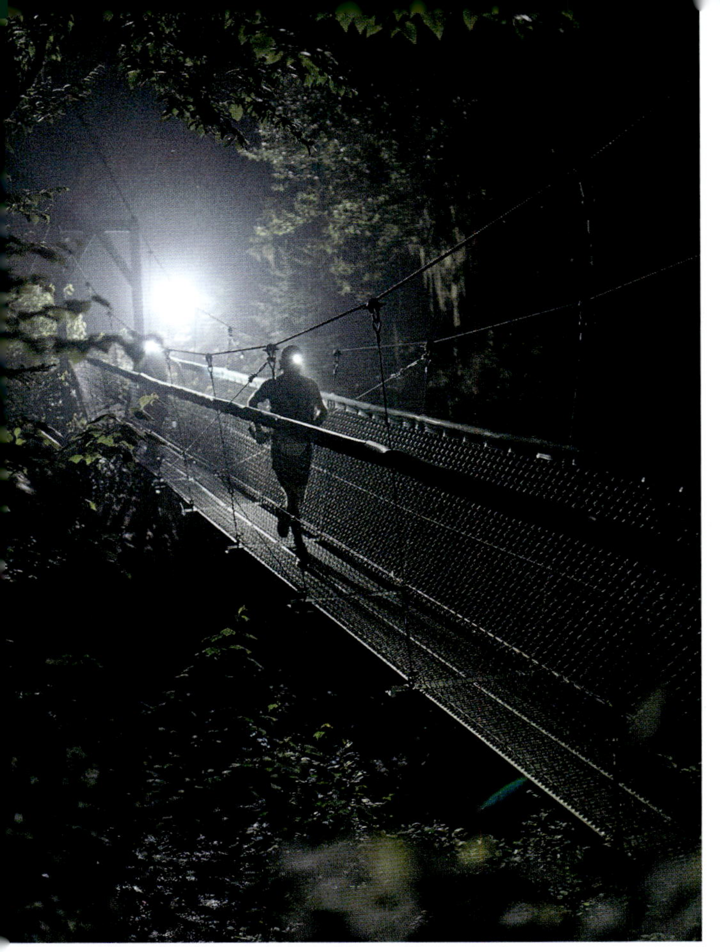

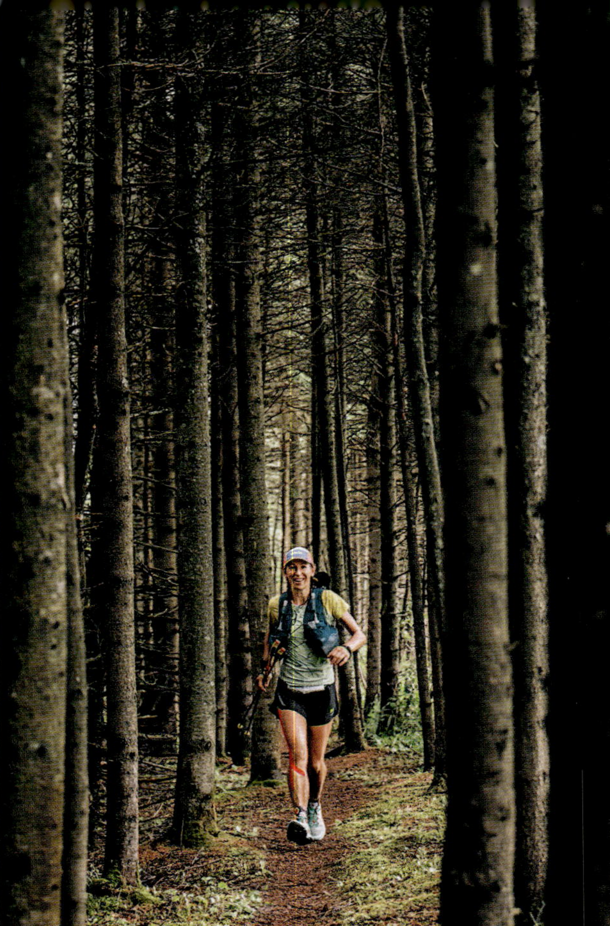

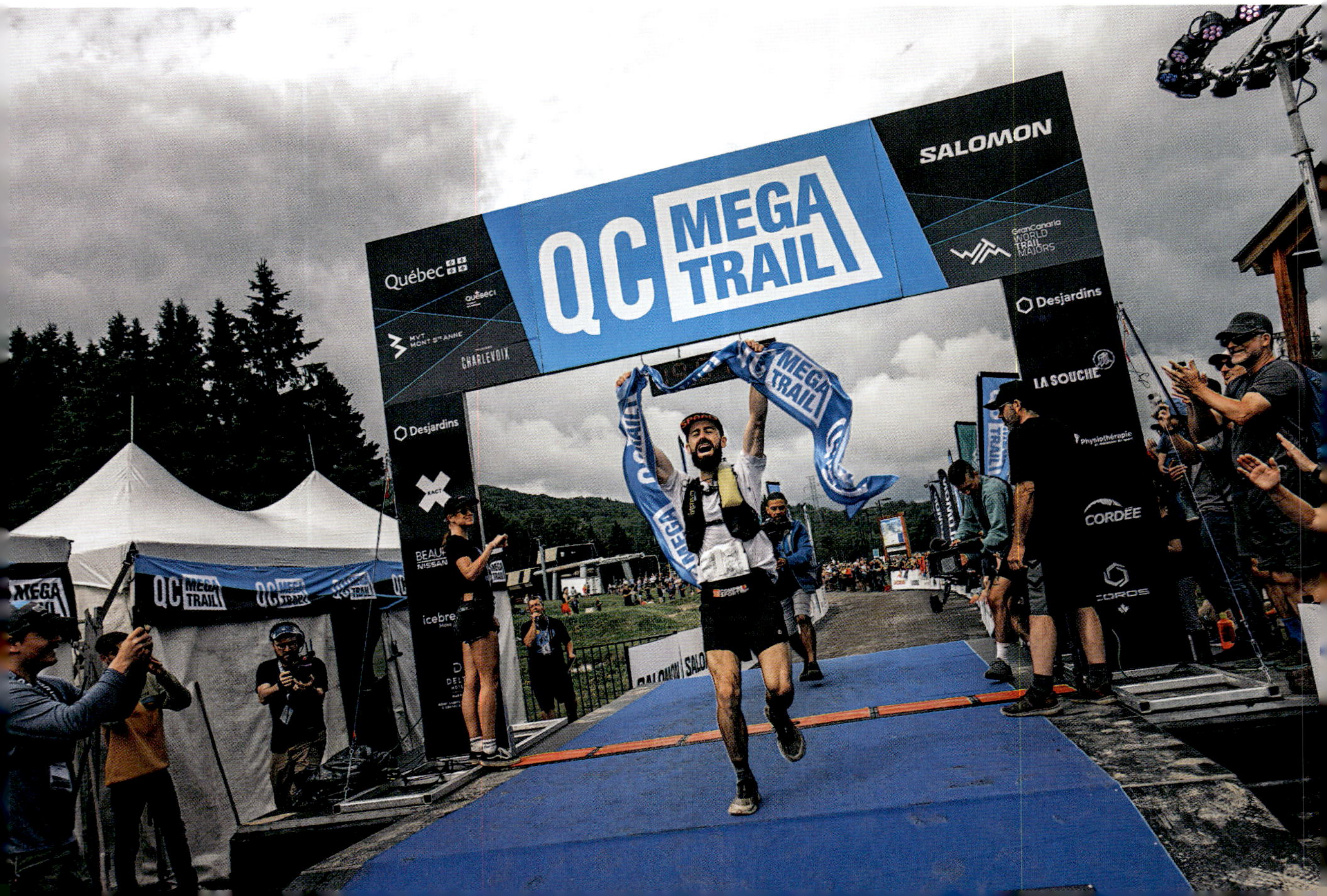
QC MEGA TRAIL
SALOMON
Québec
CHARLEVOIX
Desjardins
LA SOUCHE
CORDÉE
GranCanaria WORLD TRAIL MAJORS

OTHER DISTANCES

OTHER DISTANCES
49¾ miles (80km); 10,794ft (3,290m) ascent
31 miles (50km); 7,546ft (2,300m) ascent
20 miles (32km); 4,757ft (1,450m) ascent
15½ miles (25km); 3,117ft (950m) ascent
9¼ miles (15km); 1,378ft (420m) ascent
3¾ miles (6km); 581ft (177m) ascent
Children's race: 2/3 mile (1km); 82ft (25m) ascent

The 15½-mile (25km) race is part of the Golden Trail National Series, and the 135 is the only race in North America officially affiliated with Grand Raid de la Réunion mountain race (also known as La Diagonale des Fous – see page 202), and is also a Western States qualifying race.

As well as a wide range of race distances on offer, the race weekend isn't just about running – those attending, whether running, cheering or crewing, can look forward to a festival that includes live music, seminars on nutrition and fuelling, a comprehensive race expo, yoga sessions, shakeout runs, a fun obstacle course challenge, and plenty of activities for families.

In the final QMT 100-mile race, which took place in 2024, both the women's and men's course records were broken. Anne Champagne took the women's course record, finishing in 24:28:27, six minutes faster than Kelsey Hogan's previous time. Jean-François Cauchon broke the men's record by a commanding 25 minutes, crossing the finish line in 19:01:28. Champagne, a Quebec local, added the win to her 2019 record at the 110km distance, dedicating to the memory of a friend who had been due to pace her in the race. In a post-race interview with *Canadian Trail Running* magazine, Champagne talked about the demands of the course, and how she had needed to dig deep during challenging sections of the race, but also of the many joys she experienced. 'I get to run all day in beautiful company on these trails,' she said. She enjoyed coming across familiar athletes and volunteers throughout the race: 'It's a really community-driven event.'

> 'The conditions were very difficult so I had a little trouble finding my flow, with people in front of me, because it was very technical. There was mud, rocks and I was slipping a lot. It wasn't quite the conditions I'm used to in California. At some point I decided to push a bit to get the trail lit, and from there I just kept going and having fun in the tough conditions.'
>
> MEIKAEL BEAUDOIN-ROUSSEAU, QMT-25 CHAMPION IN 2023

PREVIOUS PAGES The stunning forest trails in the Sentier des Caps de Charlevoix, somewhere between the summit of Massif and Cap à l'Abbatis.

ABOVE LEFT A runner on 2023 the QMT-100 mile crosses the suspension bridge on the Louise-Gasnier Trail near the first-aid station.

ABOVE RIGHT The start of the Mestachibo Trail through stunning woodland. This runner still has many kilometres to go before reaching the finish line at Mont-Sainte-Anne.

LEFT Jean-François Cauchon winning the 2024 edition of the Quebec Mega Trail 100-miler.

OTHER US AND CANADIAN HIGHLIGHTS

VERMONT 100 ENDURANCE RACE

WEST WINDSOR, VERMONT, USA

RACE STATISTICS

MONTH: July
DISTANCE: 100 miles (161km)
TOTAL ASCENT: 17,000ft (5,182m)
TIME ALLOWED: 30hr

WEBSITE: www.vermont100.com

The VT100 has a long history; starting in the 1960s as a horse endurance trail, over the years it became a race, then in 1989 runners were invited to compete. Now it's the only remaining 100-miler which includes a concurrent horse race.

The 100-mile (161km) and 62-mile (100km) races follow an undulating mixture of dirt roads and horse trails, through areas of forest interspersed with great views of the Green Mountains. It's hilly but without any major climbs.

The race is a major fundraising event for VT Adaptive, a charity which empowers people of all abilities through year-round inclusive sports and recreational programming regardless of their ability to pay. VT100 was the first trail race to recognize visually and mobilit- impaired runners in their own awards category.

Please note, the course crosses a lot of private land, and therefore you can't train on the same trails.

CANYONS ENDURANCE RUNS BY UTMB

AUBURN, SIERRA NEVADA RANGE, USA

RACE STATISTICS

MONTH: April
DISTANCE: 100 miles (161km)
TOTAL ASCENT: 18,514ft (5,643m)
TIME ALLOWED: 36hr

WEBSITE: canyons.utmb.world

Starting in Auburn, an old gold-rush town and the birthplace of mountain ultras, the route winds through the northern California foothills of the Sierra Nevada range. It shares some of the most legendary and challenging sections of the Western States Trail, passing Deadwood, the Swinging Bridge via the Devil's Thumb descent, Michigan Bluff, Foresthill, Cal Street and No Hands Bridge.

Interestingly the 100-mile (161km) race has a net descent, starting at China Wall at 5,106ft (1,529m) and finishing in Auburn at 1,266ft (386m); you'll ascend 18,514ft (5,643m) but descend 22,244ft (6,780m). The 62-mile (100km) race has a similar net descent, but the 31-mile (50km) and 15½-mile (25km) races are loops.

The Canyons Endurance Runs are part of the UTMB World Series; top-three finishers will win an entry to run at the series finals, UTMB Mont-Blanc in France.

RIGHT Mountain Quarries Railroad Bridge, Canyons Endurance Runs.

GRAND TO GRAND ULTRA

GRAND CANYON, USA

RACE STATISTICS

MONTH: September
STAGE RACE: Six stages over seven days
DISTANCE: 171 miles (275km)
TOTAL ASCENT: 15,499ft (5,207m)
TIME ALLOWED: 87hr

WEBSITE: www.g2gultra.com

Starting on the north rim of the Grand Canyon and finishing at the Pink Cliffs, you'll run through geological time, exploring one of the seven natural wonders of the world.

The Grand to Grand Ultra was America's first self-supported stage race. Competitors race six stages across the Utah and Arizona desert. Stage 3 is the long one, covering a challenging 53¼ miles (85.7km); Stage 6 is the shortest at 8 miles (13km); the other stages are between 26 and 31 miles (42 and 50km). You'll run through the high desert, experiencing slot canyons, buttes, mesas and hoodoos. The desert is rich in wildlife and plants: look out for cacti, Big Horn sheep and the endangered California Condor, America's largest bird.

Runners can choose to be supported (with food and kit transported by the organizers each day) or self-supported (you carry all food and equipment needed for the duration of the race). You can also run as a team of two or three.

ABOVE A runner negotiating the slot canyons in the Grand to Grand Ultra.

GRAND MESA ULTRAS

GRAND MESA NATIONAL FOREST, COLORADO, USA

RACE STATISTICS

MONTH: July
DISTANCE: 50 miles (80.5km)
TOTAL ASCENT: 3,971ft (1,210m)
TIME ALLOWED: 15hr

WEBSITE: www.bestslopeevents.com

Described as 'Good old-fashioned Colorado mountain trail races run at high elevation', the Grand to Grand course uses as many of the fun singletrack trails as possible. There are tricky rocky ascents and fast swoopy forest tracks. You'll be running through pine and aspen forest, past wildflower-rich alpine meadows and along the banks of mountain streams and lakes. In the gaps between the trees, the views across the Grand Mesa National Forest are stunning.

This is a figure-of-eight course that follows the high ridge, with an average elevation of a vertigo-inducing 10,400ft (3,170m) above sea level. The course highpoint is 11,189ft (3,410m) on the summit of Crag Crest. The trail is well-marked and you'll find five aid stations.

There are also 34-mile (55km) or 18½-mile (30km) races on the same day, both of which have a higher average elevation than the 50-miler (80.5km).

ABOVE The Grand Mesa 50-mile ultra race in 2019.

ARROWHEAD ULTRA 135

ARROWHEAD, NORTHERN MINNESOTA, USA

RACE STATISTICS

MONTH: January
DISTANCE: 135 miles (216.5km)
TOTAL ASCENT: 5,056ft (1,541m)
TIME ALLOWED: 60hr

WEBSITE: www.arrowheadultra.com

The race follows the Arrowhead State Trail from International Falls, Minnesota, to Highway 77 on Lake Vermillion (near Tower). The trail crosses wetland in the summer, so is more popular with snowmobiles when frozen and snow covered. It's well maintained with good signage and basic shelters approximately 12 miles (19km) apart.

The first half of the route is relatively flat, while the next half is wilder and hillier with more forest. It's not uncommon to see moose and wolf tracks as well as lynx, fox and hare.

Winter temperatures in this area can dip to -60°F (-51°C), but it's also possible for the weather to warm up and the trail to thaw, which brings its own problems. Kit choice for this race is life-saving rather than time-saving.

You are permitted to race on skis or by bike; on-foot entrants can run traditionally or with a kick sled/push sled. Normally bikes are fastest, followed by ski then foot.

ABOVE Competitors can tackle the frozen length of the Arrowhead State Trail on foot, bike or skis.

TIGER CLAW 50

THE ISSAQUAH ALPS, WASHINGTON, USA

RACE STATISTICS

MONTH: May
DISTANCE: 31 miles (50km)
TOTAL ASCENT: 8,800ft (2,682m)
TIME ALLOWED: 10hr

WEBSITE: www.runtigerclaw.com

Tiger Mountain, standing at 3,004ft (915.5m), is the highest peak in the Issaquah or Issy Alps. This rugged Pacific Northwest terrain is beautiful but tough to run, with steep hills and technical trails under a lush canopy of trees and mosses. The Tiger Claw crew have come up with a cracking race format with three different loops to run. Each loop climbs the mountain by a different trail and then descends back to the start, and you have to run all three loops, but it's up to you in which order you run them.

The Pink loop follows the Tiger Mountain Trail. It's a local favourite training run, but most people don't run the other trails on the same day! The Pink loop is about 4¾ miles (7.5km) to the top with 2,700ft (823m) of ascent. The White loop follows the brutal Section Line trail – it's only 3 miles (4.8km) but packs in 2,400ft (731.5m) of ascent. The Yellow loop follows the Poo Poo Point Trail (named after the noise the loggers' lunch whistle made); it's 6 miles (9.6km) with 3,000ft (914m) of climbing.

If you don't fancy the Tiger Claw then you could try the Ascent – it's only 5½ miles (8.8km), but it manages to pack a hefty 2,500ft (762m) of ascent and the same amount of descent!

JFK 50 MILE

HAGERSTOWN, MARYLAND, USA

RACE STATISTICS

MONTH: November
DISTANCE: 50 miles (80.5km)
TOTAL ASCENT: 1,350ft (412m)
TIME ALLOWED: 13hr

WEBSITE: www.jfk50mile.org

The JFK 50 Mile was first held in 1963, one of numerous 50-mile (80.5km) events held around America as part of President John F. Kennedy's push to bring the country back to physical fitness. JFK was assassinated in November 1963 and most of the events stopped, but this race has lived on, with 2024 marking the 62nd edition.

The point-to-point, horseshoe-shaped course runs on a mixture of roads and trails, following technical sections of the Appalachian Trail initially, then a long, flat section of canal towpath. You're well looked after, with 14 checkpoints en route. The course and support lead to some quick times; Hayden Hawks ran 5:18:42 in 2020 and Sarah Biehl ran 6:05:42 in 2022. The majority of runners finish in around ten hours.

ABOVE Camille Herron crosses the line of the 2016 JFK 50-Mile race to win the women's race.

SELF-TRANSCENDENCE 3100

JAMAICA, QUEENS, NEW YORK, USA

RACE STATISTICS

MONTH: August–October
STAGE RACE: 52 days
DISTANCE: 3,100 miles (4,989km)
TOTAL ASCENT: n/a
TIME ALLOWED: 18hr per day

WEBSITE: 3100.srichinmoyraces.org

Sri Chinmoy was a spiritual teacher, athlete, artist, musician, poet and humanitarian. His emphasis on self-transcendence and the triumph of the human spirit led him to conceive this race; which aims to create a physical and spiritual journey for the athletes.

In the words of the race organizers: 'For those runners who are Sri Chinmoy's students, the 3100-Mile Race represents an affirmation of his teachings on self-transcendence, an opportunity to manifest the hidden potential of the soul in a practical and dynamic way.'

It's the longest certified road race in the world; runners must cover 3,100 miles (4,989km) over 52 days. They do this by running laps of a flat 0.5488-mile (0.9km) block in the Jamaica neighbourhood of Quuens, New York City, running hundreds of loops around a sports field, playground and high school. The course is open from 6am to midnight each day; to complete the race, athletes must cover an average of 59½ miles (95.9 km) per day.

Ashprihanal Aalto from Finland holds the record for both the fastest completion (40 days 9 hours) and the most finishes (14). Tsai Wen-Ya holds the women's record of 45 days +12:28:44 run in 2023.

WASATCH FRONT 100 MILE ENDURANCE RUN

WASATCH MOUNTAINS, UTAH, USA

RACE STATISTICS

MONTH: September
DISTANCE: 100 miles (161km)
TOTAL ASCENT: 24,000ft (7,315m)
TIME ALLOWED: 36hr

WEBSITE: www.wasatch100.com

This beautiful tour of Wasatch Mountains runs point-to-point from East Mountain Wilderness Park to Soldier Hollow. You run on a mixture of dirt roads, single- and double-track trails and rough tracks through forests, open country and canyons. The course is marked and there are 14 aid stations, but people still manage to get lost. The race organizers describe the race as a study in contrasts: 'peaks and valleys; trail and scree; heat and cold; wet and dry; summer and winter; day and night; Desolation Lake and Point Supreme; "I can't" and "I will!"'

As if the distance and elevation gains weren't challenging enough, the temperature can reach 100°F (38°C) with the sun reflecting up at you from the light-coloured soil, so the race crew recommend that on sunny days you 'carry more water than you expect to need'.

The Wasatch 100 is the final and only mandatory race in the Grand Slam of Ultrarunning. Athletes who wish to complete this challenge must finish any three of the following races and then finish the Wasatch 100 within the same calendar year. The other races are the Old Dominion 100 Mile Endurance Run, Western States 100 Mile Endurance Run, Vermont 100 Endurance Race and Leadville Trail 100 Run.

TAHOE RIM TRAIL

CARSON CITY, NEVADA, USA

RACE STATISTICS

MONTH: July
DISTANCE: 100 miles (161km)
TOTAL ASCENT: 8,000ft (2,438m)
TIME ALLOWED: 36hr

WEBSITE: www.trter.com

The TRT runs on high alpine and sub-alpine forest road and singletrack in the Sierra Nevada Mountains. The race slogan is a 'Glimpse of Heaven . . . A Taste of Hell'. Eleven-time finisher Ismael Macias defines the course as 'brutal yet beautiful' and everyone raves about the brilliant aid stations . . . Todd Vogel (nine-time finisher) says, 'What sets the race apart goes beyond its spectacular scenery and fun and engaging running. Every aid station here – the core ones are like mini villages – is a party just for you!'

A 62-mile (100km) and a 31-mile (50km) race runs over the same weekend. The looped trails begin and end at 4,888ft (1,490m) in Carson City, the lowest point on the course. The highest point, on all distances, is just below the summit of the 9,214-ft (2,808m) Snow Valley Peak, where you'll be treated to amazing views.

ABOVE Runners enjoying the spectacular scenery on the Tahoe Rim Trail around Lake Tahoe.

COCODONA 250

BLACK CANYON CITY – FLAGSTAFF, ARIZONA, USA

RACE STATISTICS

MONTH: May
DISTANCE: 250 miles (402km)
TOTAL ASCENT: 40,143ft (12,236m)
TIME ALLOWED: 125hr

WEBSITE: www.cocodona.com

The Cocodona 250 is a whopping point-to-point trail-running adventure, featuring some of the best trails in Arizona. Run from Black Canyon City up into the Bradshaw Mountains, over Mount Union, and snake down into Prescott. You'll continue over Mingus Mountain into the town of Jerome and then through Sedona's stunning red rock formations and high desert vistas. The final section runs high in the pine forests, finishing up and over Mount Elden and into downtown Flagstaff.

Despite having 125 hours available, the course records are held by Haroldas Subertas 59:50:55 in 2024 and Sarah Ostaszewski 72:50:27 in 2023. The majority of runners finish in around 110 hours.

Race Director Steve Aderholt says, 'This race captures both the beauty and the suffering of the human condition. We designed a race to test the limits of human endurance and in the end, we found the depth of the human spirit. It is so beautiful to watch, but even better to participate in.'

The Sedona Canyons 125-mile (201km) and Elden Crest 38-mile (61km) races are run during the same week, following some of the same magnificent trails.

LEFT Granite dells during the 2024 Cocodona 250.

BIG DOG'S BACKYARD ULTRA

BIG FARM IN SHORT CREEK, TENNESSEE, USA

RACE STATISTICS

MONTH: October
DISTANCE: 4.167 miles (6.706km) per yard (lap)
DAY LOOP TOTAL ASCENT: 475ft (145m)
NIGHT LOOP TOTAL ASCENT: 100ft (30½m)
TIME ALLOWED: One yard (lap) per hour until only one runner remains

WEBSITE: bigsbackyardultra.com

Backyard ultras were invented by Gary 'Lazarus Lake' Cantrell, founder of the notorious Barkley Marathons (see page 138). Big Dog's Backyard Ultra takes place on Cantrell's Big Farm. It's named after his dog and the yard he normally occupies. The race is held on a 4-mile (6.706km) course, known as a Yard. Competitors must complete one yard (lap) per hour, consecutively, until there is only one runner left to complete a lap. There is no predefined end point. The final runner is marked as the winner and only finisher; the second place runner is known as the assist.

The distance means runners race exactly 100 miles (161km) per 24 hours. The current record is 110 laps (458 miles/737km), set by Belgian runners Merijn Geerts, Ivo Steyaert and Frank Gielen during the Backyard Ultra World Team Championship in 2024. The female World Record is 87 laps (362½ miles/583km), by Meg Eckert at the same event.

YUKON ARCTIC ULTRA

WHITEHORSE, CANADA

RACE STATISTICS

MONTH: February
DISTANCE: 398 miles (640km)
TOTAL ASCENT: 18,045ft (5,500m)
TIME ALLOWED: 288hr

WEBSITE: www.arcticultra.de/home

This epic race claims to be the world's coldest and toughest ultra. It follows the Yukon Quest Trail for 211 miles (340km) or 398 miles (640km) in the Arctic winter. Conditions are super-tough, with temperatures averaging between 17.5°F and –16.5°F (–8°C and –27°C) during the short 7.5 hours of daylight; the nights are colder and temperatures have dropped to –58°F (–50°C)! Racers choose to travel across the snowy landscape on foot, XC-ski or fatbike. Bikes are often the fastest, followed by foot, then ski, but even the fastest racers will be out for well over 100 hours. The race is waymarked and supported, but checkpoints are between 27 miles (44km) and 46½ miles (75km) apart, so competitors must be very self-sufficient. The mandatory kit list reflects this, including a sleeping bag rated to –40°F (–40°C), expedition down jacket, multi-fuel stove and fire lighting equipment.

The Yukon Arctic Ultra is a partner race to the Lapland Arctic Ultra in Sweden (see page 92).

SQUAMISH 50

SQUAMISH, WESTERN CANADA

RACE STATISTICS

MONTH: August
DISTANCE: 50 miles (80.5km)
TOTAL ASCENT: 11,483ft (3,500m)
TIME ALLOWED: 17hr

WEBSITE: www.squamish50.com

Gary Robbins, Geoff Langford and the team have worked hard to create a 50-mile (80.5km) race which highlights the absolute best running terrain in Western Canada. Over 90 per cent of the course runs on technical singletrack trails. Much of the area is forested, but the trails still offer incredible views across glaciated peaks and straight out over the Pacific Ocean. The race is well flagged so you can concentrate on the running, and there are seven expertly managed aid stations with a supportive atmosphere from the crew and locals. In previous years they've had young ones dressed up in costumes high-fiving runners, at 6:15am!

The Squamish 50 is a weekend of ultrarunning; the 50-mile (80.5km) and kids' races are on the Saturday, with the 31-mile (50km) or 14¼-mile (23km) courses on Sunday. You can even run both the 50-mile and 31-mile over the weekend to earn a coveted 50/50 cap.

RIGHT A 50-km runner near the top of the Angry Midget trail. Squamish 50-mile runners take this route as well.

CENTRAL AND SOUTH AMERICA

CENTRAL AND SOUTH AMERICA INTRODUCTION

The ultrarunning feats of Mexico's Tarahumara, or Rarámuri, of the Copper Canyons in Chihuahua were made famous by Christopher McDougall's 2009 bestseller, *Born to Run*. For hunting, competition and prayer, the Rarámuri cover vast distances on foot, often wearing sandals with tyre treads as soles; running is simply part of their way of life. In 1926, an ultramarathon was held in Mexico as part of the Central American Games with Rarámuri runners Tomas Zafiro and Leoncio San Miguel running 100km (62 miles) from Pachuca to Mexico City in 9 hours and 37 minutes. Today, the Ultra Marathon Caballo Blanco (see page 180), established by Micah True (also known as Caballo Blanco – the white horse) of *Born to Run* fame in 2003, takes place over 80.5km (50 miles) each spring. Originally attended by a few Rarámuri athletes, the race now attracts over 1,200 runners from over 20 countries.

With its roots in ancient, pre-Colombian Mexican and Incan cultures, long-distance running was foundational to the cultures and lifestyles of Central and Southern American people. Ultrarunning here has much more recently seen a gradual increase in popularity, with races tending towards the adventurous end of the spectrum, often crossing long distances over multiple days.

The Latin American Trail Circuit (LATC) was founded in 2003 by three ultrarunning friends with the aim of promoting the visibility of trail running in Mexico and countries in Central America, South America and the Caribbean. The Circuit includes nine of the region's most iconic races, showcasing some of its impressive and varied geography, including Mexico's mountains, the temperate rainforests of southern Chile, Colombia's canyons, the high Andes in Peru, and El Salvador's rugged volcanic peaks. El Salvador is a relative newcomer to the trail running world. Only ten years ago, this was a country where running would have been considered unsafe but, following governmental changes, today both tourism and trail running are booming.

The Jungle Ultra (see page 166), organized by UK-based team Beyond the Ultimate as part of its global race series, explores Peru's Manu National Park, tackling 230km (143 miles) of heat and humidity, river crossings, tangled undergrowth and altitude over five stages, descending from the high altitude cloud forest to the Amazon basin.

From the jungle to the desert, the Atacama Crossing (see page 170) is part of RacingThePlanet's 4 Deserts Ultramarathon Series, which includes the Namib Race (Namibia), the Gobi March (Mongolia) and The Last Desert (Antarctica), plus an extra race in a different location each year.

PREVIOUS PAGES French runner Sophie Didou who eventually finished 3rd in the 2023 La Transtica Extreme.

BELOW A runner tackling leg-sapping soft sand in the Atacama Crossing.

The race series was founded by US ultrarunner Mary K Gadams, who founded RacingThePlanet in 2002. First held in 2004, the Atacama Crossing takes on 250km (156 miles) over six stages across Chile's Atacama Desert – officially recognized as the driest place on earth. Along the way, runners encounter rock-hard salt flats, soft sand and high dunes, freezing slot canyons and river crossings, all at an average altitude of 2,500m (8,200ft).

The Argentinian Patagonian province of Neuquén hosts the annual non-stop, self-sufficient adventure trekking race of La Misión (see page 176), billed by its organizers as a challenge rather than a race. With no fixed stopping points and with runners required to be entirely self-sufficient, the event, which offers distances of between 40 and 200km (25–124 miles), starts in Villa la Angostura in the south of the province and tours the rugged and mountainous Nahuel Huapi National Park. Another non-stop epic is the Brasil 135 Ultra (see page 182), sister race to Badwater 135, which follows the spectacular Caminho da Fé (Path of Faith) through the Serra da Mantiqueira mountains of southestern Brazil.

THE JUNGLE ULTRA

MANU NATIONAL PARK, PERU

Deep in the rainforest of Peru's Manu National Park, the Jungle Ultra tackles 230km (143 miles) of heat and humidity, river crossings, tangled undergrowth and altitude over five stages, descending from the high altitude Cloud Forest to the Amazon basin. Competitors can expect GPS tracking, checkpoints and camps with medical and support staff, drinking water on the course and hot water for preparing food at all camps, but otherwise are expected to be self-sufficient for the duration of the race. Nights are spent in hammocks in the jungle, and temperatures range from 5°C (41°F) in the evenings to 30°C (86°F) during the day.

Stage 1 descends 2,290m (7,513ft), starting at Wayqecha Biological Research Station at an altitude of 3,000m (9,842ft), following rocky mountain tracks with stunning views down to the rainforest. Tough climbs – including some requiring a rope to pull yourself up – and long descents lead through five fascinating and distinct ecosystems.

Stage 2 starts with a descent through jungle into an area of hut settlements, where local villagers watch the runners pass. The middle section delves into the depths of the jungle, with steep muddy climbs and descents, river crossings and heat. Runners discover the jungle's fascinating flora and fauna, much of which bites or stings.

RACE STATISTICS

MONTH: May–June
STAGE RACE: Five stages in five days
DISTANCE: 230km (143 miles)
TOTAL ASCENT: 4,000m (13,123ft)
HIGHEST POINT: 2,740m (8,989ft)
STARTERS 2024: 35 (8 female, 27 male)
FINISHERS 2024: 28 (6 female, 22 male)
TIME ALLOWED: Varies for each stage, according to conditions
FEMALE COURSE RECORD: Eleonoora Hintsa Figueiredo 35:23:00 (2024)
MALE COURSE RECORD: Vicente Jaun García 27:40:00 (2016)
FIRST RUN: 2012
ENTRY FEE: £3,000

WEBSITE: www.beyondtheultimate.co.uk/race/jungle-ultra

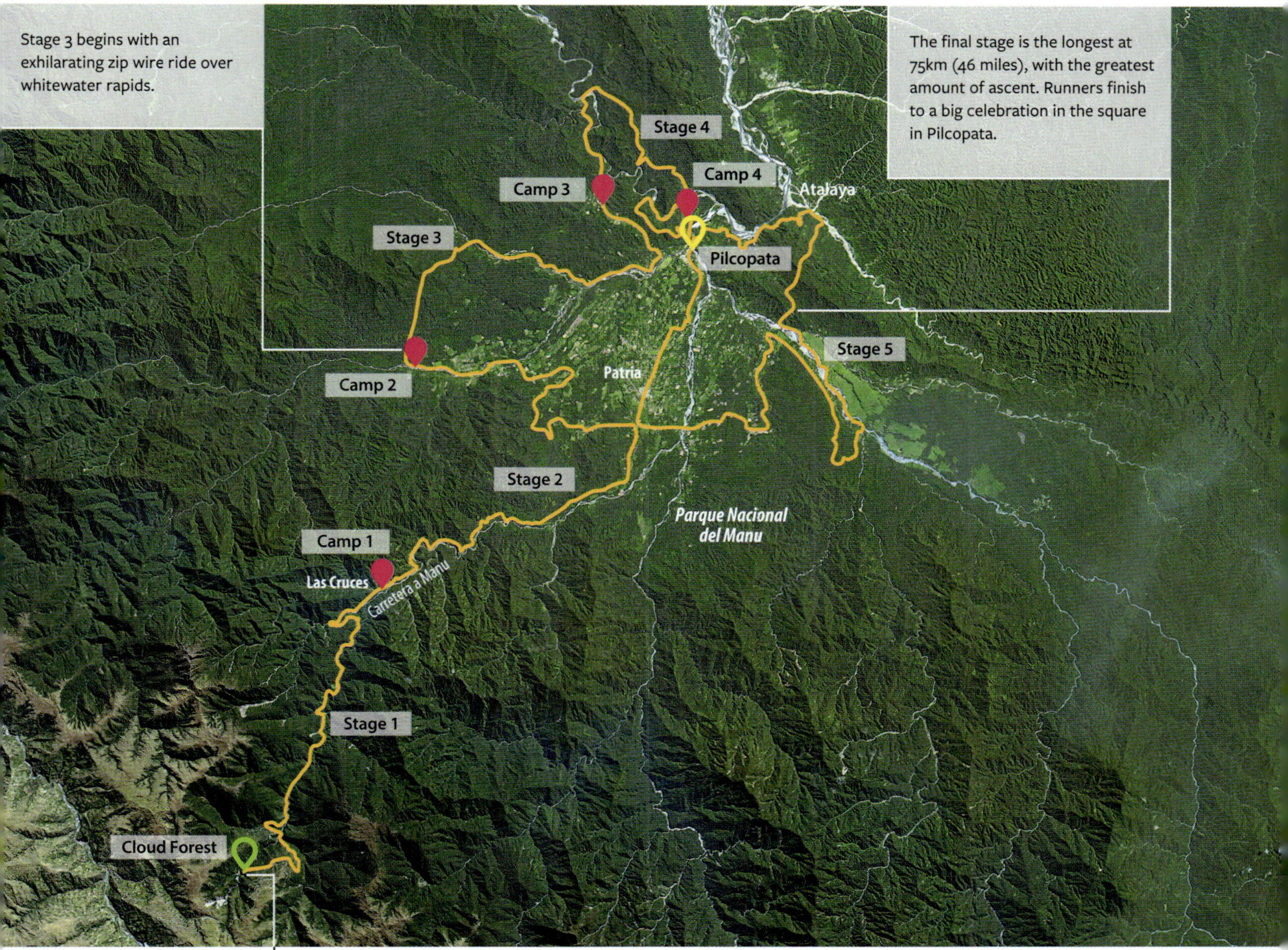
Stage 3 begins with an exhilarating zip wire ride over whitewater rapids.
The final stage is the longest at 75km (46 miles), with the greatest amount of ascent. Runners finish to a big celebration in the square in Pilcopata.
Stage 4
Camp 4
Atalaya
Camp 3
Stage 3
Pilcopata
Camp 2
Patria
Stage 5
Stage 2
Parque Nacional del Manu
Camp 1
Las Cruces
Carretera a Manu
Stage 1
Cloud Forest

The race starts at an altitude of 2,740m (8,989ft), with runners descending a whopping 2,290m (7,513ft) during the first stage.

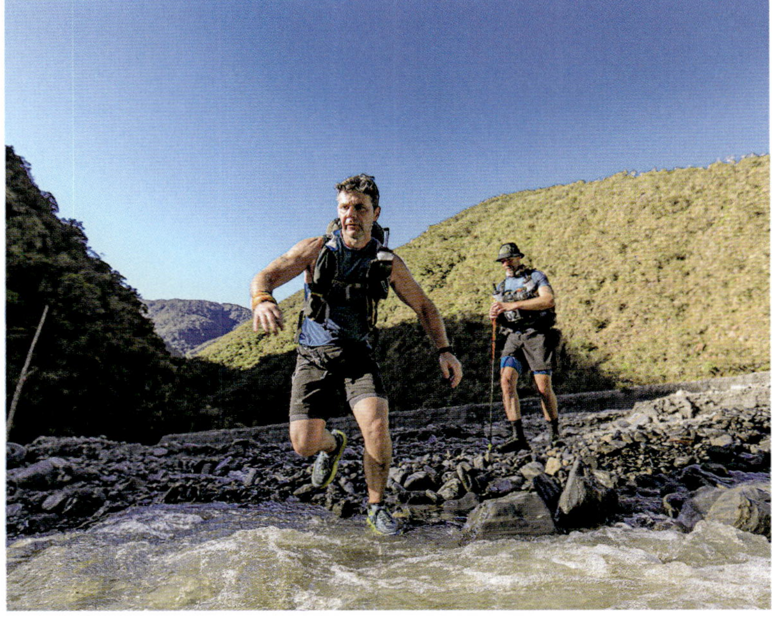

RIGHT At the start of Day 3, runners cross rivers and streams.

LEFT One of many river crossings in the Jungle Ultra.

STAGE DETAILS

Stage 1 Cloud Nine: 34km (21 miles); 730m (2,395ft) ascent
Stage 2 Amazonia: 42km (26 miles); 520m (1,706ft) ascent
Stage 3 Solo Aguanta: 26km (16 miles); 610m (2,000ft) ascent
Stage 4 The Lull: 34km (21 miles); 980m (3,215ft) ascent
Stage 5 The Long One: 75km (46½ miles); 1,280m (4,200ft) ascent

Stage 3 begins with a zip wire over a wide river with whitewater rapids, followed by many more crossings of smaller rivers and streams. Leaving the canopy, runners pass through open terrain exposed to the elements – as draining in its own way as the jungle. The day ends in the village of Santa Rosa de Huacaria, with local children accompanying runners across the line.

Stage 4 is notoriously tough, with steep climbs and descents, mud, scrambles and river crossings all in high humidity and a cut-off to make at checkpoint 3. For those who make it through, the hardest climb of the race awaits, with runners competing for the title of King/Queen of the Hill. The day ends at the lodge and research station, Villa Carmen.

Stage 5 is the longest of the race at 75km (46½ miles) and, like stage 4, has over 1,000m (3,280ft) of descending and a mid-stage cut-off to contend with. Runners set out before sunrise, passing through dense jungle with river crossings and steep, muddy terrain to negotiate. The race finishes in the main square of Pilcopata, where celebrations await.

Competitors can also expect a post-race celebratory meal, while Beyond the Ultimate has partnered with the Knoydart Forest Trust to help support their conservation as a means of offsetting carbon from air travel.

> 'The Jungle Ultra is a race like no other. Endless river crossings, sweltering heat, humidity and slinging your own hammock at the end of the day, this race challenges you mentally and physically right from beginning to end. BTU do a fantastic job in super challenging conditions. The Jungle Ultra keeps me coming back year after year. It's the ultimate challenge.'
>
> CAROLIN BOTTERILL, FIVE-TIME JUNGLE ULTRA FINISHER

The Jungle Ultra is part of Beyond the Ultimate's Global Race Series: four extreme stage races set in some of the world's most remote places: the Ice Ultra crosses the Arctic Circle; the Jungle Ultra ventures through the Amazon Rainforest; the Desert Ultra crosses the Namib Desert; and the Mountain Ultra climbs the Tian Shan Mountains in Kyrgyzstan.

ABOVE On Day 5, a runner is followed by a Peruvian street dog who stayed with them for almost 20 miles.

BELOW A runner uses a rope to help with a steep climb out of the riverbed.

ATACAMA CROSSING

ATACAMA DESERT, CHILE

The Atacama Crossing is part of the 4 Deserts Ultramarathon Series, which includes the Namib Race (Namibia), the Gobi March (Mongolia) and The Last Desert (Antarctica), plus an extra race in a different location each year. The race series was founded by US ultrarunner Mary K Gadams, who founded RacingThePlanet in 2002.

First held in 2004, the Atacama Crossing is a 250km (156 miles) stage race run across Chile's Atacama Desert – officially recognized as the driest place on earth. Over six stages, competitors must navigate rock-hard salt flats, soft sand and high dunes, freezing slot canyons and river crossings. An average altitude of 2,500m (8,200ft) adds thin, dry air to the list of challenges. The desert's unique landscape of salt lakes, volcanoes, lava flows and sand dunes has been compared to that of Mars, and was used as a filming location for the television series *Space Odyssey: Voyage to the Planets*, and by NASA as a testing site for the Mars rover. As they traverse the desert, runners experience dark, starry nights in the foothills of the Andes, the vast, snow-capped mountains rearing above. The race route goes through the Salar de Atacama, Moon Valley and Valle de la Muerte, finishing in the Town Square of San Pedro de Atacama.

Known for its chilled vibe and great post-race pizza and hospitality, San Pedro de Atacama has been the host town for the Atacama Crossing since the beginning. An oasis town located in the middle of the Atacama Desert, it has a permanent population of just 2,500 people.

RACE STATISTICS

MONTH: March–April
STAGE RACE: Six stages in seven days
DISTANCE: 250km (156 miles)
TOTAL ASCENT: 2,813m (9,230ft)
HIGHEST POINT: 3,200m (10,500ft)
STARTERS 2023*: 115 (33 female, 82 male)
FINISHERS 2023*: 82 (24 female, 58 male)
TIME ALLOWED: Varies and is updated daily during the race
FEMALE COURSE RECORD: Anne-Marie Flammersfeld 29:49:53 (2012)
MALE COURSE RECORD: Rob Forbes 21:20:46 (2022)
FIRST RUN: 2004
ENTRY FEE: $4,100

WEBSITE: www.racingtheplanet.com/atacamacrossing

*Not held in 2024 but due to go ahead in 2025

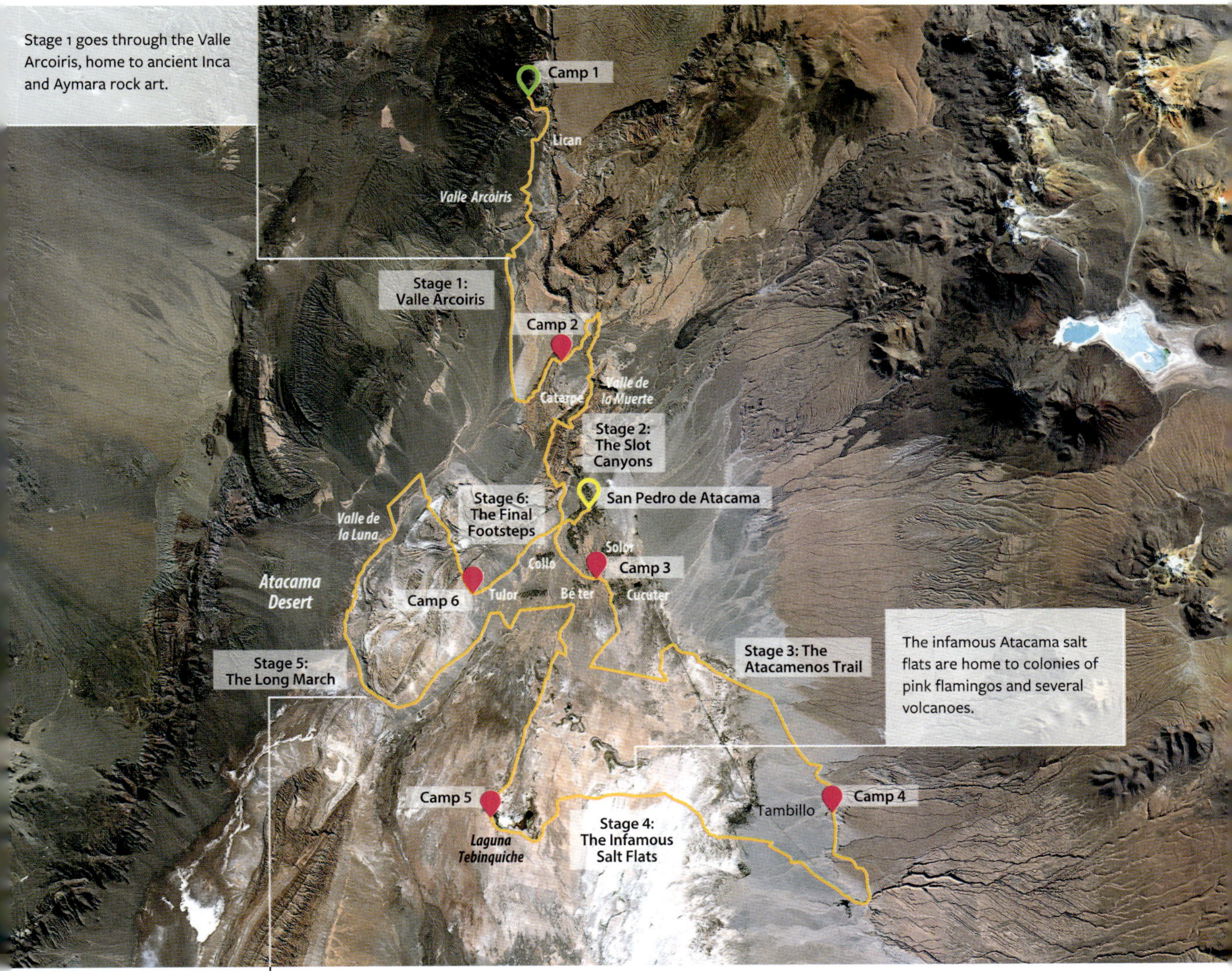

Stage 1 goes through the Valle Arcoiris, home to ancient Inca and Aymara rock art.
Camp 1
Lican
Valle Arcoiris
Stage 1: Valle Arcoiris
Camp 2
Catarpe
Valle de la Muerte
Stage 2: The Slot Canyons
San Pedro de Atacama
Stage 6: The Final Footsteps
Valle de la Luna
Solor
Collo
Camp 3
Atacama Desert
Camp 6
Tulor
Be ter
Cucuter
Stage 3: The Atacamenos Trail
The infamous Atacama salt flats are home to colonies of pink flamingos and several volcanoes.
Stage 5: The Long March
Camp 5
Laguna Tebinquiche
Stage 4: The Infamous Salt Flats
Tambillo
Camp 4

Runners have 2 days to complete Stage 5: The Long March at 81km (50 miles). Those who finish earlier gain themselves more rest time.

ELEVATION PROFILE

STAGE 1
STAGE 2
STAGE 3
STAGE 4
STAGE 5
STAGE 6
3,200M (10,500FT)
0.00km/miles
250km (156 miles)

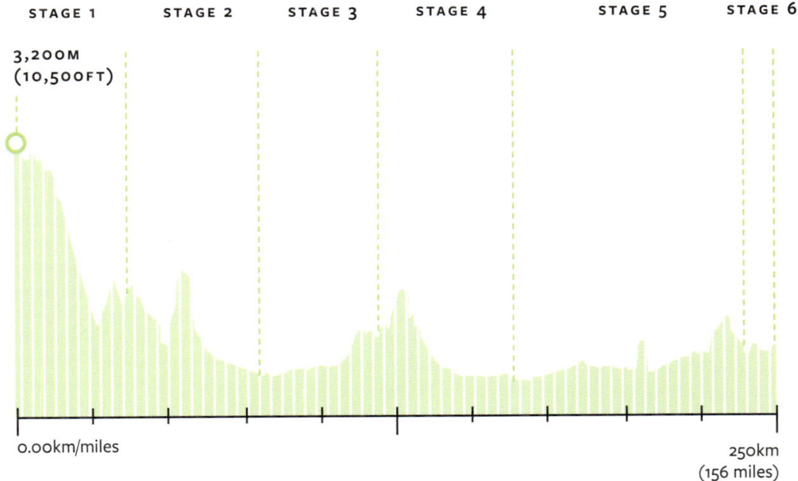

LEFT Rainbow Valley, the first campsite of the Atacama Crossing.

STAGE DETAILS

Stage1 Valle Arcoiris: 35.3km (22 miles); 427m (1,401ft) ascent

Stage 2 The Slot Canyons: 37.5km (23½ miles); 657m (2,156ft) ascent

Stage 3 The Atacamenos Trail: 39.8km (25 miles); 287m (942ft) ascent

Stage 4 The Infamous Salt Flats: 44.4km (27¾ miles); 492m (1,614ft) ascent

Stage 5 The Long March: 81km (50¼ miles); 855m (2,805ft) ascent

Stage 6 The Final Footsteps: 12km (7½ miles); 95m (312ft) ascent

Its picturesque streets cluster around a pretty tree-lined plaza and churc, and it boasts a great range of hotels and self-catering options. Those participating in the Atacama Crossing are advised to arrive a few days early so they can acclimatize to the altitude and heat – the town lies at 2,400m (7,875ft) above sea level, with the race starting at 3,000m (9,850ft). As well as making the most of the many attractions, including El Tatio Hot Springs with its bubbling mud, steamy soil and spectacular geysers, the Atacama, with its vast, dark, star-speckled skies, is one of the best places in the world for stargazing.

The Atacama Salt Flats are also home to colonies of nesting pink flamingos and many sacred Incan sites, as well as several volcanoes including the Licancabur Volcano, which was a ceremonial centre during the Incan period.

Due to the Atacama's proximity to the Andes Mountain range, runners may experience extreme weather during their crossing, including strong winds, rain in the mountains and large variations in temperature. from –1°C (30°F) at night to over 35°C (95°F) during the day.

The Atacama Crossing is a self-supported race, with competitors carrying everything they need for the duration of the race. Backpacks weigh in at between 7 and 14kg (15½–31lb). Runners must be thoroughly prepared for the harsh conditions of this race, and the mandatory equipment lists 35 different items, allowing competitors to manage most eventualities out on the route.

The race attracts a diverse field from across the world, including elite and recreational runners. Only around 20 per cent of competitors expect to run the entire course, with 60 per cent combining running with walking, and 20 per cent walking the entire course. Finishing times range between 25 and 70 hours. In the most recent edition, 42 countries were represented, with 30 per cent of the field being women.

PREVIOUS PAGES Valle de la Luna or Moon Valley on Stage 5, The Long March.

ABOVE A canyon in the Atacama Desert on Stage 1.

BELOW Valle de la Muerte (Valley of Death), aka Mars Valley, on Stage 2.

LA MISIÓN

VILLA LA ANGOSTURA, ARGENTINA

In the words of its organizers:
It's not a race.
It's not an ultra trail.
It's... The Mission

La Misión (The Mission) is a non-stop self-sufficient adventure trekking race, starting in Villa la Angostura, located in the south of the Argentinian Patagonian province of Neuquén. and touring the Nahuel Huapi National Park. This vast, protected area is known for its many lakes, including Nahuel Huapi, its largest glacial lake. The Andes form the park's western border, among whose peaks rises Mount Tronador, a dormant volcano. Villa la Angostura is a picturesque village located on the coast of Lake Nahuel Huapi, surrounded by high mountains and extensive forests, home to rare pudu deer. It's a region of beautiful landscapes that, as well as being an outstanding place to run, offers skiing, adventure sports (including water sports), trekking, wildlife watching and warm hospitality.

The organizers ensure that the trails used during the race are well maintained, and the route is well marked along the way and easy to follow, with minimal tape used for route marking.

RACE STATISTICS

MONTH: February
DISTANCE: 160km (99½ miles)
TOTAL ASCENT: 8,200m (26,903ft)
HIGHEST POINT: 1,900m (6,234ft)
STARTERS 2024: 89 (22 female, 67 male)
FINISHERS 2024: 60 (9 female, 51 male)
TIME ALLOWED: 72hr
FEMALE COURSE RECORD: Laura Moratorio 30:01:00 (2022)
MALE COURSE RECORD: Jose Francisco Dragone 20:32:00 (2018)
FIRST RUN: 2011
ENTRY FEE: $330

WEBSITE:
www.lamisionrace.com

The final climb gains the highest point in the race – Oconnor at 1,900m (6,234ft).

The race is self-sufficient but runners can access a drop bag at Villa Traful, 80km (49 miles) into the race.

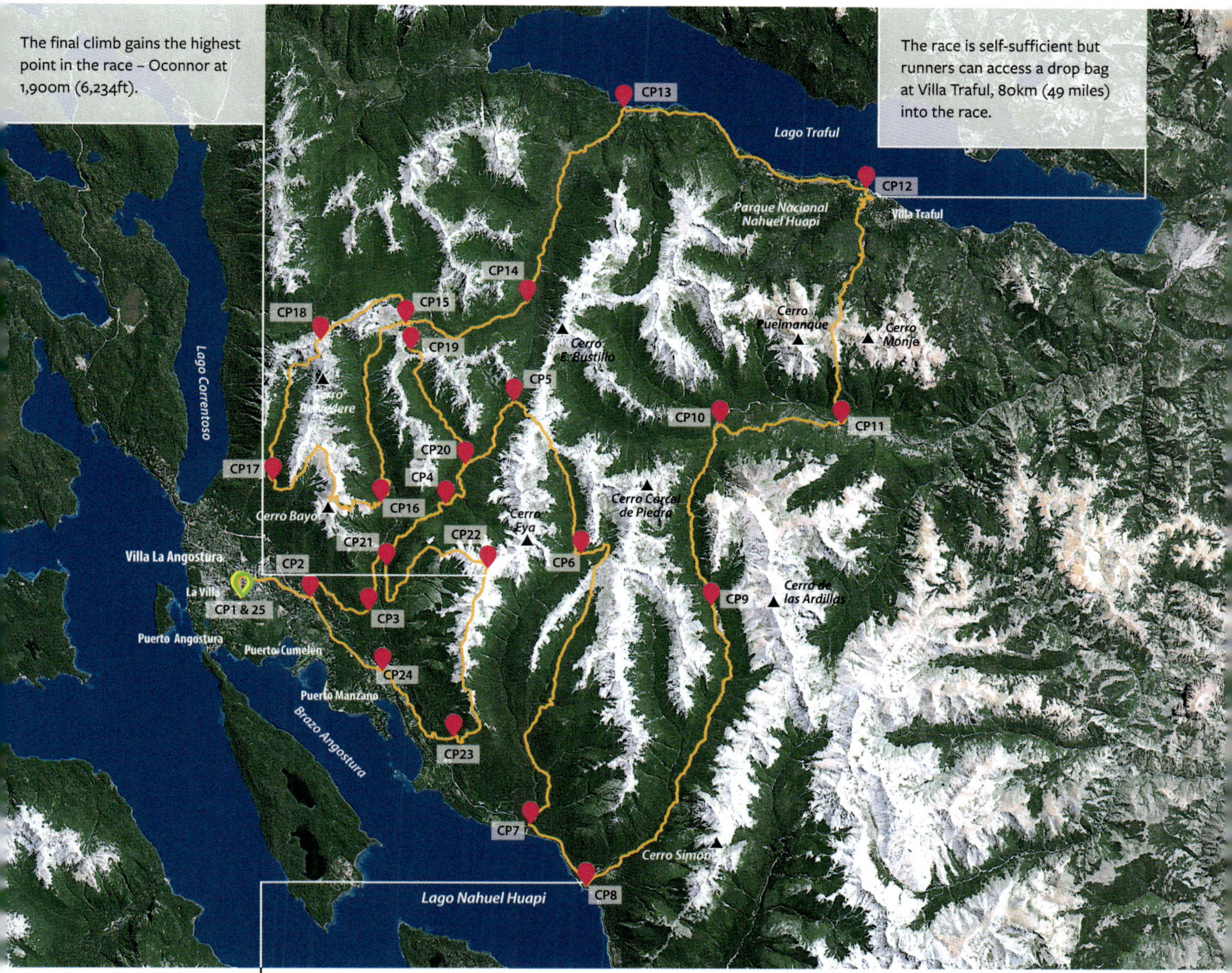

The route visits the peaceful shores of Lago Nahuel Huapi – the largest glacial lake in the Nahuel Huapi National Park.

ELEVATION PROFILE

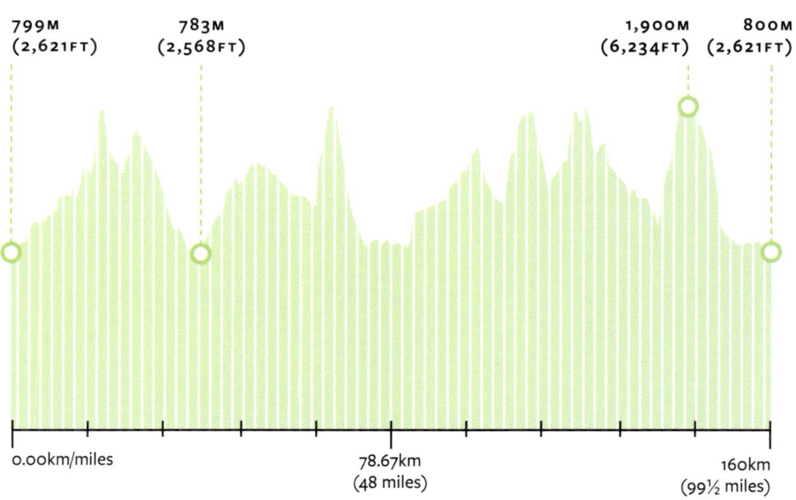

LEFT Lake and mountain views in La Misión.

La Misión was conceived as an authentic, long-distance trekking race. Competitors climb five mountains of almost 2,000m (6,500ft), linked by long, forested valleys scored through by streams and rivers. It's a wonderfully varied route, with stark contrasts between the lush lower sections and the moonscape mountain ridges and plateaus.

With adventure at its heart, La Misión is, in the words of its organizers, 'a true multi-day mountain trekking race in total self-sufficiency'. There are no mandatory stops, so when, where and how long to stop for is up to individuals. Runners must be 100 per cent self-sufficient for the duration of the race, carrying all the mandatory equipment and the food they will consume with the exception of a drop bag. This is accessed once during the 160km (99½ miles) race and twice during the 200km (124 miles) event and can contain spare food, clothing and equipment, although the full mandatory equipment list must be carried at all times. Regular wild water sources provide plenty of opportunities for refilling water bottles. Everyone will spend at least one night on the course, most will spend two nights, and the back-of-the-pack runners in the 160km and 200km events will spend three nights. The 160km event is the classic event – a challenging mission for even the most experienced runners. The 200km might be mission impossible.

OTHER DISTANCES
200km (124 miles); 10,000m (32,808ft) ascent
120km (74½ miles); 5,000m (16,404ft) ascent
80km (49¾ miles); 3,800m (12,467ft) ascent
40km (25 miles); 1,500m (4,921ft) ascent

FAR LEFT Traversing the ridges of Cerro O'Connor, where runners spend more than 7km (4 miles) above 1,900m (6,234 feet). The panoramic view of the Andes mountains is immense.

LEFT During the race, competitors constantly cross rivers and streams of the purest water. This is one of the many crossings of the Cataratas stream.

ABOVE One of the many checkpoints of La Mision; runners spend up to 3 nights on the mountain.

Despite being held in February, when the Patagonian weather is generally good, rain and strong winds aren't uncommon during the race and there is sometimes snowfall in the mountains. The mandatory kit list is therefore extensive and comprehensive, ensuring competitors can deal with any conditions or incidents along the route.

Currently, the vast majority of entrants are from South America, with Argentinian runners generally dominating the podiums. But La Misión has recently become part of the TORX® eXperience – the organization behind some of the world's most challenging ultras, including the original Tor des Géants (see page 38). Completing the 120km (74½ miles), 160 or 200km event qualifies runners to enter Tor des Géants, which may bring more nationalities to experience the many joys and challenges of La Misión.

OTHER CENTRAL AND SOUTH AMERICAN HIGHLIGHTS

ULTRA MARATHON CABALLO BLANCO

URIQUE, CHIHUAHUA, MEXICO

RACE STATISTICS

MONTH: March
DISTANCE: 80km (50 miles)
TOTAL ASCENT: 3,050m (10,000ft)
TIME ALLOWED: 11hr to enter the final loop

WEBSITE: www.truemessages.org/ultra-caballo

The Ultra Caballo Blanco was created to share the exceptional beauty of the copper canyons and the running culture of the Raramuri (Tarahumara) people. Micah True, known as El Caballo Blanco (the white horse), invited international athletes to race with the Raramuri. The income from the race would help support the community, and the prizes would be a motivation to maintain the running traditions. True Messages, the non-profit organization which manages the race, continues this aim, raising money to support the local culture and fund community educational programmes to encourage an active lifestyle.

Since the first event in 2003 the race has grown and now over 1,200 international and 800 local athletes compete each year. There are the much celebrated children's races known as the Caballitos Runs, a half-marathon, marathon, the headline 80km (50 miles) Ultra and a challenging 100-miler. All the distances start and finish in Urique, sharing some of the same trails and canyons.

The 80km Ultra follows ancient trails and ridgelines, with spectacular views down into the canyons. Sections of the trail descend into deep canyons, crossing rivers and running past waterfalls. The Sierra Tarahumara is the largest and deepest canyon system in North America. Some of the trails are technical and rocky with steep ascents and descents, but there are also easier sections where you can marvel at the scenery. Most runners find the heat – up to about 35°C (95°F) – and lack of shade the hardest aspect of the race; there are regular water stations, but it's best to carry water and take sun cream.

To truly experience the magic of the copper canyons and the culture of the Raramuri people, a week-long run camp is offered, with the race at the end. Over the week, guests can run every day, exploring the trails with the experienced camp hosts and the Raramuri endurance runners. There will be the chance to attend cultural events and festivities, experiencing local food and customs in the run-up to race day but the week isn't mandatory, and all races can be entered as standalone events.

LA TRANSTICA

VILLA NUEVA–MANZANILLO, COSTA RICA

RACE STATISTICS

MONTH: November

STAGE RACE: Prologue plus five stages, six days

DISTANCE: 200km (124 miles)

TOTAL ASCENT: 9,300m (30,512ft)

TIME ALLOWED: Is stated each day if necessary

WEBSITE: www.latranstica.org

La Transtica crosses Costa Rica, from the Pacific Ocean to the Caribbean Sea. The course is designed to be an adventure, where runners discover the country's geology, flora, fauna and local culture.

You can run the Extreme or the Adventure version of the race; both cross the country in five stages, plus a prologue. The route starts in Playas del Pacifico in Villa Nueva and finishes in Manzanillo. The Extreme covers around 200km (124 miles), with five stages between 28km and 48km (17½ and 30 miles). The Adventure covers 117km (72¾ miles) on shorter days of between 18km and 28km (11 and 17½ miles).

The whole adventure takes ten days; this includes the prologue, race, internal travel and some sightseeing. There is the possibility of adding extra days to spend more time exploring Costa Rica.

The race supports the association El Niño, which provides very substantial assistance to children in schools in Costa Rica.

ULTRA FIORD

SOUTHERN PATAGONIA, CHILE

RACE STATISTICS

MONTH: February

DISTANCE: 55km (34 miles)

TOTAL ASCENT: 3,600m (11,811ft)

TIME ALLOWED: 15hr

WEBSITE: www.ultrafiord.com

Ultra Fiord is a fully waymarked race running through the magical world of the fjords in southern Patagonia. All the race distances pass through wild territory, through forests, around mountains, and along rivers and lakes with views of glaciers and snow-topped peaks. This is a summer race, but the high altitude and mountainous terrain mean that you may end up crossing extended areas of snow. The tough 55km (34 miles) course takes you to an altitude of 1,180m (3,871ft) with lots of ascents.

Alongside the 55km (34 miles) race there are 42km (26 miles), 30km (18½ miles) and 16km (10 miles) distances. All the courses run loops from the base camp at Río Serrano and include regular, well-stocked aid stations to keep you fuelled and motivated.

Ultra Fiord is part of the Racing Patagonia project, created in 2002 by Stjepan Pavicic to help promote the amazing running in the area and contribute to the sustainable development of tourism and the local community.

FAR LEFT A Raramuri runner racing the Ultra Marathon Caballo Blanco in traditional costume.

LEFT Runners in La Transtica cross Costa Rica from the Pacific Ocean to the Caribbean Sea.

BRAZIL 135 ULTRA

ÁGUAS DA PRATA–PARAISÓPOLIS, BRAZIL

RACE STATISTICS

MONTH: January
DISTANCE: 239.7km (149 miles)
TOTAL ASCENT: 7,305m (23,967ft)
TIME ALLOWED: 60hr

WEBSITE: www.brazil135.net

The Brazil 135 follows one of the hardest sections of the Caminho da Fé (Path of Faith) through the Serra da Mantiqueira mountains. You'll run through one of the remaining belts of Atlantic coastal rainforest. It's considered to be the hardest footrace in Brazil.

The trail starts in Águas da Prata and immediately climbs the biggest hill on the course, reaching an altitude of 1,642m (5,387ft) and then descending back to around 830m (2,723ft). This pattern of ascent and descent continues, but the following summits are lower. The 193km (120 miles) aid station is in Paraisópolis, with the final section running an out-and-back route to Luminosa.

An intriguing rule allows you to stop at 'decision points' along the route without incurring a DNF. This effectively means that although the full distance is a whopping 239.7km (149 miles), you could aim to finish at any of the following distances: 88.5, 128.75, 161, 193, or 217km (55, 80,100, 120 or 135 miles).

Brazil 135 is a sister race to the American Badwater 135.

PATAGONIA RUN

SAN MARTÍN DE LOS ANDES, NEUQUÉN, PATAGONIA, ARGENTINA

RACE STATISTICS

MONTH: April
DISTANCE: 161km (100 miles)
TOTAL ASCENT: 9,230m (30,282ft)
TIME ALLOWED: 41½hr

WEBSITE: www.patagoniarun.com

The race is in the Lanín National Park at the foot of the Andes mountains. The park is a protected area for the araucaria trees and is home to pumas and condors. The landscape is breathtaking, and the course makes the most of this, with stunning alpine trails and many highpoints from which to appreciate the views. There is often snow on the higher areas of the trail and it can be cold, especially overnight.

The 100-miler starts high at about 1,250m (4,100ft) in the Chapelco Ski Resort, and climbs straight up to the race's maximum altitude of 1,959m (6,427ft) on Filo Chapelco. After a few more climbs, you descend to the Pas Puentes de Luz at 730m (2,395ft), 55km (34 miles) into the race. Another series of climbs follows, topping out at 1,765m (5,791ft) on the Cumbre Co. Colorado and returning to 655m (2,149ft) at about 120km (74½ miles). The final section takes you up to 1,650m (5,413ft) on Cumbre Co. Quilanlahue before descending on by now very tired legs to the finish at 650m (2,132ft) in San Martín.

This festival of running lasts from Wednesday to Sunday, with races throughout the week. The Vertical Km, 10km and 21km races are on Wednesday; the 42km on Thursday; the 110km and 161km start on Friday; and a 70km race starts on Saturday. The races are all finished on Sunday morning, and are followed by the awards ceremonies.

CHICAMOCHA CANYON RACE

CHICAMOCHA CANYON, SANTANDER, COLOMBIA

RACE STATISTICS

MONTH: June
DISTANCE: 175km (109 miles)
TOTAL ASCENT: 9,258m (30,374ft)
TIME ALLOWED: 50hr

WEBSITE: www.chicamochacanyonrace.com

This race follows a big loop of the Santander region, running on ancient paths, across rugged terrain and through a range of vegetation and habitats. You'll climb to over 2,000m (6,500ft) in the mountains and descend to around 400m (1,300ft) deep in the canyons. The trail drops into the canyons three times, crosses four rivers and will expose you to high daytime temperatures, which can reach 40°C (104°F).

It's a tough and unforgettable race with incredible scenery. The eighth edition of the 175km (109 miles) course will be run in 2025, and no one has gone under 24 hours yet. The fastest times are by Maximilien Vanicatte, who ran 24:16:06 in 2023, and Jennifer Herringdine, who ran 28:50:11 in 2019; the majority of finishers take between 40 and 50 hours.

The route is fully waymarked, with 15 water stations and 6 fully stocked aid stations.

80km (49¾ miles), marathon and half-marathon distances are also available on the same day.

LEFT A runner on the marathon course during the 2024 Chicamocha Canyon Race.

AFRICA

AFRICA INTRODUCTION

East Africa's distance running prowess is clear across the world in road and track competitions. Since 2003, the men's marathon World Record has been held by a runner from either Kenya or Ethiopia; similarly for the women's World Record since 2017 (without male pacemakers) or 2019 (with male pacemakers). Books such as Adharanand Finn's *Running with the Kenyans* and Michael Crawley's *Out of Thin Air* have brought the culture and practices of East African running to readers across the world.

Historically, ultrarunning has offered little in the way of prize money or sponsorship to elite runners, meaning the sport was predominantly participated in by those who had other jobs and not as a career, as is the case with elite road and track athletes. But times are changing, ultrarunning is proving itself an exciting spectator sport, brought to viewers by live footage from spectacular destinations, and the brands, and therefore sponsors, are getting on board. With increases in the value of sponsorship packages and prize money, more top-class elite runners are being drawn to the sport, and up-and-coming ultrarunners are increasingly able to make the sport a viable career choice. A 2024 race analysis of over 1 million runners in the journal *Nature* found that East African runners are already the fastest over the 50km (31 miles) distance. As ultrarunning grows, so does the potential for a more diverse – and faster – elite field.

Africa as a continent, however, has a rich history of ultrarunning. The 87km (54 miles) Comrades Marathon (see page 198) is the world's oldest and biggest ultramarathon, drawing fields of around 23,000 runners from across the globe to the KwaZulu-Natal province of South Africa in June each year for more than 100 years. Frist held in 1986, the Marathon des Sables (see page 188) – Marathon of the Sands – is one of the original staged ultramarathons, and something of an institution in the ultra world. Over seven days, competitors traverse 240km (150 miles) of the Sahara Desert in southern Morocco, tackling heat, dunes and leg-sapping soft sand.

Africa's strikingly diverse landscapes make for some truly unique races. Billed as the world's toughest flat ultramarathon, the Salt Pans Ultra 100km (see page 194) takes runners across Botswana's breathtaking and extremely challenging Sua Pans, part of the expansive Makgadikgadi Salt Pans. As much of a contrast to the flat expanses of the salt pans as it's possible to imagine, La Diagonale des Fous – the crossing of fools – (see page 202) takes place in the French department of La Réunion, an island in the Indian Ocean some 680km (420 miles) to the east of Madagascar. The main race makes a complete south-to-north crossing of the island, from its tropical, beach-holiday coasts complete with palm trees and lagoons to its savagely steep

PREVIOUS PAGE Giant dunes faced during the 2024 Marathon des Sables Legendary event, Morocco.

BELOW Seemingly endless salt plains and high heat during the Salt Pans Ultra, Botswana.

and technical volcanic interior. Notoriously tough, with varying weather conditions and a relatively high level of objective danger in the mountains, this is a race for those seeking a challenge of a lifetime, and one that also draws a deep elite field to its start line.

Elsewhere in the continent, the Addo Elephant Trail Run (see page 213) is set in the Addo Elephant National Park in the Eastern Cape Province. Founded in 2005, it is South Africa's oldest 100-mile trail run. Offering an immersive alternative to the traditional 4x4-based safari, UltraMARAthon (see page 210) came into existence in 2020 when a group of runners created an event to support conservation and community initiatives in the greater Mara area. So far the project has supported the Mara Elephant project, the rangers who manage the reserves, improved local healthcare provision and increased awareness of the area.

MARATHON DES SABLES

SOUTHERN MOROCCAN SAHARA, MOROCCO

Marathon des Sables – Marathon of the Sands – is one of the original staged ultramarathons, and something of an institution in the ultra world. The six-stage, 240km (150 miles) stage race is held annually in the Sahara Desert in southern Morocco. The route changes a little each year, but the longest single stage is always Stage 3 (days three and four), when runners have two days to cover the distance. The longest 'long' stage was in the 2009 edition of the race, when it covered 91km (56½ miles).

Billed as one of the toughest footraces on earth (although today it has many rivals for this title), MDS was first held in 1986. The concept was conceived by French concert promoter Patrick Bauer who, two years previously, had traversed the Sahara Desert on foot and alone. Bauer covered 350km (214 miles) in 12 days without encountering a single oasis or desert community, and realized the route's potential as an endurance race.

Twenty-three runners participated in the race in that first year, with French runners Bernard Gaudin and Christiane Plumere taking the men's and women's wins respectively.

By 2009 the field had grown to over 1,000 runners, and the Solidarité Marathon des Sables association was created, aiming to give back to the local communities by developing projects in health, education and sustainable development in Morocco. Competitor numbers have remained similar since.

RACE STATISTICS

MONTH: April
STAGE RACE: Six stages in seven days
DISTANCE: 240km (150 miles)
TOTAL ASCENT: 1,814m (5,951ft)
HIGHEST POINT: 914m (2,999ft)
STARTERS 2024: 1,009 (215 female, 794 male)
FINISHERS 2024: 781 (194 female, 587 male)
TIME ALLOWED: 82hr
FEMALE COURSE RECORD: Nathalie Mauclair 23:36:40 (2017)
MALE COURSE RECORD: Rachid El Morabity 18:33:28 (2022)
FIRST RUN: 1986
ENTRY FEE: €3,890

WEBSITE:
www.marathondessables.com

Stage 6 is the shortest, followed by an awards ceremony and gala evening, plus a recovery day in Ouarzazate.

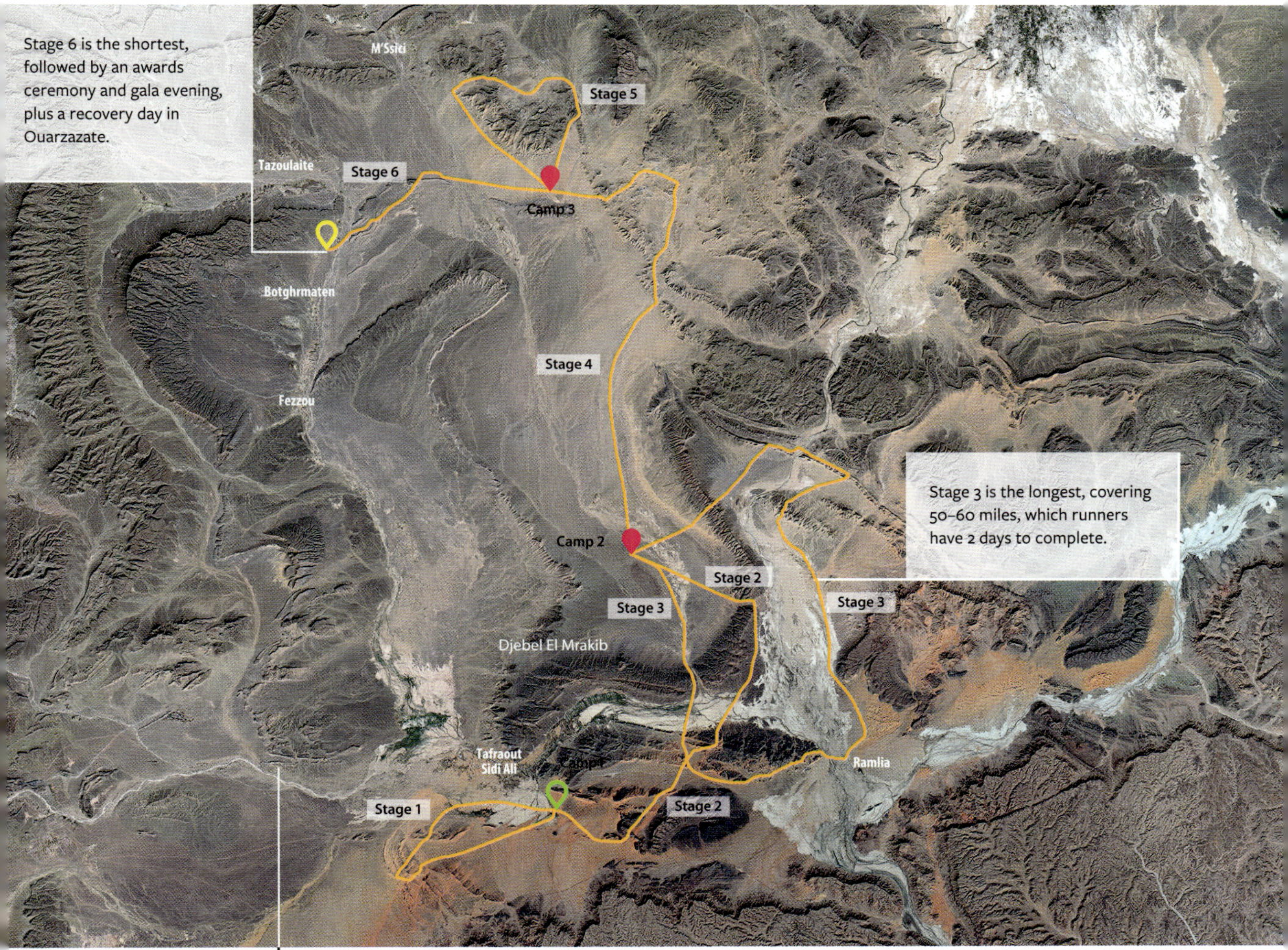

Stage 3 is the longest, covering 50–60 miles, which runners have 2 days to complete.

The Sahara covers 8.6 million sq km (3.3 million sq mi), making it the largest hot desert in the world.

ELEVATION PROFILE (STAGES 1–3)

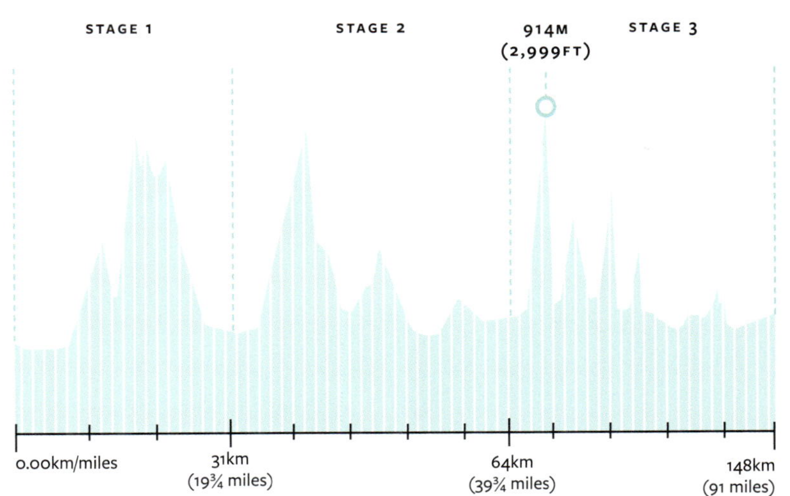

LEFT Stage 4 of the 2024 Marathon des Sables. Runners cover 6 stages in 7 days – a total of 150 miles.

Today, there are three options for competitors to choose from: Marathon des Sables The Legendary: 240km/150 miles in the Sahara Desert in Morocco; the Marathon des Sables: 70, 100 or 120km spread over three stages, or the MDS Trek: four stages with a total distance of up to 120km (74½ miles), offering a more accessible adventure with extra comfort.

Camp life is an important part of the MDS experience, and the overnight camp village, with Berber tents that sleep up to eight erected by the race crew in readiness for runners, offers a place to eat, rest and share experiences with other participants.

The MDS Legendary and MDS are self-sufficient during the stages, and runners must bring and carry all food for the full duration of the event. On the MDS Trek, meals are provided in the morning and evening, as well as a packed lunch on stage days. Water supply is fully managed by the organization to meet competitors' needs throughout all of the races.

In 1994 Mauro Prosperi, a former Olympian from Sicily, hit the headlines after straying 299km (186 miles) off route during a sandstorm. He was lost for ten days before being found in Algeria, following a well-publicized search of the desert, having reportedly resorted to drinking his own urine in order to survive.

2024 ROUTE (ROUTE CHANGES SLIGHTLY EACH YEAR)

STAGE 1: 31km (19¼ miles); 186m (610ft) ascent
STAGE 2: 33km (20½ miles); 315m (1,033ft) ascent
STAGE 3: 84km (52 miles); 878m (2,881ft) ascent (over 2 days)
STAGE 4: 40km (24¾ miles); 232m (761ft) ascent
STAGE 5: 32km (20 miles); 144m (472ft) ascent
STAGE 6: 21km (13 miles); 59m (193ft) ascent

FACT FILE

- Chris Moon from Lanarkshire became the first amputee to complete the Marathon des Sables in 1996. Moon had lost his right arm and leg while supervising the clearing of landmines in Mozambique.
- Dima and Lama Hattab, Jordanian twins, were the first female Middle Eastern participants in the race, in 2001.
- Explorer Sir Ranulph Fiennes became the oldest Briton to complete the Marathon des Sables, in 2015, at age 71, raising over £1 million for the Marie Curie charity. However, in 2017 David Exell became the oldest Brit to complete the race, at 75.
- Cactus became the first dog to complete the Marathon des Sables in 2019. A stray dog, Cactus, started joining in with the runners during the second stage of the race and then went on to complete the remaining stages of the race. Cactus was awarded the official race number 000 and received his finishers' medal.

PREVIOUS PAGES The mobile finish line and overnight camp.

ABOVE The start of one of stages during the 2024 edition of the race.

BELOW Soft sand and miles of rocky desert landscape makes racing tough for MDS Legendary competitors.

SALT PANS ULTRA

MAKGADIKGADI SALT PANS, BOTSWANA

Billed as the world's toughest flat ultramarathon, the SPU 100 takes runners across Botswana's breathtaking Sua Pans, part of the expansive Makgadikgadi Salt Pans.

With the race spanning just over 100km (62 miles) on the map, the challenge of keeping going in a straight line means most runners end up covering some extra distance. It starts at the southern edge of Sua Pan, venturing deep into the salt pans, where awe-inspiring scenery and gruelling conditions battle for attention. Depending on the rainy season, runners could face conditions ranging from rock-hard, dry, ankle-breaking terrain to sections of sticky, slippery mud – it's truly a test of mental and physical endurance in one of the planet's most unique landscapes.

RACE STATISTICS

MONTH: September
DISTANCE: 102.6km (63¾ miles)
TOTAL ASCENT: 26m (85ft)
HIGHEST POINT: 921m (3,022ft)
STARTERS 2024: 32 (4 female, 28 male)
FINISHERS 2024: 8 (0 female, 8 male)
TIME ALLOWED: 17hr
FEMALE COURSE RECORD: Christili Muller 15:08:03 (2023)
MALE COURSE RECORD: Tyler Rocha 11:37:16 (2024)
FIRST RUN: 2019
ENTRY FEE: €320

WEBSITE: www.saltpansultra.com

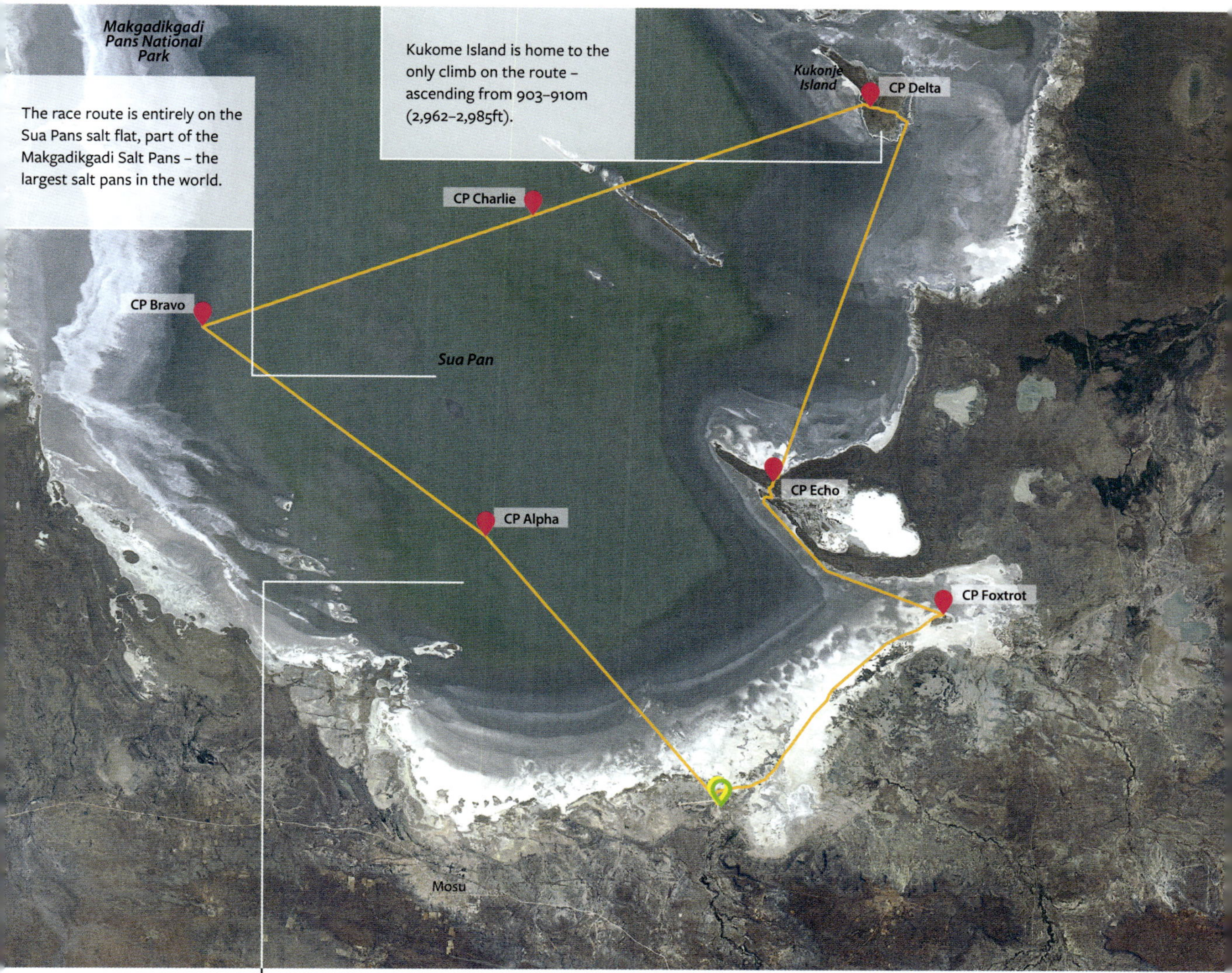

Makgadikgadi Pans National Park

The race route is entirely on the Sua Pans salt flat, part of the Makgadikgadi Salt Pans – the largest salt pans in the world.

Kukome Island is home to the only climb on the route – ascending from 903–910m (2,962–2,985ft).

Kukonje Island

CP Delta

CP Charlie

CP Bravo

Sua Pan

CP Echo

CP Alpha

CP Foxtrot

Mosu

With a dry, salty environment, temperatures exceeding 40°C (104°F) and no shelter, good hydration is essential. Aid stations provide runners with water and sports nutrition/hydration products.

ELEVATION PROFILE

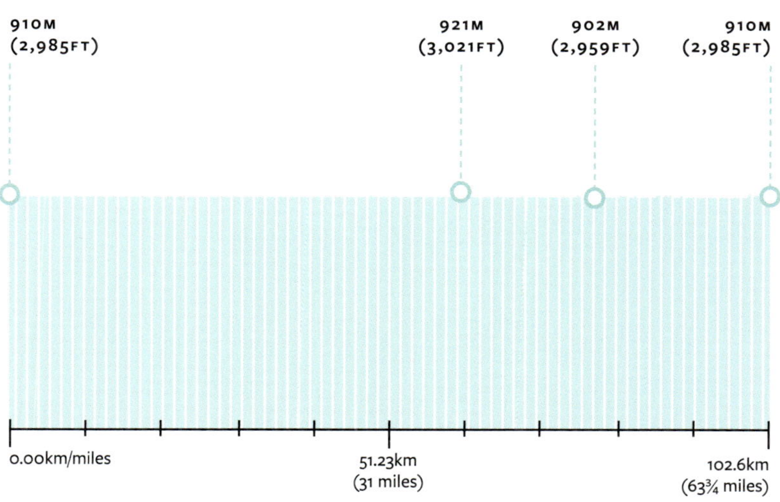

LEFT Runners supporting each other on the vast, open spaces of Botswana's Sua Salt Pans.

ABOVE Runners face miles of pancake-flat salt pans and scrub. It's the home of elephants and lions but you're unlikely to meet them in the heat of the day.

'Yes, the Salt Pan Ultra is wild. In 2022 when I first shot the event [as a photographer] I came across elephant tracks on the pans (plenty of elephants in the area), some of the aid station guys had elephants near them and had just left when I got there, so sadly I didn't get to capture them on images. Maybe this year. And there were lion tracks on the trail route. So yes it's basically as wild as it can get. However, the likelihood of any runner bumping into a "large and furry" is highly unlikely as the runners reach the areas they could bump into them when it's really hot already. The last two years temperatures have been around 40°C [104°F]. I think they measured 45 degrees in 2022. So it is a pretty brutal event. But honestly, if I ran trails this one would be on my bucket list. I have the honour of covering the event. And stopping in the middle of the pan to take a moment and enjoy the peace and solitude and if the wind isn't blowing, true silence, and your breathing and heartbeat suddenly become loud is simply out of this world.'

GARETH ROBERTS, PHOTOGRAPHER

OTHER DISTANCES

Like its big sister, the SPU100, the SPU50 offers a challenging adventure across Botswana's stunning Makgadikgadi Salt Pans. Though shorter, it is still a formidable challenge, ideal for those wanting a shorter option or considering the full distance in the future. Starting at the southern edge of Sua Pan, the 50km route delves deep into the pans, sampling everything the 100km has to offer over half the distance.

53.5km (33 miles), 29.5m (97ft) ascent

When it comes to the Salt Pans Ultra, flat isn't necessarily easy, and the race has a finisher rate of just 20–40 per cent. Legendary ultrarunner Harvey Lewis explains what makes this unique race so challenging:

> 'First, it's off-trail. There are no course markings. You'll definitely want to wear your trail shoes, and I wore gaiters as well. Perhaps 10–15 per cent has a smooth surface that doesn't require you to change your stride, but the majority of time you need to lift your feet a little higher or there are substantial places where it feels like you are running in an inch of snow.
>
> Second, navigating. While you have the benefit of electronics, and it's required as part of the mandatory gear that every runner has the map & route GPX file downloaded on their device, it's not as easy as it may seem. Without any reference points on a 360-degree horizon, it's hard not to do some zigzagging and to run the tangent. I found myself looking down at my watch every few minutes and pulling out my photo with a better map every mile. It just throws off the rhythm a bit. Third place, Matthew Cross, had his navigation go out while he was in a sandstorm and only collected his bearings seeing Tyler and me as small specks in the distance. There are beacons every runner wears to track the runners, but navigation is still a good challenge on the unmarked course.
>
> Third, the aid stations were great and volunteers very helpful, but the distance between aid stations of 15km per station and then 18km between Echo and Foxtrot mean that runners are likely out in the elements for 2–3 hours between aid stations. Runners must carry 3 litres of liquids (I was carrying typically 3.5 to 4 litres in the warmer part of the day). While ice wasn't guaranteed at the aid stations I did find it this year. Still, what ice I had melted in a couple miles and the drinks were warm making them tougher to drink.
>
> Fourth, the heat! There was wind that pushed the warm air into you mixed with the salty environment just made everything dry. If a runner can finish quickly enough they may avoid the worst of it, but by 3pm the temperature is 44°C. There are a few areas on the course where you run past a few baobab trees, but across 98 per cent of the course there is absolutely no shade or escape from the heat. I would suggest for this race to cover one's full body from the sun. I wore shorts with calf sleeves and also had my hands exposed. While I wore sunblock, I do believe it would have drained me less.
>
> You might ask why one should run a race like this. While it is really a challenging course, it's absolutely surreal and the Makgadikgadi Pan is like no other place on the planet – there is a raw beauty to the wilderness there. It's not for the faint of heart and one should have some experience with heat as well as respect for the environment and potential danger of making bad choices. The race was one of the best organized, especially for the value that I have ever experienced.'

COMRADES MARATHON

DURBAN–PIETERMARITZBURG, SOUTH AFRICA

The Comrades Marathon is the world's oldest and biggest ultramarathon, drawing fields of around 23,000 runners from across the globe to take on the 87km (54 miles) route in the KwaZulu-Natal province of South Africa in June each year. 2021 marked the 100th anniversary of the race, which continues to hold a prominent position on the ultramarathon calendar. Being an on-road race, it's known for drawing the fastest elites – often those with strong marathon running credentials – and the podium places are hotly contested.

The race start and finish alternate between Pietermaritzburg and Durban each year. Pietermaritzburg is 878m (2,880ft) above sea level, and Durban is at sea level, on the Indian Ocean coast. As a result, Durban to Pietermaritzburg is known as the 'up run', whereas the route from Pietermaritzburg to Durban is known as the 'down run'. 'Down' years tend to be quicker, but notoriously hammering on the legs. The race is run on the roads of KwaZulu-Natal province, taking in a series of hills known as 'The Big Five'. On 'up' years these are tackled in the following order: Cowies Hill, Fields Hill, Botha's Hill, Inchanga and Polly Shortts. The highest point of the race is at the Umlaas Road interchange, at an altitude of 870m (2,850ft) above sea level. Runners are well catered for along the route, with around 40 official refreshment stations providing a range of food and drinks, as well as a number of physiotherapy and first aid stations located at strategic points.

RACE STATISTICS

MONTH: June

DISTANCE: 87.6km (54½ miles)

TOTAL ASCENT: Down run 1,238m (4,062ft); up run 1,913m (6,276ft)

HIGHEST POINT: 870m (2,850ft)

STARTERS 2024: 22,517 (4,484 female, 18,033 male)

FINISHERS 2024: 17,301 (3,296 female, 14,005 male)

TIME ALLOWED: 12hr

FEMALE COURSE RECORD: DOWN: Gerda Steyn 5:44:54 (2023), UP: Gerda Steyn 5:49:46 (2024)

MALE COURSE RECORD: DOWN: Tete Dijana 5:13:58 (2023), UP: Leonid Shvetsov 5:24:49 (2008)

FIRST RUN: 1921

ENTRY FEE: South Africa citizens 1,200 Rand, SA residents & rest of Africa entrants 2,000 Rand, international entrants 4,500 Rand

WEBSITE: www.comrades.com

The Umlaas Road interchange is the highest point on the course at 870m (2,850ft).

The Wall of Honour at halfway overlooks the Valley of 1000 Hills. Runners and their supporters can purchase a memorial block to commemorate their achievement.

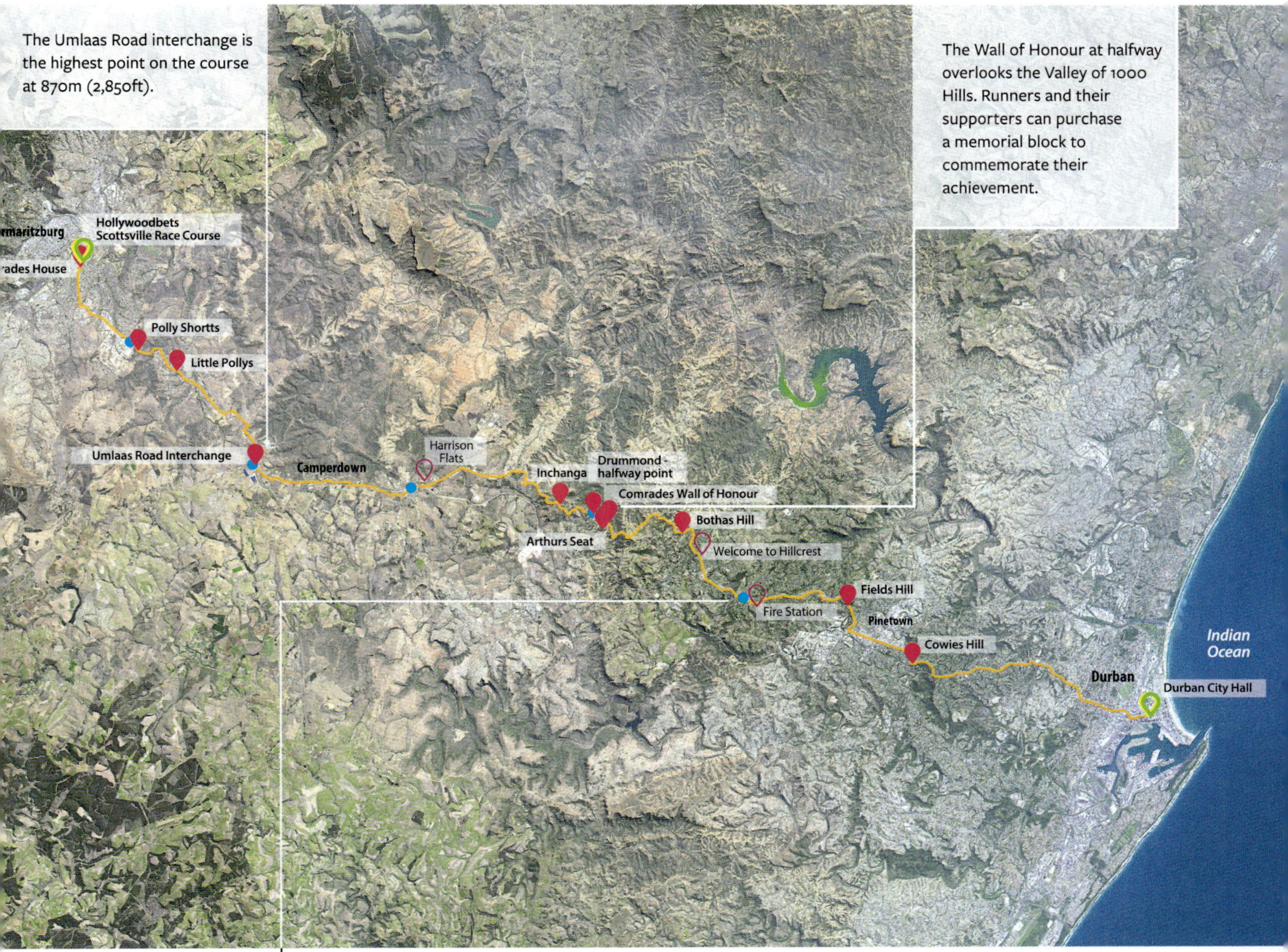

rmaritzburg
Hollywoodbets Scottsville Race Course
rades House
Polly Shortts
Little Pollys
Umlaas Road Interchange
Camperdown
Harrison Flats
Inchanga
Drummond - halfway point
Comrades Wall of Honour
Arthurs Seat
Bothas Hill
Welcome to Hillcrest
Fire Station
Fields Hill
Pinetown
Cowies Hill
Durban
Durban City Hall
Indian Ocean

The race has strict cut-off points along the route (see blue dots). The overall maximum time allowed is 12 hours.

ELEVATION PROFILE

19M (62FT)
8M (26FT)
870M (2,850FT)
641M (2,103FT)
0.00km/miles
43.43km (27 miles)
87.6km (54½ miles)

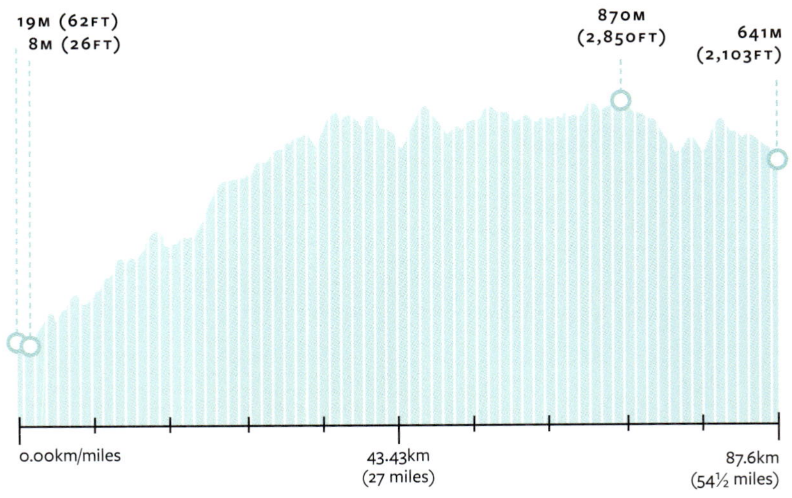

LEFT The start line of the 2023 Comrades Marathon.

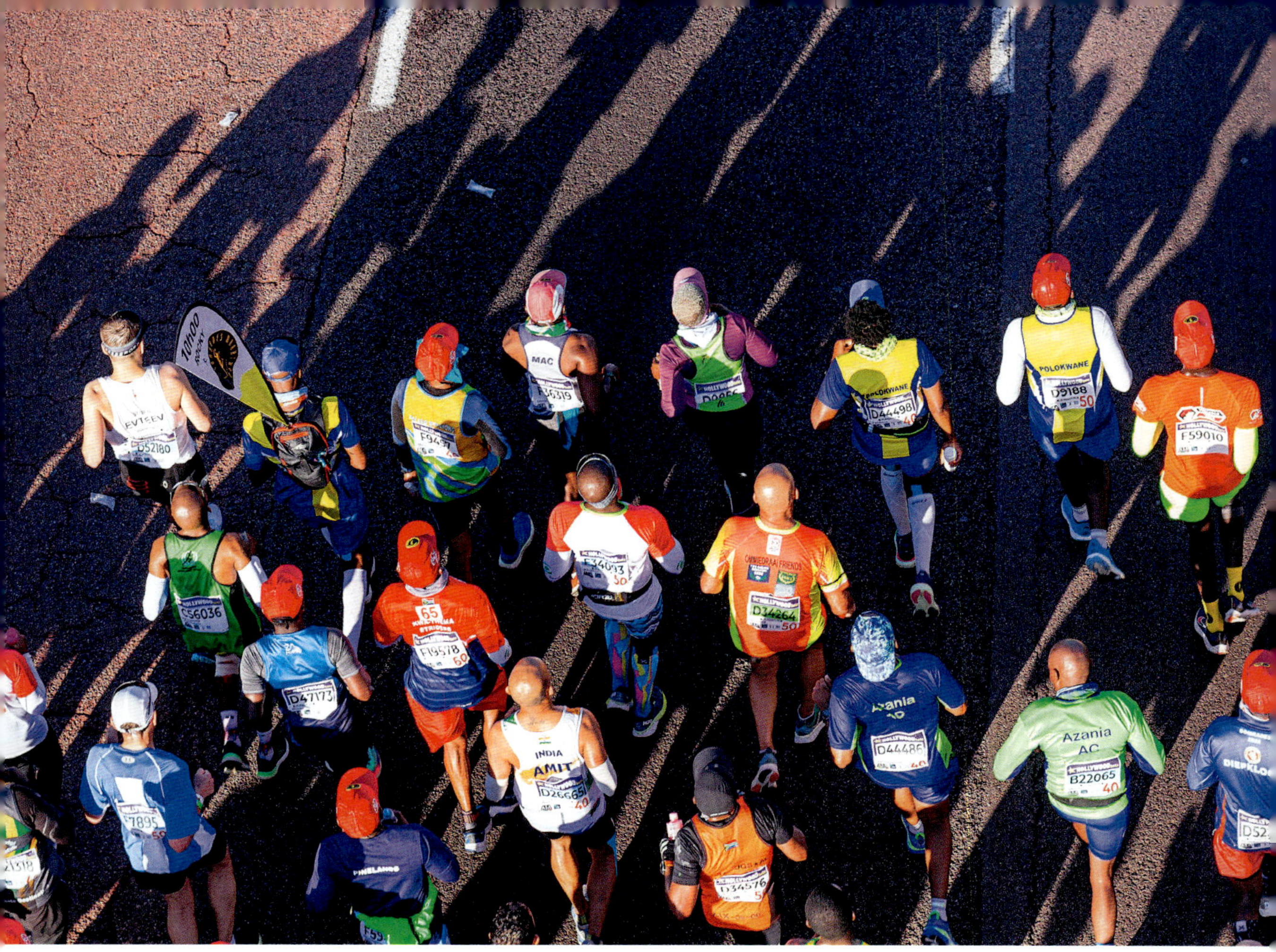
POLOKWANE
Azania
AC
B22065
INDIA
AMIT

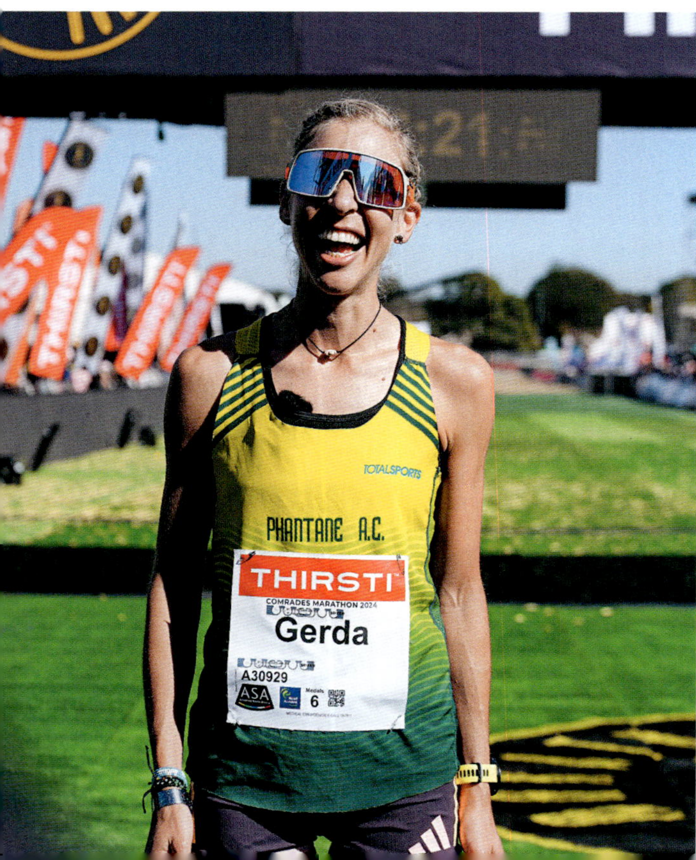

TOTALSPORTS
PHANTANE A.C.
THIRSTI
COMRADES MARATHON 2024
Gerda
A30929
ASA

MyLife
MyLife
MyLife

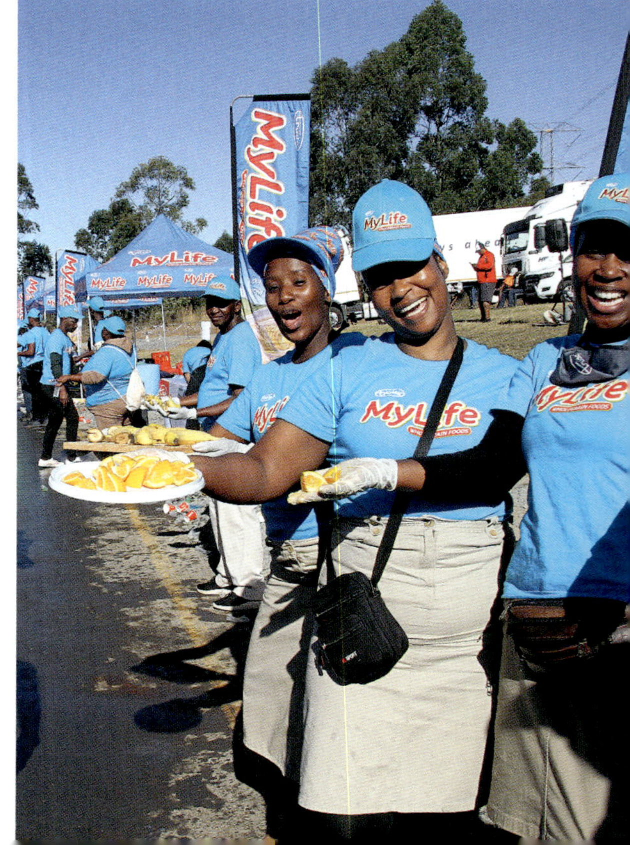

The first Comrades was organized by Vic Clapham, a British soldier who had emigrated to South Africa. Seeking a way to honour those who died fighting in World War I, he proposed an endurance challenge that would symbolize the physical and mental challenges of wartime.

The League of Comrades of the Great War, an organization of former soldiers, opposed the plan at first but eventually agreed to sponsor the race in 1921; it started with 34 runners. At first only white men could run in the race, with women and people of colour permitted from 1975.

Most years, over 10,000 runners reach the finish within the allowed time of 12 hours. The cut-off is notoriously strict, with runners being stopped even if they are only a few metres from the finish. The cut-off was increased from 11 hours in 2003 and interestingly, as participation has increased since the 1980s, the average finish times for both male and female runners, along with the average age of finishers, have increased substantially.

The race has been held every year since its inception with the exception of 1941 to 1945 due to World War II, and 2020 and 2021 due to the coronavirus pandemic, resuming in 2022 with a field of 15,000 entrants. The top ten men and women across the line receive a coveted gold medal, while all those who cross the line within the cut-off time receive a finishers' medal. A very select few runners wear a coveted Green Number. To be a member of the Green Number Club, first introduced in 1972, a runner must have achieved three wins, five golds (top ten finishes) or more than ten finishers' medals. Green Numbers also have advance access to entries, which open a day before general entries.

While the average Comrades time is increasing, record times, particularly in the women's race, are still being broken. In recent years, Gerda Steyn broke both the down (2023) and up (2024) course records.

ABOVE LEFT 10-hour pacesetters and fellow runners setting off on the 2023 edition of the Comrades Marathon.

FAR LEFT Women's record holder (Up and Down directions), Gerda Steyn, after winning in 2024.

LEFT Enthusiastic aid station support at the 2023 Comrades Marathon.

GRAND RAID DE LA RÉUNION: LA DIAGONALE DES FOUS

RÉUNION ISLAND, FRANCE

La Diagonale des Fous – the crossing of fools – takes place in the French department of La Réunion, an island in the Indian Ocean lying 680km (420 miles) to the east of Madagascar. A place of contrast, the coastal regions capture the essence of a tropical island, with white sandy beaches, coconut trees and the turquoise water of the lagoon edged by a coral reef. Yet inland, volcanic activity beneath the seabed has created an entirely different landscape, where rugged mountain giants rise skyward from the earth. The summit of the mighty Piton des Neiges reaches an airy 3,069m (10,069ft). Piton de la Fournaise (2,632m/8,635ft) is still an active volcano, erupting regularly, although harmlessly.

At the island's centre, huge geological collapses have formed three vast cirques – Mafate, Cilaos, Salazie – open to the sea via narrow gorges. These cirques are crossed by hiking trails, linked by waterfalls and gorges, creating a dramatic arena for the unfolding drama of La Diagonale des Fous, one of five races of varying distances that take place during the island's annual festival of trail running, Grand Raid de la Reunion.

RACE STATISTICS

MONTH: October
DISTANCE: 175km (109 miles)
TOTAL ASCENT: 10,150m (33,300ft)
HIGHEST POINT: 2,474m (8,153ft)
STARTERS 2024: 2,839 (359 female, 2,480 male)
FINISHERS 2024: 2,013 (226 female, 1,787 male)
TIME ALLOWED: 66hr
FEMALE COURSE RECORD: Courtney Dauwalter 24:37:47 (2022)
MALE COURSE RECORD: François D'Haene 22:58:30 (2013)
FIRST RUN: 1989
ENTRY FEE: €210

WEBSITE: www.grandraid-reunion.com

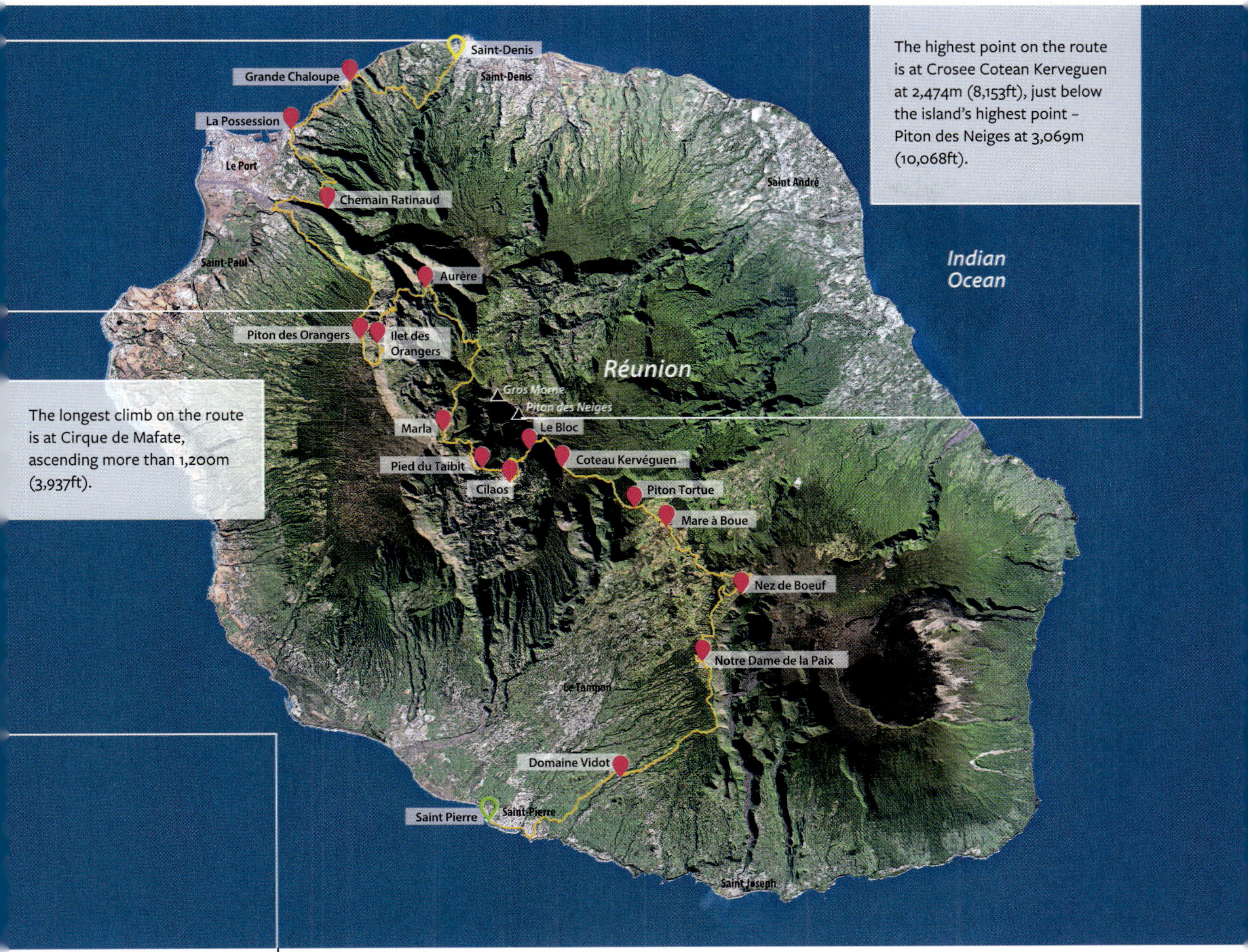

The highest point on the route is at Crosee Cotean Kerveguen at 2,474m (8,153ft), just below the island's highest point – Piton des Neiges at 3,069m (10,068ft).

The longest climb on the route is at Cirque de Mafate, ascending more than 1,200m (3,937ft).

Runners can expect a warm welcome and their coveted 'I Survived' t-shirt at the finish in Saint-Denis. The city is the most populous on the island, of all French overseas departments and 19th in all of France.

ELEVATION PROFILE

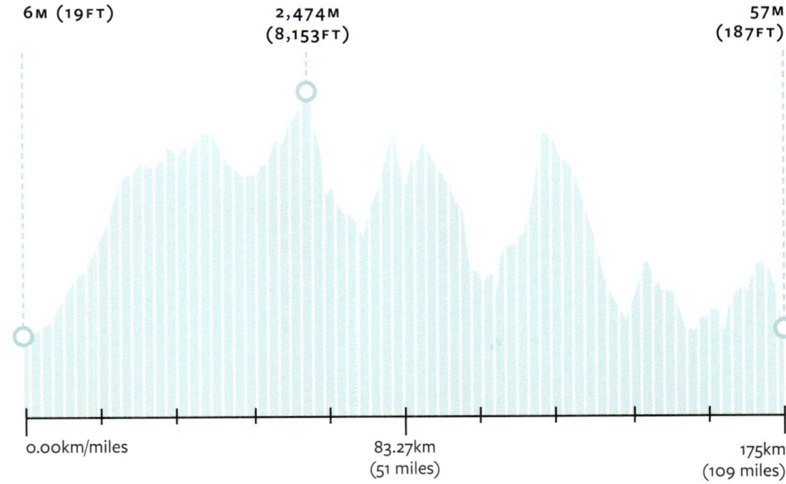

FAR LEFT Beautiful section of shaded trail on the 2023 Diagonale des Fous.

LEFT Nicolas Gourdon speeding to victory in the 2023 Trail de Bourbon.

PREVIOUS PAGES River crossing choices at Grand Raid de la Réunion – to take shoes and socks off or not?

ABOVE The coveted Grand Raid de la Réunion finishers' medal.

Every year, runners from all over the world gather here to pit themselves against the extreme landscape and climate.

Réunion residents are passionate about trail running, with nearly half of participants each year being locals, and those who aren't running the race enthusiastically supporting along the way. Some 20,000 people watch the start and around 10 per cent of the island's population show up to watch the race unfold at some point along its route. The local TV and radio stations also provide non-stop race coverage for the duration of the race, as well as live streaming for online viewers across the world.

First held in 1989, 'Diag' is considered one of the world's toughest mountain ultras, drawing elite and recreational runners to test themselves against its savage course. The route crosses the heart of Réunion Island from south to north, traversing an array of different landscapes including the lush forests and steep rocky ridges of Réunion Island National Park, a UNESCO World Heritage Site. Setting out at 9pm from Saint Pierre, on the island's southern coast, the atmosphere is a party, charged with nervous excitement, the long line of runners illuminated by headtorches as they wind their way up the first of many climbs. The longest climb ascends 1,200m (3,937ft) up to the edge of the famous Cirque de Mafate.

As they make their crossing, runners must not only tackle the distance, but also contend with rapidly changing weather conditions, particularly at higher altitudes, and rough and technical terrain.

OTHER DISTANCES

The Trail de Bourbon: 100km (62 miles); 6,090m (19,980ft) ascent

The Mascareignes: 70km (43½ miles); 4,000m (13,123ft) ascent

The Metis Trail: 50km (31 miles); 2,500m (8,202ft) ascent

Zembrocal Trail (four-stage relay): 151km (94 miles); 9,130m (29,954ft) ascent

Narrow trails edge precipitous drops, cross rivers and ravines, and scale high mountain peaks, and the race has seen three fatalities since it began. The weather, which can be savagely hot in the valleys and stormy up high, can quickly turn the course into an even more formidable challenge, with slippery rocks and muddy sections common.

While the race is tough, it's well known for its strong community spirit and warm, friendly island welcome that unites participants, volunteers and residents alike. The organizers make it clear that solidarity and mutual encouragement are as important as individual performance, with runners supporting each other through difficult times, and building camaraderie through shared effort and respect for the hardships en route. The race finishes in Saint-Denis, on the island's north coast, where emotions often run high, with runners overwhelmed with a sense of triumph and accomplishment, broken down and yet made stronger by their adventure.

As the race organizers put it: 'The Diagonale des Fous is not only an ultra-trail race, it is an inner journey, an exploration of oneself through the UNESCO World Heritage-listed Réunion National Park. The vertiginous Pitons, Cirques and Remparts symbolize the human capacity to overcome the most difficult obstacles.'

Over the years there have been some hard-fought races and memorable winners in the Diagonale des Fous, with the results list reading like a who's who of ultrarunning. Kilian Jornet took the win in 2010 and 2012. France's François D'Haene has won the race four times – in 2013, 2014, 2016 and 2018, the latter alongside compatriot Benoît Girondel. D'Haene also lined up at the 2023 edition of the race, a last-minute entry after more than a year off with injury, sporting a hand-drawn bib. Another joint win saw Ludovic Pommeret and Daniel Jung finishing the Diagonale des Fous hand in hand in 2021.

Courtney Dauwalter won the 2022 edition, finishing fourth in the overall standings and setting a new women's course record, making her the first woman to have won Western States, Hardrock 100, UTMB and Diagonale des Fous. Katie Schide took the women's title in 2023, with that year's Hardrock 100 champion Aurélien Dunand-Pallaz victorious in the men's race – both leading the field from the start.

OTHER AFRICAN HIGHLIGHTS

BOA VISTA ULTRA-TRAIL

BOA VISTA ISLAND, CAPE VERDE ARCHIPELAGO

RACE STATISTICS

MONTH: December
DISTANCE: 150km (93 miles)
TOTAL ASCENT: 1,322m (4,337ft)
TIME ALLOWED: 40hr

WEBSITE: www.boavistaultratrail.com

The island of Boa Vista lies 450km (280 miles) off the west coast of Africa. While best known for its beaches, turtles and traditional music, it also hosts a cracking set of trail races. Run the 150km (93 miles) Ultra which loops the whole island, the 75km (46½ miles) Salt Marathon that loops the west of the island and finishes on one of the salt pans, or the 42km (26 miles) Eco Marathon that stays in the north and loops the coastal beaches and inland desert.

In December, temperatures range between around 30°C (86°F) in the day and 10°C (50°F) at night and it's very unlikely to rain. It is sandy underfoot so kit to cope with the sun, the change in temperatures and anything to reduce sand getting into your shoes is necessary.

All three races share sections of the pristine beach and inland trails. You'll be running on dirt tracks, salt pan, sand dunes and beach. There are 15 checkpoints on the 150km (93 miles) route with water on course, but runners must be self-sufficient in terms of food and navigation.

The races have been held since 2000, but don't often attract a large field. The fastest times are held by Jailson Manuel Duarte Oliveira (17:13:00 in 2023) and Marta Poretti (21:17:00 in 2011) but most people finish much closer to the 40 hour cut-off.

RIGHT The Atlas Mountains mark the boundary between the Sahara's ocean and desert climates, and make a stunning backdrop in the Trans Atlas Ultra.

TRANS ATLAS MARATHON

THE HIGH ATLAS, MOROCCO

RACE STATISTICS

MONTH: May
STAGE RACE: Four stages in four days
DISTANCE: 167km (104 miles)
TOTAL ASCENT: 8,000m (26,247ft)
TIME ALLOWED: 12–14hr per day

WEBSITE: www.transatlasmarathon.net

The TAM Ultra-Trail is a high-altitude stage race held in the high Atlas mountains. It was created by Mohamad and Lahcen Ahansal, famous brothers who have won 15 editions of the Marathon des Sables (see page 188) between them.

These mountains mark the boundary between the northern oceanic climate and the desert climate of the Sahara. The highest mountain in the region is Jbel Toubkal at 4,167m (13,671ft), the race reaches around 3,500m (11,483ft), and the camps are between 1,800m (5,905ft) and 2,300m (7,546ft). Temperatures in the area tend to be between 5°C (41°F) (at the top of mountain passes) and 30°C (80°F) in the valleys. It can get down to 0°C (32°F) overnight, so a warm sleeping bag is on the kit list. The trail is well marked, following dirt roads, tracks and some technical rocky, arid, mountainous terrain.

The race is run over four stages between 30km (18½ miles) and 55km (34 miles). Runners are provided with a good breakfast and dinner but must carry their own lunch and snacks. The overnight camps are set up ready for the runners and include showers, cooking facilities and power.

The TAM Challenge is a shorter version of the race, running approximately 80km (49¾ miles), with 4,000m (13,123ft) of ascent over four stages. Runners start at the same time, on the same course; you finish at one of the earlier checkpoints and a 4x4 transports you to the camp.

Ultra MARAthon

MAASAI MARA, KENYA

RACE STATISTICS

MONTH: November
DISTANCE: 50km (31 miles)
TOTAL ASCENT: 342m (1,122ft)
TIME ALLOWED: 8½ hr

WEBSITE: www.ultramarathon.co.ke

The UltraMARAthon came into existence in 2020 when a group of runners created an event to support conservation and community initiatives in the greater Mara area. So far the project has supported the Mara Elephant project, the rangers who manage the reserves, improved local healthcare provision and increased exposure to the area, bringing in much-needed paying tourists.

The race loops the Lemek Conservancy on rough roads, grassy plain and tracks. It's not particularly hilly but races at an altitude of over 1,500m (4,900ft) so you may notice the effects of altitude. Average temperatures are a pleasant 26°C (79°F) and the average finishing time is just shy of five hours.

The main draw is the wildlife and beautiful scenery. A previous competitor put this perfectly:

'Unlike traditional safari experiences where you are safely tucked away in a vehicle, the UltraMARAthon places you in the heart of the wilderness. Every step of the race brings a visceral sense of connection to the environment around you.'

ULTRA X TANZANIA

AFRICAN GREAT LAKES REGION, TANZANIA

RACE STATISTICS

MONTH: February
STAGE RACE: Five stages in five days
DISTANCE: 223.8km (139 miles)
TOTAL ASCENT: 5,439m (17,845ft)
TIME ALLOWED: approx. 56hr. Exact cut-off communicated at the start of each stage

WEBSITE: www.ultra-x.co/tanzania

This five-stage ultra is set in the remote backcountry of northern Tanzania, in the southern shadow of Mount Kilimanjaro. The course climbs part-way up the Kili as the trail passes through savannah and forest and along the shore of lakes teeming with amazing wildlife.

During the race you'll camp in three different pre-erected campsites in Namalok Nature Reserve, Marangu and Lake Chala where there will be a big BBQ around the campfire. The stages are between 31.2km (19 miles) and 58.4km (36 miles) long, but the fully supported nature means you only have to carry the day's kit and there are aid stations every 10km (6¼ miles).

The whole event package takes place over eight days, with options to extend your stay and take part in a safari or climb Kilimanjaro after the race.

Ultra X have a series of races around the world; competitors who complete any of the events qualify for the Ultra X World Rankings. This is based on the total distance raced , and there are prizes and rewards for regular competitors.

LEFT Runners can expect to see incredible wildlife, including herds of giraffe, crossing the Masai Mara.

THE DESERT ULTRA

NAMIB DESERT, NAMIBIA

RACE STATISTICS

MONTH: November
STAGE RACE: Five stages in five days
DISTANCE: 250km (155 miles)
TOTAL ASCENT: 1,210m (3,970ft)
TIME ALLOWED: Varies with conditions and is confirmed at the start of each day

WEBSITE: www.beyondtheultimate.co.uk/race/desert-ultra

The Namib Desert is one of the oldest and driest deserts in the world. Some regions receive less than 2mm of precipitation per year, and it's estimated to have been arid for between 55 and 80 million years. Daytime temperatures can reach 50°C (122°F) and fall to freezing at night. It's dusty and sandy scrubland and sand dunes terrain. A challenging environment to run in.

The Desert Ultra covers around 250km (155 miles) in five stages. Runners are self-sufficient, carrying all their clothing, food, sleeping gear and equipment for the duration of the race. Boiling water and tents are provided at the camps, and water is available at every checkpoint.

The first three stages are between 42km (26 miles) and 50km (31 miles) each, starting at the base of Spitzkoppe Mountain and generally descending across sandy or rocky plains, dry river valleys and coarse grassland. Look out for elephants, lions, zebras and giraffes. Stage 4 is shorter at just 22km (13¾ miles), a gentle day (although it is uphill) to prepare you for the 92km (57 miles) Stage 5.

Stage 5 starts with sand dunes and finishes at the remote rhino conservation outpost where you'll celebrate the finish.

The Desert Ultra is part of the Beyond the Ultimate global race series.

RIGHT The Runyanga Ultra Trail takes runners through Zimbabwe's Eastern Highlands..

RUNYANGA ULTRA-TRAIL

EASTERN HIGHLANDS OF ZIMBABWE

RACE STATISTICS

MONTH: September
DISTANCE: 162km (101 miles)
TOTAL ASCENT: 5,600 (18,373ft)
TIME ALLOWED: 45hr

WEBSITE: www.runyangaultra.run

Founded in 2023, the RuNyanga Ultra Trail is Zimbabwe's first-ever 100-mile Ultra Trail run, taking place in the majestic Eastern Highlands of Zimbabwe. With 30km (18½ miles), 50km (31 miles), 50-mile (80.5km) and 100-mile (161km) races on offer, the weekend will see over 300 athletes take on the challenge.

RuNyanga is a new race, which started in 2023 and is organized by the people who run the Addo Elephant Trail Run. The course follows a big loop of Nyanga National Park in Zimbabwe's Eastern Highlands, and climbs Mount Nyangani (2,593m/8,507ft), the highest point in the country. You'll run through areas of rainforest and the ecologically important forest-grassland and shrubland. Nyanga is home to a remarkable diversity of mammals, including a small antelope called the blue duiker, and Samango monkeys which are only found here.

The 50 mile, 50km and 30km races run loops of the national park over the same weekend; both the 50 mile and 50km routes also climb Mount Nyangani. They use some of the same aid stations as the 100-miler and all events share the same prizegiving and buckle ceremony.

RMB ULTRA-TRAIL CAPE TOWN

CAPE PENINSULA, SOUTH AFRICA

RACE STATISTICS

MONTH: November
DISTANCE: 164km (102 miles)
TOTAL ASCENT: 7,516m (24,659ft)
TIME ALLOWED: 45hr

WEBSITE: www.ultratrailcapetown.com

The Mother City (Cape Town) occupies the land between the two oceans and Table Mountain National Park. The UTCT 100 crosses the beautiful northern mountains to run in the more remote mountains of the southern Cape. It's a technical course with lots of steep ascent and descent and a genuine mountain feel; add to this the changeable summer weather, which often starts in single digit temperatures but climbs considerably during the day, and you can see why it's billed as a tough day out.

The event offers a distance to suit every trail runner – as well as the 100-miler you can run 100km (62 miles), 55km (34 miles), 35km (21¾ miles), 23km (14¼ miles) or 16km (10 miles). The other distances run sections of the northern mountain trails, including Table Mountain and other sections, which form part of the iconic natural World Heritage Site and one of the New 7 Wonders of Nature.

The RMB Ultra-trail Cape Town is one of the ten World Trail Majors.

LEFT Robbie Simpson, winner of the 2024 PT55km race at Ultra-Trail Cape Town.

RIGHT Runners following trails through Addo Elephant National Park.

ADDO ELEPHANT TRAIL RUN

ADDO ELEPHANT NATIONAL PARK, EASTERN CAPE PROVINCE, SOUTH AFRICA

RACE STATISTICS

MONTH: March
DISTANCE: 161km (100 miles)
TOTAL ASCENT: 5,500m (18,045ft)
TIME ALLOWED: 40hr

WEBSITE: www.addo.run

Founded in 2005 this is South Africa's oldest 100-mile trail run. It's set in the Addo Elephant National Park in the Eastern Cape Province of South Africa. It's a remote trail in the African wilderness, running through the bush and sharing the tracks with kudu, impala, baboons, ostriches, bushbuck, black-backed jackals, mountain reedbuck, red hartebeest, mountain zebra, warthogs and eland. Addo is the only National Park in the world that's home to the big seven: elephant, lion, leopard, rhino, buffalo, southern right whale and the great white shark. If you extend your stay, you can visit the areas of the park where these animals live.

Temperatures in this region are normally between 20°C (68°F) and 30°C (86°F) during the day; lots of the trails are open so it's important to bring a hat and use sunscreen. The race is waymarked with fully stocked checkpoints every 8–12km (5–7½ miles). Underfoot you'll be running on dirt roads, rocky trails and awesome singletrack through the bush.

There are also 80km (50 miles), 50km (31 miles) and 21km (13 miles) races on the same weekend. All are point-to-point races on the same or similar trails.

27
GOBI MARCH
(MONGOLIA)

ASIA

ASIA INTRODUCTION

In the Japanese tradition of Tendai Buddhism, the Marathon Monks of Mount Hiei run the 29km (18 miles) loop around Mount Hiei for 100 days in a row, wearing white robes – the colour that symbolizes death – and sandals, stopping 250 times for prayer. This is the first stage in a potential seven-year, 1,000-day trial of endurance for those wishing to continue on the path to Enlightenment. During the seventh and final year, the very few Marathon Monks who are still able to continue cover 84.5km (52½ miles) a day for 100 days. While it sounds extreme, it's not unusual for ultra-endurance challenges to be self-transcendent, even spiritual experiences for those who take part.

Mountain running in Japan has been popular for decades with the country, hosting tough races such as the Mount Fuji Climbing Race, the Hasetsune Cup and the super-tough Trans Japan Alps Race. Ultra trail races started to grow in popularity in the 2000s, when the OSJ Ontake 100km (62 miles) and the Shinetsu Five Mountains Trail 110km (68 miles) were first held. As 100-mile races gained popularity across the world, Japan followed suit, with the inaugural Ultra Trail Mount Fuji (UTMF) attracting 850 starters. With the likes of US ultrarunning superstar Courtney Dauwalter lining up, the rebranded Mount Fuji 100, part of the World Trail Majors series, has established itself as a major player on the global ultrarunning stage. Mount Fuji 100 (see page 242) offers runners from adventurers to elites the opportunity to experience Japanese culture and the magical landscapes around the legendary mountain, which oversees the proceedings, its conical, snow-capped summit providing a glorious backdrop.

Thailand hosts another incredible Asian mountain race: the TRANS-INT 160 (see page 238) in Chiang Mai, Thailand's second-largest city. This point-to-point race travels 175km (108¾ miles) through the beautiful Doi Inthanon National Park, home to Doi Inthanon, the Himalayan 'Roof of Thailand' where runners reach an elevation of 2,565m (8,415ft). With 10,000m (32,800ft) of total elevation gain, and many technical trails, this is a tough but spectacular race, and part of the UTMB world series.

Chinese ultrarunning has seen a rapid rise over the past few years and the national team now includes some of the best in the world. China hosts Ultra-Trail Mount Yun (see page 234), one of the UTMB world series's newest races, which takes in the trails of Mount Yun in the northern Chinese province of Shanxi.

For a more immersive Himalayan experience, the Mustang Trail Race (see page 228) covers 166km (103 miles) of high-altitude mountain trails and passes over eight stages, allowing runners to stop the clock to visit places of

PREVIOUS PAGES A runner passes part of the Ovgon Khiid Monastery and Stupas on Stage 3 of the Gobi March, Mongolia.

BELOW Four Sisters Ultra Tour on Mount Siguniang.

spiritual and historical interest along the way. Boasting the smallest field of any ultra featured in this book, the incredible Mongolia Sunrise to Sunset (see page 224) is an annual charity run that has been taking place since 1999, making it one of Asia's oldest ultramarathons. Runners start and finish at Camp Toilogt on the shores of pristine Lake Khovsgol, exploring Northern Mongolia's Khovsgol National Park including running through traditional nomadic yurt villages and a climb up to Chichee Pass at 2,300m (7,550ft). Proceeds from the event support environmental projects in Khovsgol National Park, and help to preserve the unique culture and lifestyle of Mongolia's nomadic people.

Other highlights in Asia include the Mount Everest Extreme Ultra (see page 246), which covers 69km (43 miles) with a net elevation loss of around 2,000m (6,560ft); the Gobi March (see page 248), a stage race through the stunning Karakorum region of Central Mongolia; and the Borneo Ultra-Trail Marathon (see page 251), which takes runners through dense jungle and cultural landscapes close to Mount Kinabalu, the highest mountain in Borneo and Malaysia, at 4,095m (13,435ft).

ULTRA X JORDAN

WADI RUM, JORDAN

Sam Heward, co-founder of Ultra X, stumbled into multi-stage racing at the age of 22, having not previously been a runner. Signing up for a desert ultra, he assumed it would be a one-off challenge but ended up having a life-changing experience. Together with his friend Jamie Sparks, organizer at the time of the Wadi Rum Ultra, Sam set up Ultra X with the aim of encouraging more people to try multi-day ultras.

Today, alongside the original Ultra X Jordan, runners have the opportunity to run 250km (155 miles) – or half that distance for those keen to try stage racing but not yet ready to average 50km per day – over five days in the following locations: Rwanda, Tanzania, England, Wales, Scotland, Finland, Slovenia, Nevada, Madeira and Morocco.

Ultra X also has a Spring Trail Series, which takes place on the Serpent Trail, a stunning route that weaves through the greensand hills, rivers, woodland and lowland heath of the UK's South Downs National Park.

Jordan holds a special place in the hearts of the team behind the Ultra X ultramarathon series as its birthplace. It was here that the Wadi Rum Ultra grew into a global ultrarunning series.

RACE STATISTICS

MONTH: September–October
STAGE RACE: Five stages in five days
DISTANCE: 220km (137 miles)
TOTAL ASCENT: 2,522m (8,274ft)
HIGHEST POINT: 1,352m (4,436ft)
STARTERS 2024: 78 (24 female, 54 male)
FINISHERS 2024: 74 (23 female, 51 male)
TIME ALLOWED: approx. 54.5hr
FEMALE COURSE RECORD: Mirthe Nieuwstraten 20:52:17 (2023)
MALE COURSE RECORD: Salameh Al Aqrah 19:04:21 (2024)
FIRST RUN: 2017
ENTRY FEE: from £1,595

WEBSITE:
www.ultra-x.co/jordan

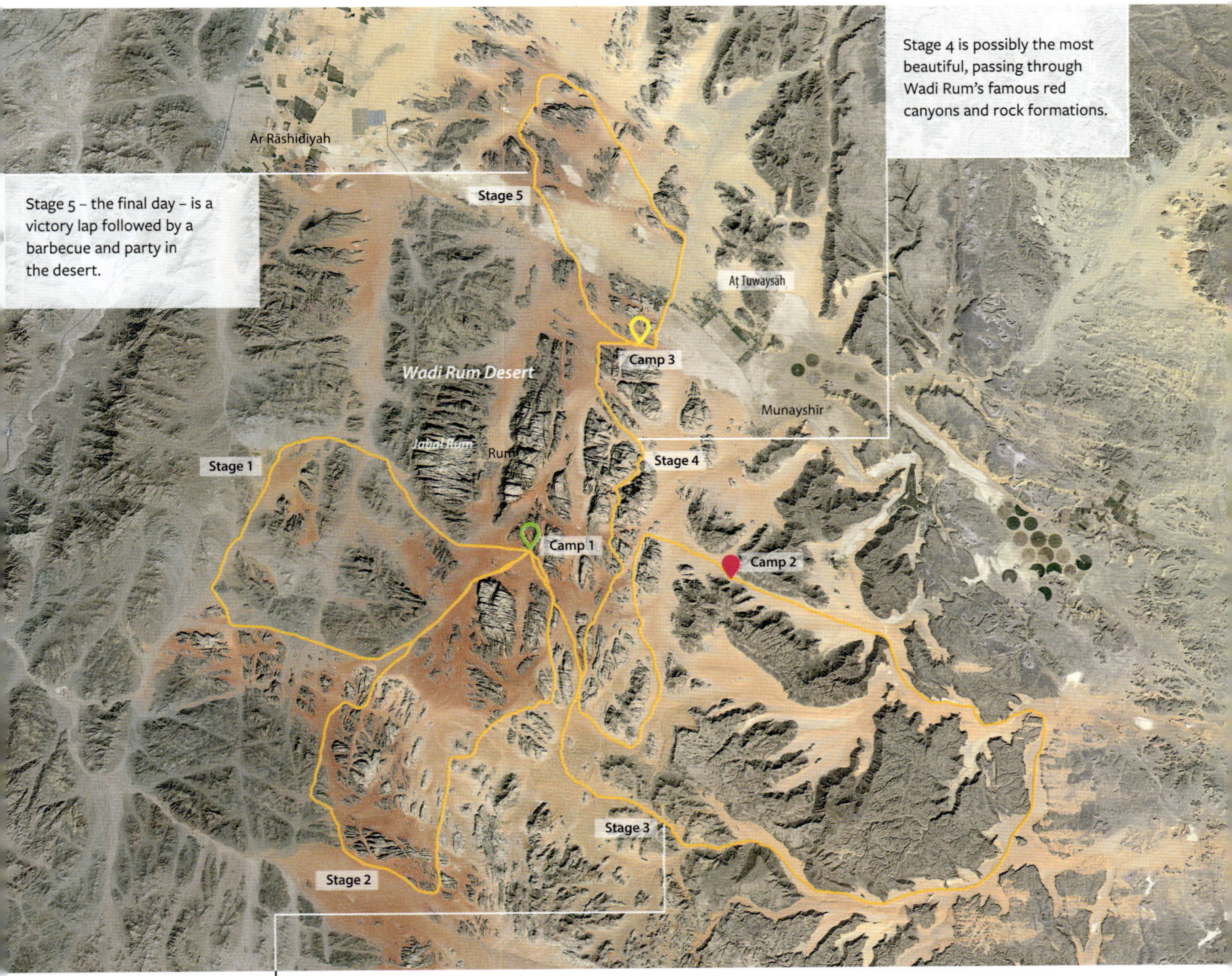

Stage 4 is possibly the most beautiful, passing through Wadi Rum's famous red canyons and rock formations.

Stage 5 – the final day – is a victory lap followed by a barbecue and party in the desert.

Stage 3 is the highest and longest stage, covering 58km (36 miles) with 883m (2,896ft) of ascent.

ELEVATION PROFILE

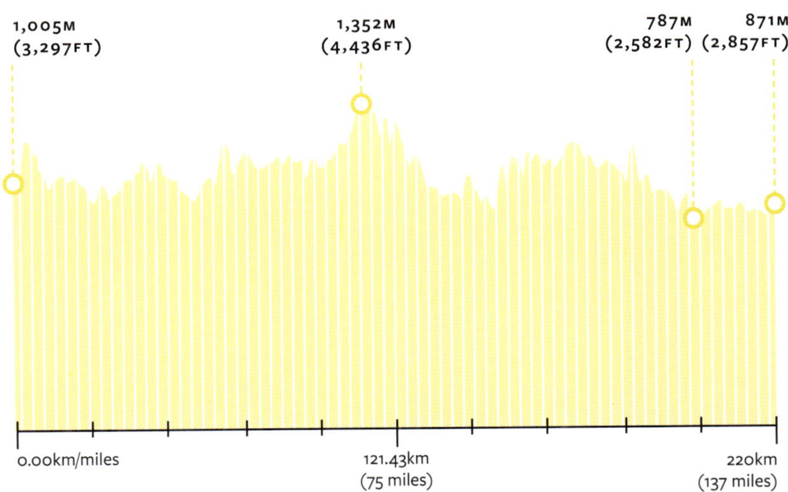

LEFT Finish line and base camp in Jordan's Wadi Rum desert.

The profound isolation and raw beauty of the place means runners who take part in the event say it's been a transformative experience and, in 2017, founders Sam Heward and Jamie Sparks began plotting how this event could be the beginning of something much bigger. Having seen the impact that a multi-stage adventure could have on people's lives, they had a dream of making the space more accessible for all.

The race takes place in the awe-inspiring Wadi Rum – the Valley of the Moon – in the Jordanian desert, which, according to Race Director Sam, is one of the most beautiful places on the planet. Here, participants are enveloped in a landscape so vast and otherworldly, surrounded by towering red rock formations, canyons and sand dunes, it feels like running on Mars. Having begun with only six participants, the race now consistently has fields of over one hundred. Daytime temperatures range between 25–35°C (77–95°F), dropping to around 15°C (59°F) overnight.

PREVOIUS PAGES Runners traverse the rugged desert terrain during Stage 2 of the 2023 race, surrounded by the breathtaking sandstone landscapes of Wadi Rum.

ABOVE Start line celebrations at Ultra X Jordan.

STAGE DETAILS

Stage 1: 38km (23½ miles); 232m (761ft) ascent

Stage 2: 40km (25 miles); 548m (1,798ft) ascent

Stage 3: 60km (37¼ miles); 883m (2,897ft) ascent

Stage 4: 48km (30 miles); 468m (1,535ft) ascent

Stage 5: 34km (21 miles); 391m (1,283ft) ascent

As with all of the Ultra X races, Jordan covers 220km (137 miles) over five days, meaning runners must prioritize self-care – in particular sorting out kit, essential footcare, massage, fuelling and hydrating for recovery from the previous day's exertions and preparation for the following day – alongside enjoying camp life in the evenings so they're ready to start again the following day. Stages start between 4am and 8am, with checkpoints approximately every 7km (4⅓ miles) offering support and medical assistance along the way. Stage 3 is considered the toughest day, covering nearly 60km (37¼ miles) with 883m (2,897ft) of ascent. For those who make it to day four, Wadi Rum's famous arch and canyon await before the victory lap of the final day, followed by a celebratory barbeque and party in the desert.

In the spirit of offering those without a vast amount of ultrarunning experience the opportunity to take part, Ultra X provides great support to runners throughout the race journey, including phone calls for registered participants to talk through kit and nutrition for their race and ask any questions they have about the specifics of participating in the event.

> 'I went to Jordan to run 250km in five days. But what I got in return was so much more. The Wadi Rum desert makes a spectacular backdrop for a multi-day ultra race. It has a unique beauty that sometimes borders on being hostile. The race is infused with local flavour and it is impossible to forget you are blessed with a unique opportunity not available to all. Running was done on clearly marked routes, although it boggles my mind how the course team could translate the hand-drawn map to real life. When you sign up for a desert race you expect to do sand running. Don't be fooled by the absence of huge sand dunes. You will run in sand for miles and miles. Full moon and starlit skies will rejuvenate you between stages. The support and medical crews do a wonderful job of keeping you safe, hydrated and in high spirits en route and at camp. If you ever consider signing up for this event be prepared to do a tough ultra, but also expect to walk away with your soul filled with wonder and new perspective.'
>
> ESTELLE GEERKENS, ULTRA X JORDAN FINISHER

MONGOLIA SUNRISE TO SUNSET

KHOVSGOL NATIONAL PARK, MONGOLIA

Mongolia Sunrise to Sunset is an annual charity run that has been taking place since 1999, making it one of Asia's oldest ultramarathons. This beautiful and isolated event has been included in the top 100 best races in the world by *Runner's World* UK and is regularly featured among the world's most beautiful races.

In the stunning Khovsgol National Park in Northern Mongolia, participants run through magical forests and vast, open lowlands; climb craggy mountain passes; and trace the peaceful shores of Lake Khovsgol, while herds of hairy yaks watch them pass. Mongolian horsemen serve as race marshals and aid station support.

Runners in both distances – the 100km (62 miles) and 42km (26 miles) – set out from Camp Toilogt along the shores of the national park's pristine alpine lake. One of the largest single bodies of drinkable fresh water in the world, it is surrounded by wildlife-rich landscapes and a population of mostly nomadic Mongol people who live in gers (Mongolian yurts) and tend herds of horses, camels, cattle and yaks. Runners may also encounter reindeer-herding Tsaatan people, and wild sheep, ibex, bear, moose, along with more than 200 species of birds.

RACE STATISTICS

MONTH: August
DISTANCE: 100km (62 miles)
TOTAL ASCENT: 2,120m (6,955ft)
HIGHEST POINT: 2,300m (7,550ft)
STARTERS 2024: 58 (20 female, 38 male)
FINISHERS 2024: 56 (18 female, 38 male)
TIME ALLOWED: 18hr
FEMALE COURSE RECORD: Mari Takemura 13:00:00 (1999)
MALE COURSE RECORD: Florian Vieux 10:03:00 (2012)
FIRST RUN: 1999
ENTRY FEE: $1,980

WEBSITE:
www.ms2s.dk

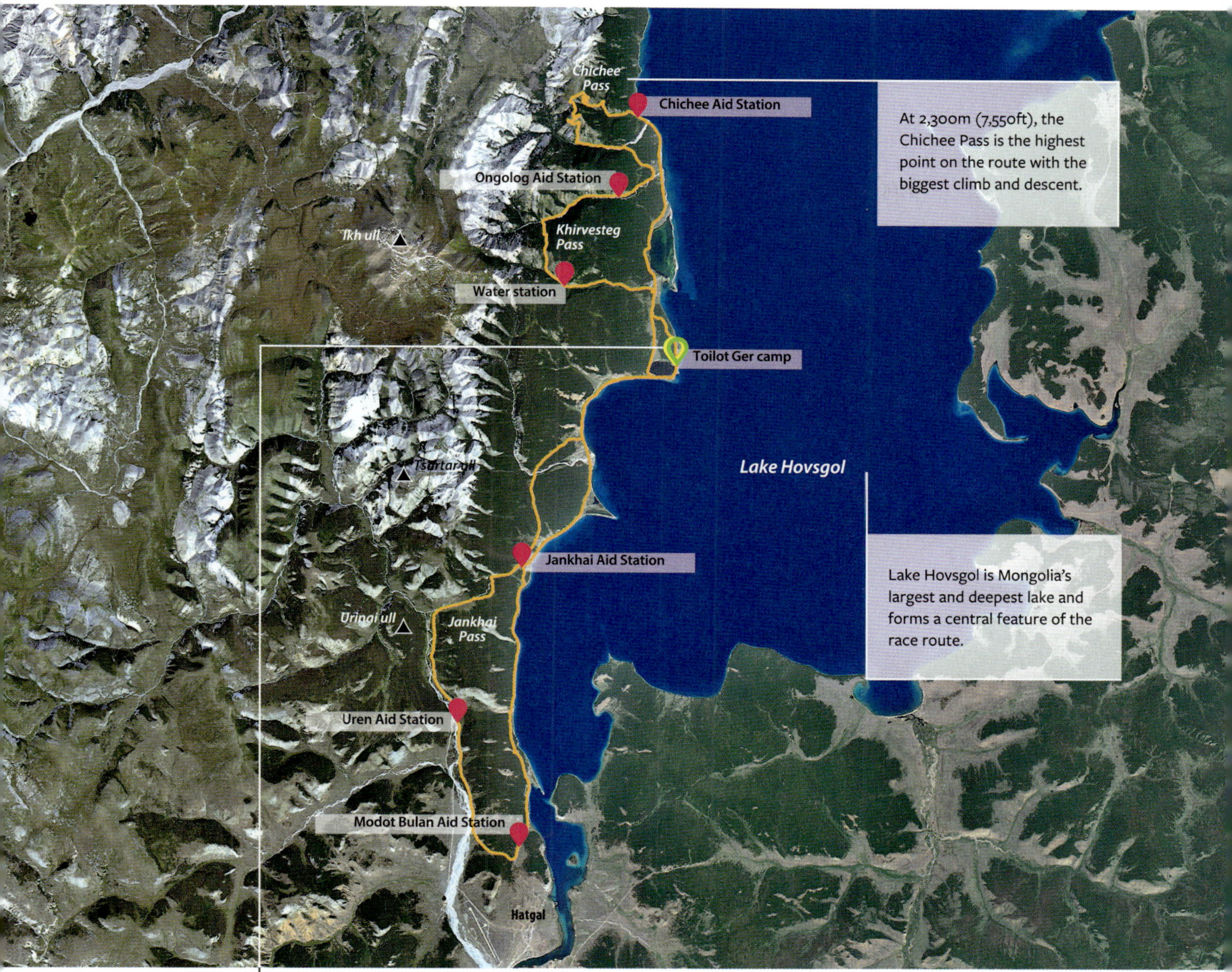

Chichee Pass
Chichee Aid Station
At 2,300m (7,550ft), the Chichee Pass is the highest point on the route with the biggest climb and descent.
Ongolog Aid Station
Ikh ull
Khirvesteg Pass
Water station
Toilot Ger camp
Tsartaruli
Lake Hovsgol
Jankhai Aid Station
Lake Hovsgol is Mongolia's largest and deepest lake and forms a central feature of the race route.
Uringi ull
Jankhai Pass
Uren Aid Station
Modot Bulan Aid Station
Hatgal

The 42km (marathon) race only completes the northern loop. Runners in the 100km race continue on to the southern loop.

ELEVATION PROFILE

1,651M (5,416FT)
2,300M (7,550FT)
1,643M (5,390FT)
1,652M (5,419FT)
0.00km/miles
50.17km (31 miles)
100km (62 miles)

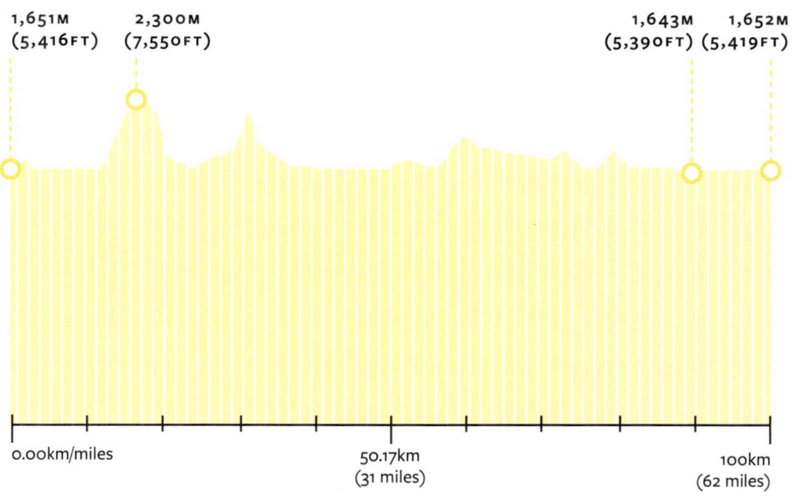

LEFT Runners in the Mongolia Sunrise to Sunset race pass through wildlife-rich lowlands tended by nomadic people.

OTHER DISTANCES

42km (26 miles);
1,400m (4,593ft) ascent

The trail winds through woods and over windblown lowlands, eventually leaving the lake to tackle a 700m (2,300ft) climb into the mountains to reach the Chichee Pass at 2,300m (7,550ft) from where there are spectacular mountain and valley views. Following ridgelines and then a long descent into a river valley, another steep climb awaits, which winds through dense forest to Khirvesteg Pass. Another steep descent returns to the lakeshore and Camp Toilogt – the finish of the marathon and the fourth aid station for 100km runners. The 100km route continues along the lakeshore to ascend Jankhai Pass, reaching a height of just under 2,000m (6,500ft). From here it's gently downhill all the way back to the lake, with the final 25km (15½ miles) along the level lakeshore.

This isn't just a race – it's an opportunity to experience a week of Mongolian culture and hospitality, and an incredible adventure. In the days before and after the race, participants spend time with the local nomadic population, sleeping in traditional Mongolian Gers and exploring the spectacular wilderness on horseback.

All proceeds from the event are used to fund environmental projects in Khovsgol National Park, in cooperation with Global Nature Fund, as well as to preserve the unique nomadic lifestyle and culture of its population.

While it's primarily an adventure, runners can expect some tough terrain. The marathon distance tackles more than 2,200m (7,200ft) of climbing, while the 100km ultra scales 3,375m (11,073ft) of ascent. But the event is designed to be achievable by most, with a generous cut-off time of 18 hours for both 42km and 100km. MS2S is a member of the International Trail Running Association (ITRA). Finishers of the 100km ultra distance get four UTMB qualifying points. MS2S is also a partner of the Asia Trail Master.

> 'Visiting the Khovsgol Lake area is like stepping into a different world. It is a paradise on earth. We work hard to keep the National Park as clean as it is, and to support the inhabitants so they can continue their unique way of life.'
>
> MS2S RACE DIRECTOR NICOLAS MUSY

> 'It was a complete success. It was an outstanding event – not to be missed. I have often been asked to name the race that I enjoyed most. My previous hesitations to name my favourite event are now replaced by a certitude: Mongolia Sunrise to Sunset.'
>
> HENRI GIRAULT – WORLD RECORD HOLDER FOR THE GREATEST NUMBER OF COMPLETED 100KM RACES (600+)

ABOVE As well as lakeshore and grassy lowlands, runners follow mountain and valley trails, climbing to an elevation of 2,300m (7,550ft) at Chichee Pass.

BELOW The race route skirts the pristine Lake Khovsgol.

MUSTANG TRAIL RACE

MUSTANG DISTRICT, NEPAL

The Mustang Trail Race is a multi-stage trail-running challenge through the wild, spiritually rich landscapes of Upper Mustang, a culturally Tibetan, trans-Himalayan region in the west of Nepal. Located behind the Greater Himalayan Range, in the rain shadow created by the Annapurna Massif, the region is a short flight or nine-hour drive from the town of Pokhara. The total distance of nearly 200km (124 miles) is split across eight stages of around 15–30km (9–18½ miles) each at altitudes between 2,900–4,300m (9,514–14,108ft) with 8,200m (26,903ft) of elevation gain. The thin air challenges many, especially in the early stages before acclimatization has fully taken place. Underfoot, the terrain is challenging, running on centuries-old trading trails that follow the safest trading route between Nepal and Tibet.

But once the running is done, runners have plenty of time to immerse themselves in the local landscape and culture, resting and recuperating at traditional teahouses or heading off to explore the region's fascinating caves, villages, monasteries and Hindu temples. During some stages of the race that pass particularly intriguing landmarks, runners are allowed to stop the clock to go and explore, restarting it when they resume the race, so there's no rush to get the day done – it's all about the experience.

RACE STATISTICS

MONTH: March–April
STAGE RACE: Eight stages in nine days
DISTANCE: 166km (103 miles)
TOTAL ASCENT: 8,200m (26,903ft)
HIGHEST POINT: 4,301m (14,111ft)
STARTERS 2024: 36 (17 female, 19 male)
FINISHERS 2024: 30 (14 female, 16 male)
TIME ALLOWED: n/a
FEMALE COURSE RECORD: Chhechee Sherpa 21:56:00 (2018)
MALE COURSE RECORD: Suman Kulung 19:08:50 (2019)
FIRST RUN: 2013
ENTRY FEE: $3,850

WEBSITE:
www.mustangtrailrace.com

Stage 2 is considered by many to be the toughest, with over 2200m of climbing and a high point of 3985m, coming before many runners are fully acclimatised to the altitude.

Stage 3 climbs to 4,301m (14,111ft) – the highest point on the entire route.

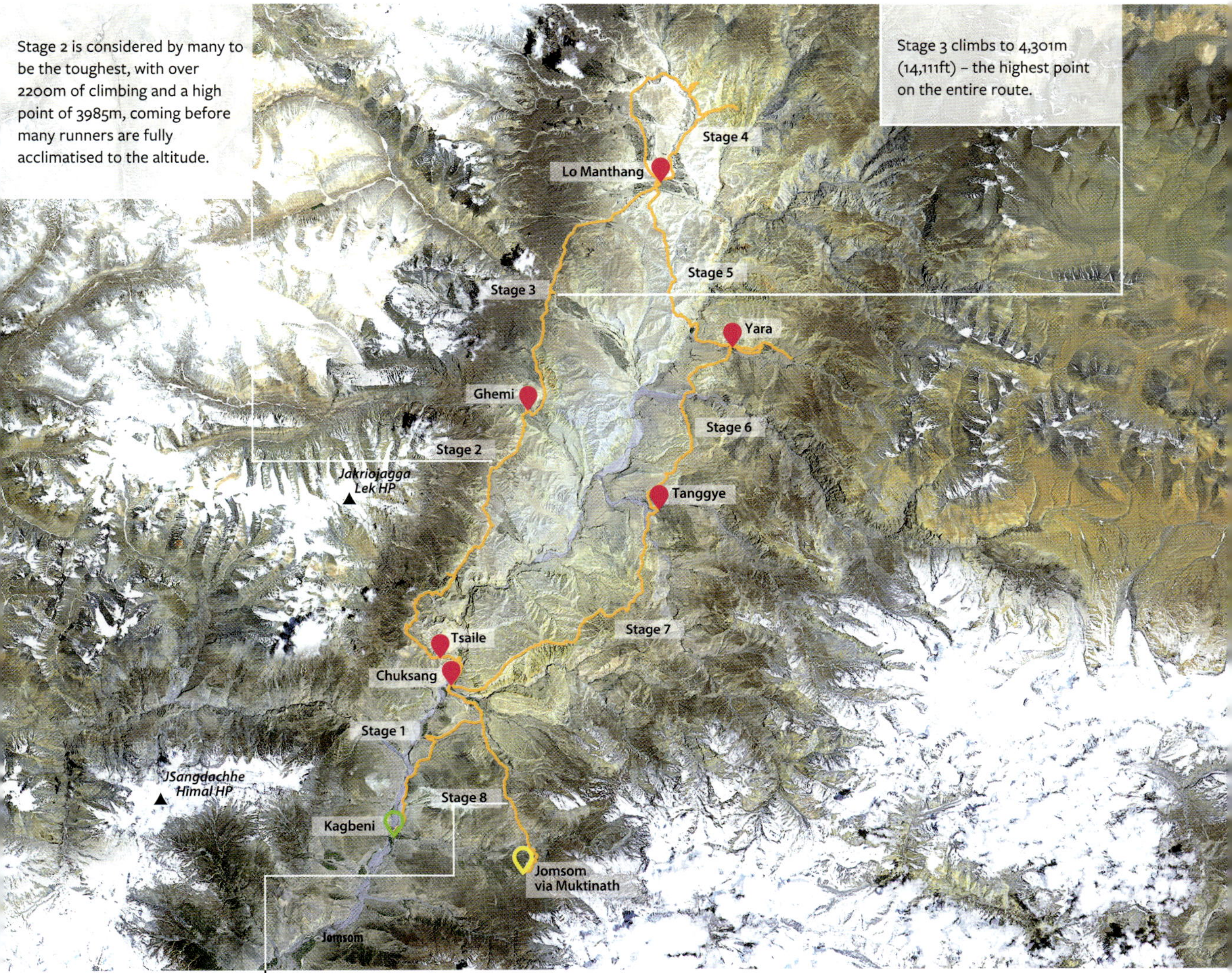

The final stage climbs to a high point of 4,030m (14,111ft) at the Gyu La before a celebration finish in Muktinath.

ELEVATION PROFILE

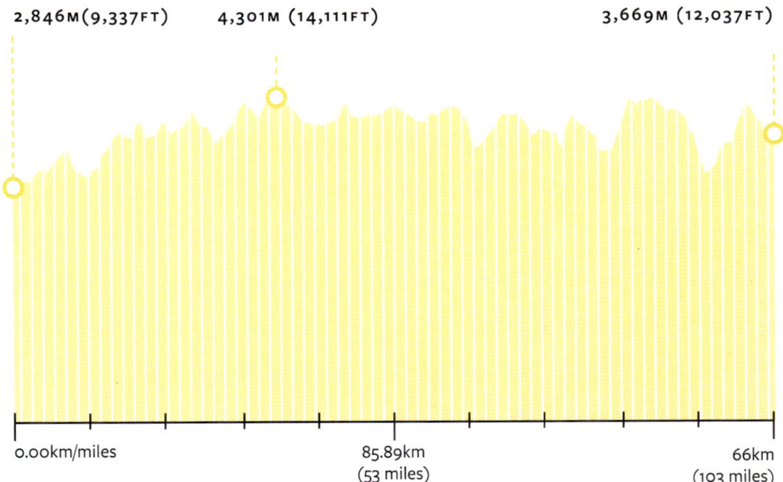

LEFT Prayer flags at the start of the Mustang Trail Race.

With its unique landscape and ancient culture, Mustang retains an air of mystery. Only opened to tourism in 1992, it remains much as it has been for centuries, a heart of Tibetan Buddhist culture where conserved monasteries and rustic caves house priceless historical treasures.

At the finish of the final stage, runners have the option to complete a full circumambulation of Mustang by running or hiking to Jomsom, two–three hours away, or taking a bus back to the hotel. So far, according to the race organizers, 90 per cent of people have chosen the latter!

Mustang is a fully supported race, with runners carrying only a light pack with the day's supplies and everything else transported by the race organizers. Nights are spent in traditional teahouses on comfortable mattresses, and hearty meals are provided. The race takes place over 12 days in total, with eight racing days, one hiking day, two travelling days, and a one-day briefing in Kathmandu.

> 'Mustang trail race will always go down as one of my favourite experiences. Over the eight stages of the race you run through some of the most spectacular vistas, visiting and staying in remote villages along the way. Running in Nepal is like no other running. It's more than a race, it's really a journey of self-discovery. The conditions are tough, with technical terrain and high altitude, there is so much mystery and uncertainty around how you will fare. But alongside that are majestic views, the development of strong friendship bonds and a love for a country that is rich in culture and warmth. Nepal stole my heart the very first time I visited back in 2013 and it's a place that I feel a real pull to return to again and again.'
>
> RENEE MCGREGOR, TWO-TIME MUSTANG TRAIL RACE FINISHER

ABOVE Three runners on Stage 3, climbing up to the Mui La to 4,100m. Annapurna I is faintly visibly through the haze.

FAR LEFT AND LEFT This area used to be the Tethys Sea some 50 million years ago. The soft rocks allow water and wind to carve out dramatic scenery.

STAGE DETAILS	
Stage 1: Kagbeni to Tsaile – 15km (9 miles); 538m (1,765ft) ascent	Kagbeni is a traditional stone-built Mustangi village standing at the entry point to the restricted area of Upper Mustang, the former Kingdom of Lo. Within the village, a maze of passageways leads to a central fort at its heart. Runners set out on jeep tracks, reaching the mud-built village of Tangbe from where there's a climb to a plateau before descending into a valley towards the beautiful village of Tetang, with its ancient salt mine. More level terrain leads along the Kali Gandaki River, edged by cliffs dotted with meditation caves. A short, steep climb leads up to the stage finish in the small and dramatically positioned village of Chele, also known as Tsaile.
Stage 2: Tsaile to Ghemi – 27.5km (17 miles); 2,202m (7,224ft) ascent	With the greatest amount of climbing and considered the hardest stage by many, especially those still to fully acclimatize, day two sets out from Tsaile and climbs steeply alongside a river gorge to the village of Samar. The climbing continues, reaching a low pass with a stunning view of the canyon landscape, before following the Pilgrims' Route on an enjoyable descent to a small monastery located within a natural cave. The trail climbs out of the gorge and up to Syangboche, Tamagaon and the Nyi La pass before another delightful descent to reach the stage finish in the pretty village of Ghemi.
Stage 3: Ghemi to Lo Manthang – 21km (13 miles); 1,097m (3,599ft) ascent	From Ghemi, runners will discover the longest prayer wall in Nepal, close to the red cliffs of Drakmar. A gradual climb through a maze of crags leads to Mui La, with grand views of the Annapurna range. On the descent, runners can visit the oldest monastery in the region, Ghar Gompa, thought to date to the eighth century. The second half of the day runs through yak grazing areas, often dotted with nomads' gers, finishing at the gates of the remote walled city of Lo Manthang.
Stage 4: Lo Manthang via Konchok Ling – 29km (18 miles); 1,063m (3,487ft) ascent	Stage 4, the longest of the week, takes in a loop to the north of Lo Manthang, passing through a mix of grazing pastures and surreal arid landscapes. After an early river crossing, a long, steady climb follows the road leading to China and Tibet. Level trails wind between ancient villages, crossing rivers to reach the caves, some featuring cave paintings in the Tibetan Buddhist style and, later on, the famous cave villages of Nyphu and Garphu. Runners return across easier terrain, following smooth trails through grazing pastures back to Lo Manthang.
Stage 5: Lo Manthang to Yara – 16km (10 miles); 650m (2,133ft) ascent	From Lo Manthang, a steady climb visits two small passes, from where runners descend through a spectacular canyon to reach the village of Dhi. The route continues along a riverbed to the finish in Yara, famous for its caves and cave paintings.
Stage 6: Yara to Tanggye – 18.3km (11 miles); 782m (2,566ft) ascent	Day six begins with a walk uphill to Ghara (3,800m/12,500ft) to reach the extraordinary cave-complex of Luri Gompa with its exquisitely painted stupa and rare 13th-century Pala style images. The race starts at the cave, descending back to Yara and traversing the southerly plateau towards a river-crossing at Damodar Khola, known for an abundance of 'Shaligrams' or ammonite fossils. Climbing from the river gains a ridge before runners descend to a plateau and on to the stage finish in Tanggye.
Stage 7: Tanggye to Chuksang – 23.9km (15 miles); 1,168m (3,832ft) ascent	Day seven begins with a crossing of the river at Tanggye Khola. The long, steady climb to Paha is rewarded with a stunning section of ridge running, the mountains unfolding all around, including stunning views to Dhaulagiri ('white mountain'), an 8,000m (26,250ft) peak, which dominates the skyline.
Stage 8: Chuksang to Jomsom via Muktinath – 15.1km (9½ miles); 1,184m (3,885ft) ascent	From Chuksang, runners make the long climb to the Gyu La (4,030m/13,222ft), visiting the fascinating mud and wood village of Tangbe along the way. Stunning views await at the top of the pass, from where an enjoyable descent on good trails leads to the finish line of the stage and the race at Muktinath.

ABOVE Serge Cofrade-Party running through the mud brick village of Chhusang.

RIGHT Runner heading to the Snow Leopard cave close to the border with Tibet.

ULTRA-TRAIL MOUNT YUN BY UTMB

XIANGNING, CHINA

Ultra-Trail Mount Yun, one of UTMB's newest races, invites runners to discover the trails of Mount Yun in the northern Chinese province of Shanxi. Across the different race distances, the race explores the natural wonders as well as the cultural and historical legacies of the area. Laozi, the founder of Taoism, once visited Mount Yun, securing the mountain's place in history. The race offers an unforgettable trail-running adventure through an enchanting emerald paradise with lush pine forest and breathtaking natural scenery surrounding the majestic Mount Yun itself.

There are four races offering Running Stones at Mount Yun by UTMB, required for entry into UTMB Mont-Blanc World Series Finals races in Chamonix (see page 20).

The 100-mile UMY race starts at midday local time on the Friday of race weekend. Finishers receive four UTMB Running Stones, with the top three gaining direct access to the following year's UTMB Mont-Blanc.

The 100k race is the DMY, departing at 9pm local time on the Friday of race weekend from Zhonghe square. With a total elevation gain of 6,536m (21,444ft), runners start off up a challenging climb, gaining the highest point in the race within the first 15km (9¼ miles). The DMY offers finishers three UTMB Running Stones, with the top three gaining direct access to the following year's CCC at the UTMB World Series Finals.

RACE STATISTICS

MONTH: April
DISTANCE: 159.2km (99 miles)
TOTAL ASCENT: 6,536m (21,444ft)
HIGHEST POINT: 1,652m (5,420ft)
STARTERS 2024: 389 (82 female, 307 male)
FINISHERS 2024: 307 (65 female, 242 male)
TIME ALLOWED: 48hr
FEMALE COURSE RECORD: Wenfei Xie 23:03:50 (2024)
MALE COURSE RECORD: Jia-Ju Zhao 17:05:57 (2024)
FIRST RUN: 2019
ENTRY FEE: $276

WEBSITE: mount-yun.utmb.world/races/100M

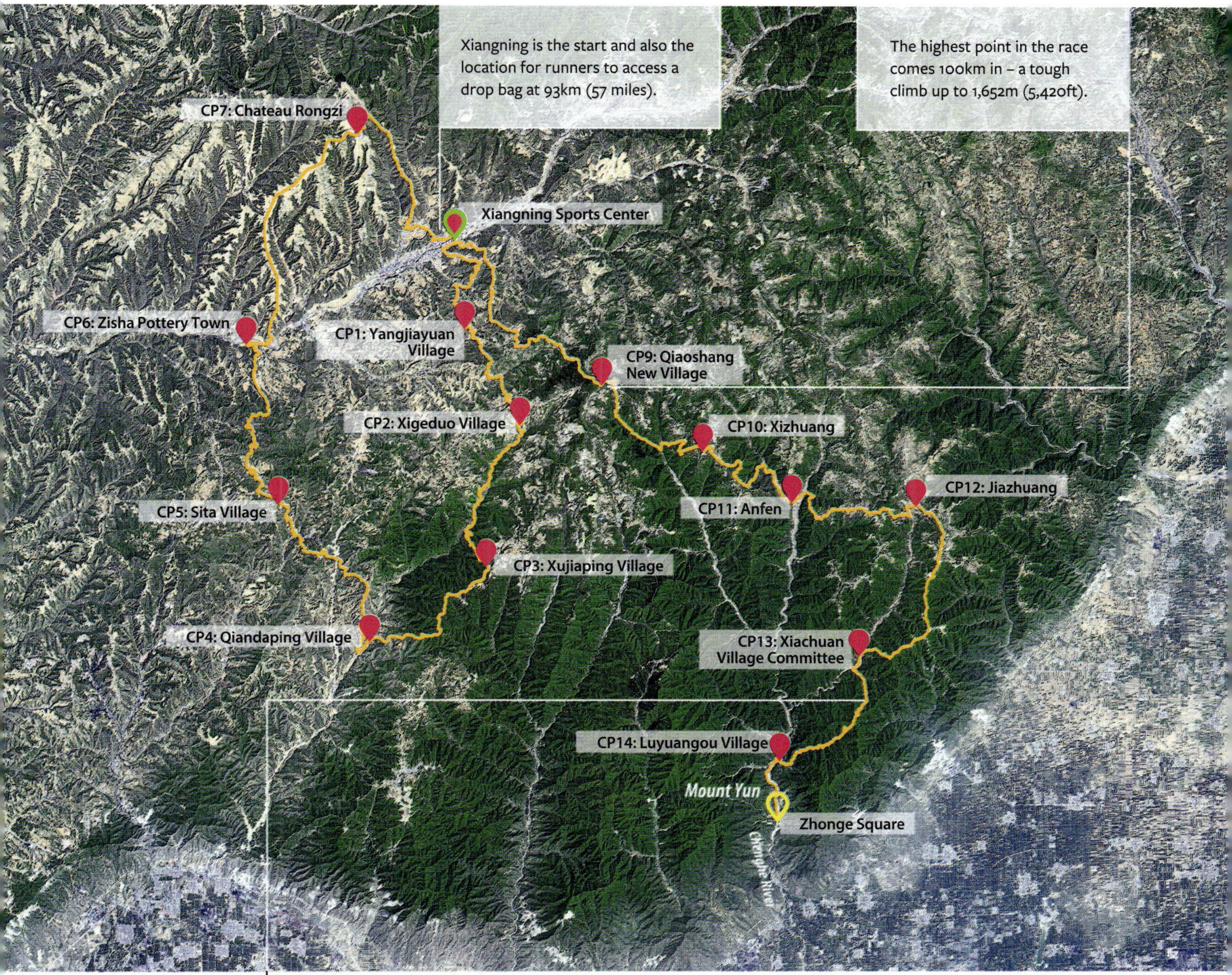

Xiangning is the start and also the location for runners to access a drop bag at 93km (57 miles).

The highest point in the race comes 100km in – a tough climb up to 1,652m (5,420ft).

CP7: Chateau Rongzi
Xiangning Sports Center
CP6: Zisha Pottery Town
CP1: Yangjiayuan Village
CP9: Qiaoshang New Village
CP2: Xigeduo Village
CP10: Xizhuang
CP5: Sita Village
CP11: Anfen
CP12: Jiazhuang
CP3: Xujiaping Village
CP4: Qiandaping Village
CP13: Xiachuan Village Committee
CP14: Luyuangou Village
Mount Yun
Zhonge Square
Chengde River

The sting in the tail is a steep climb and descent at 152km (94 miles) – then it's downhill all the way to the finish.

ELEVATION PROFILE

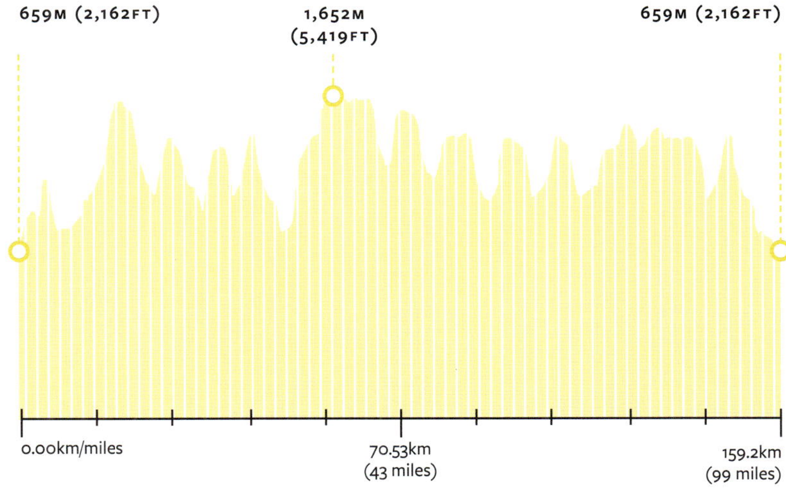

LEFT Zhang Huqing looking strong in the 100-mile UMY, 2024.

OTHER DISTANCES

DMY 100k: 96.8km (60 miles); 4,356m (14,291ft) ascent
TMY 70k: 68.4km (42½ miles); 2,570m (8,432ft) ascent
MMY 50k: 48.3km (30 miles); 2,407m (7,897ft) ascent
NMY 30k: 29.7km (18½ miles); 1,751m (5,745ft) ascent
EMY 20k: 21.1km (13 miles); 1,389m (4,557ft) ascent
LMY10k: 11.8km (7¼ miles); 1,040m (3,412ft) ascent
YMY10k: 8.9km (5½ miles); 561m (1,840ft) ascent
KMY 3k: 3km (2 miles); 250m (820ft) ascent

The 50k MMY starts on Saturday at 8am local time, also from Zhonghe square. It has 2,718m (8,917ft) of elevation gain, offers two UTMB Running Stones, and gives the first three finishers guaranteed spots in the following year's OCC.

The 20k EMY departs an hour after the MMY at 9am local time. It has 6,536m (21,444ft) of elevation gain, featuring two main climbs, and offers runners one UTMB Running Stone.

Highlights of the main race include the Five Dragon Palace, a Taoist temple in Ruicheng, also known as King Guangren's Temple. Built in 831 AD during the Tang Dynasty, it is the oldest surviving Taoist temple in China. Jade Emperor Tower is one of the most spectacular buildings in the Mount Yun range, positioned at an altitude of 1,629m (5,344ft), and the ancient village of Ta'erpois, known for its cave dwellings. It's also an opportunity to experience the many fascinating cultural influences of the region, from the influences of Confucianism, Buddhism and Taoism to the local traditional street food.

Ultra-Trail Mount Yun was the second Chinese event to join the UTMB World Series, after Ultra-Trail Ninghai, which takes place in the Zhejiang province on China's east coast in April. As China's ultrarunning team grows stronger each year, more and more athletes are taking part in UTMB World Series Finals.

Jiaju Zhao, UMY 100-mile men's race winner in 2024, told Trail Running Spain: 'The terrain at Ultra-Trail Mount Yun by UTMB is highly varied, many different types of cliffs, caves and even cave dwellings. I even had an urge to stop at one of them to get a nap. Also, I was very excited to finish during EMY 20K start as all runners there were cheering and encouraging me. Overall, I would like to praise the organization – I really enjoyed running the UMY 100M – there is almost no hard surface, such a big part of the race is running through green areas. I am looking forward to being back next year to break my own record.'

LEFT Eventual winner of the UMY, Zhao Jiaju, during the 2024 event.

TRANS-INT 160 BY UTMB

CHIANG MAI, THAILAND

Held under the name Doi Inthanon until 2024, Chiang Mai Thailand is a UTMB World Series Major, meaning finishers receive double Running Stones, increasing their chances of securing a place at the UTMB World Series Finals in Chamonix, should they wish to take part.

This point-to-point race, part of the UTMB World Series, travels 175km (108¾ miles) through glorious Thai landscapes, including the famous Doi Inthanon National Park. Here, runners will pass spectacular waterfalls, follow peaceful trails, visit remote villages and climb to airy viewpoints. Also known as 'The Roof of Thailand', Doi Inthanon is part of the Himalayan mountain range, with elevations ranging between 800m (2,625ft) and 2,565m (8,415ft), including Doi Inthanon Mountain, the highest mountain in Thailand. With 10,000m (32,800ft) of total elevation gain, and many technical trails, this is a tough race. Chiang Mai, sometimes written as Chiengmai or Chiangmai, is the largest city in northern Thailand, and the second largest city in Thailand. It is 700km (435 miles) north of Bangkok in a mountainous region.

Runners will continue to remote Ob Khan National Park, known for its river and deep gorges, and popular Doi Suthep-Pui National Park, with its waterfalls, temples and trail network. The finish line awaits at the Provincial Administrative Organization Park in Chiang Mai.

RACE STATISTICS

MONTH: December
DISTANCE: 175km (108¾ miles)
TOTAL ASCENT: 10,000m (32,800ft)
HIGHEST POINT: 2,065m (6,775ft)
STARTERS 2024: 359 (60 female, 299 male)
FINISHERS 2024: 233 (35 female, 198 male)
TIME ALLOWED: 48hr
FEMALE COURSE RECORD: Antonina Iushina 24:23:52 (2024)
MALE COURSE RECORD: Can-Hua Luo 20:25:33 (2024)
FIRST RUN: 2020
ENTRY FEE: 11,500 THB

WEBSITE:
chiangmai.utmb.world

From Doi Inthanon National Park runners pass through Ob Khan National Park, known for its stunning rivers and deep gorges.

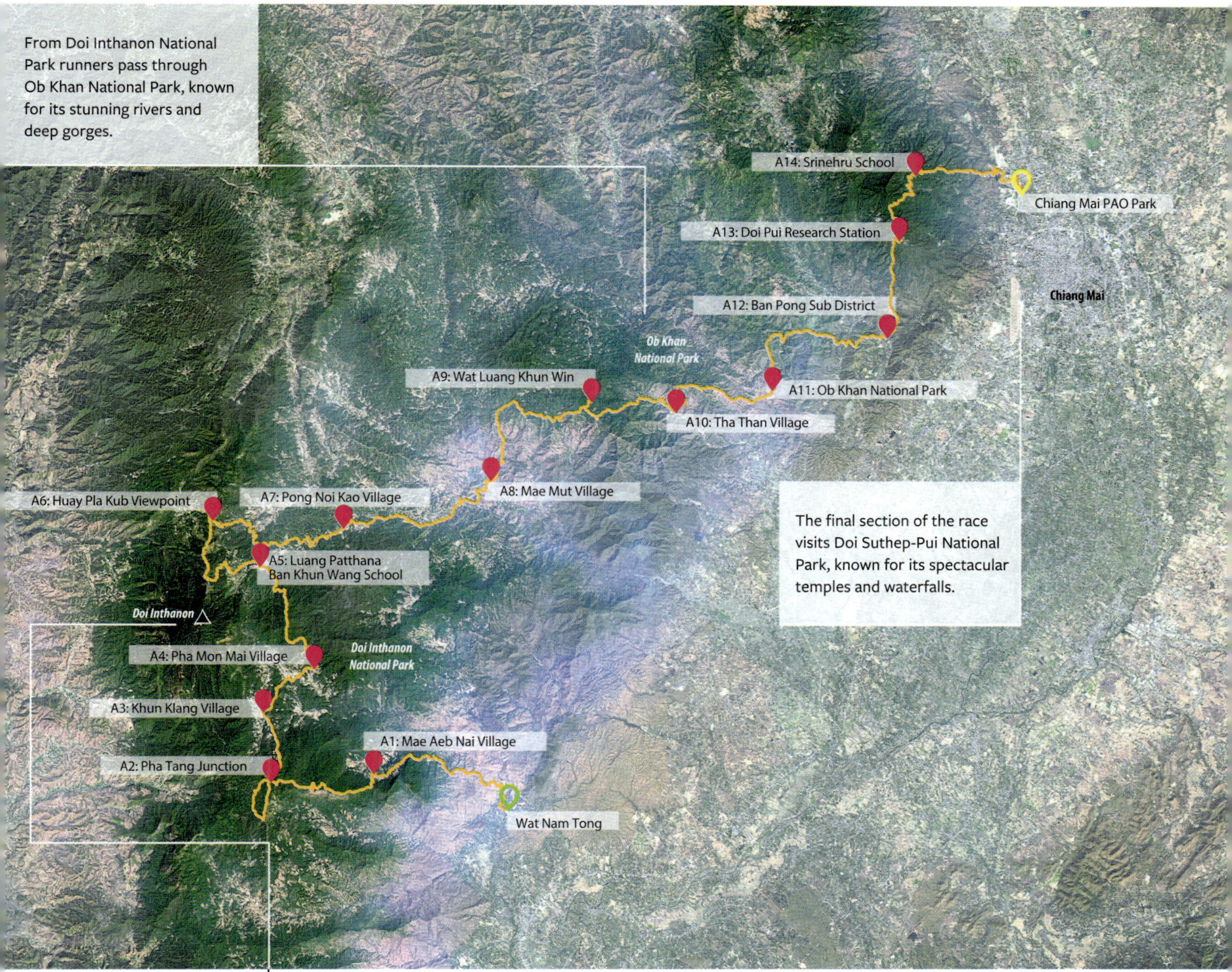

A14: Srinehru School
Chiang Mai PAO Park
A13: Doi Pui Research Station
Chiang Mai
A12: Ban Pong Sub District
Ob Khan National Park
A9: Wat Luang Khun Win
A11: Ob Khan National Park
A10: Tha Than Village
A8: Mae Mut Village
A6: Huay Pla Kub Viewpoint
A7: Pong Noi Kao Village
A5: Luang Patthana Ban Khun Wang School
Doi Inthanon
A4: Pha Mon Mai Village
Doi Inthanon National Park
A3: Khun Klang Village
A1: Mae Aeb Nai Village
A2: Pha Tang Junction
Wat Nam Tong

The final section of the race visits Doi Suthep-Pui National Park, known for its spectacular temples and waterfalls.

The highest point on the route lies below the summit of Doi Inthanon at 2,065m (6,775ft).

ELEVATION PROFILE

306m (1,003ft)
299m (980ft)
2,065m (6,774ft)
320m (1,049ft)
0.00km/miles
86.00km (53 miles)
175km (108¾ miles)

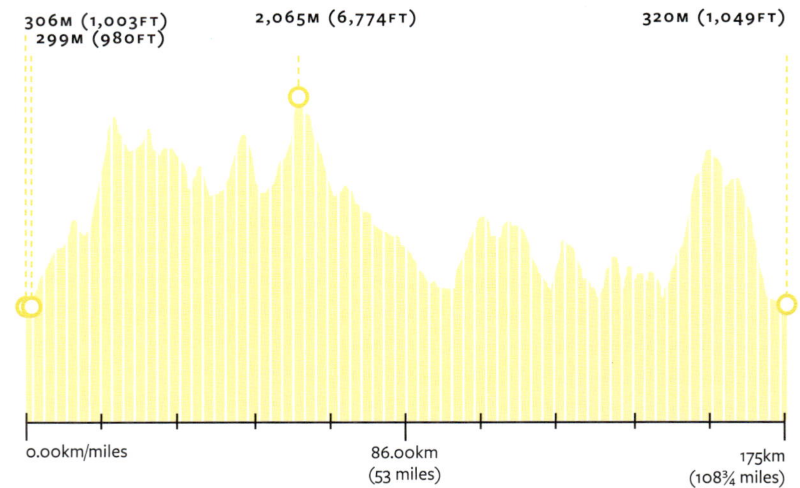

LEFT The race runs through wild National Parks, villages and temples.

OTHER DISTANCES

Elephant 100: 93km (57¾ miles); 5,380m (17,585ft) ascent

Hmong 50: 53km (33 miles); 3,040m (9,974ft) ascent

Suthep 20: 24km (15 miles); 1,190m (3,904ft) ascent

Chedi 10: 12km (7½ miles); 300m (984ft) ascent

TRANS-INT 160 is the only route over the race weekend that follows a point-to-point trail, starting at the foothills of Doi Inthanon in the Doi Inthanon National Park and visiting Ob Khan National Park and Doi Suthep-Pui National Park before finishing at the Royal Park Rajapreuk. All other distances – Elephant 100, Hmong 50, Suthep 20 and Chedi 10 – are looped courses, starting and finishing at the Royal Park Rajapreuk. Free transport is provided by the organizers to shuttle runners between the start and finish of the 160. Trans-Int gains finishers eight Running Stones for entry to the UTMB World Series Finals races, Elephant six Stones, and Hmong four Stones.

Though the race takes part just after the rainy season, humidity is still high and rainfall is possible. The timing of the race showcases the forests, jungles, rivers and waterfalls at their fullest. Fascinating wildlife abounds, with Indian muntjacs, wild boars, Assam macaques, Indochinese serows, Asian golden cats, Malayan porcupines and Asian black bears among many others.

Runners can expect full race support in line with all UTMB-branded races, with sports nutrition and hydration alongside authentic Thai food at aid stations.

In the 2022 edition of the race, Canadian runner Jenny Quilty won the women's 100-mile race in 15th place overall and nearly an hour ahead of her nearest female rival, Wenfei Xie of China.

Quilty, who is based in British Columbia, told Run 247, 'It was beautiful to go through all the villages. I was on one of the ridges at sunrise and it was just magical. The trails here are like nowhere else.'

LEFT Gediminas Grinius tackling a steep descent on his way to 2nd place at the 2023 Trans-Int 160.

RIGHT The race start, in Chiang Mai park.

MOUNT FUJI 100

JAPAN

Rising from the island of Honshu, Mount Fuji is an active volcano and an iconic sight, with its conical, snow-capped summit. Standing at 3,776m (12,389ft), it is the tallest mountain in Japan, the second-highest volcano located on an island in Asia (after Mount Kerinci on the Indonesian island of Sumatra) and the seventh-highest island peak on earth.

The Mount Fuji 100 ultramarathon was first held in 2012, when it was known as Ultra-Trail Mount Fuji (UTMF). But Japanese runners had been testing themselves against the mountains for decades before that in tough races such as the Mount Fuji Climbing Race (founded in 1913, a challenging 21km /13 miles with a brutal 3,000m/9,850ft ascent); the Hasetsune Cup (founded in 1993, a demanding 70km/43½ miles with over 4,200m/13,800ft of ascent); and the super-tough Trans Japan Alps Race (founded in 2002, which takes in a massive 27,000m/88,600ft of ascent over its 415km- (258 mile-) route.

While there were established road ultras in Japan, including the renowned Lake Saroma 100km (62 miles) ultramarathon, which was established in 1987, trail ultras didn't take off until the late 2000s, when the rise of ultrarunning in Europe and the US inspired the first 100km trail races. These included the OSJ Ontake (100km) in 2008 and the Shinetsu Five Mountains Trail (110km/68 miles) in 2009. As 100-mile (161 km) races gained popularity across the world, Japan followed suit, with the inaugural UTMF attracting

RACE STATISTICS

MONTH: April
DISTANCE: 166.6km (103½ miles)
TOTAL ASCENT: 7,038m (23,090ft)
HIGHEST POINT: 1,567m (5,141ft)
STARTERS 2024: 2,279 (289 female, 1,990 male)
FINISHERS 2024: 1,442 (182 female, 1,260 male)
TIME ALLOWED: 45hr
FEMALE COURSE RECORD: Courtney Dauwalter 19:21:22 (2024)
MALE COURSE RECORD: Hirokazu Nishimura 18:15:32 (2022)
FIRST RUN: 2012
ENTRY FEE: 45,000 JPY

WEBSITE: www.mtfuji100.com

Shojiko
Lake Motosu
Fujiyoshida
Fujiyoshida
Oshino
Nijyumagari
Fujihokuroku Park Gymnasium
Mount Fuji Meisui Stadium
Yamanakako Kirara
Lake Yamanaka
Fumoto
Mount Fuji
Fujinomiya
Gotemba
Fujinomiya
Kodomonokuni

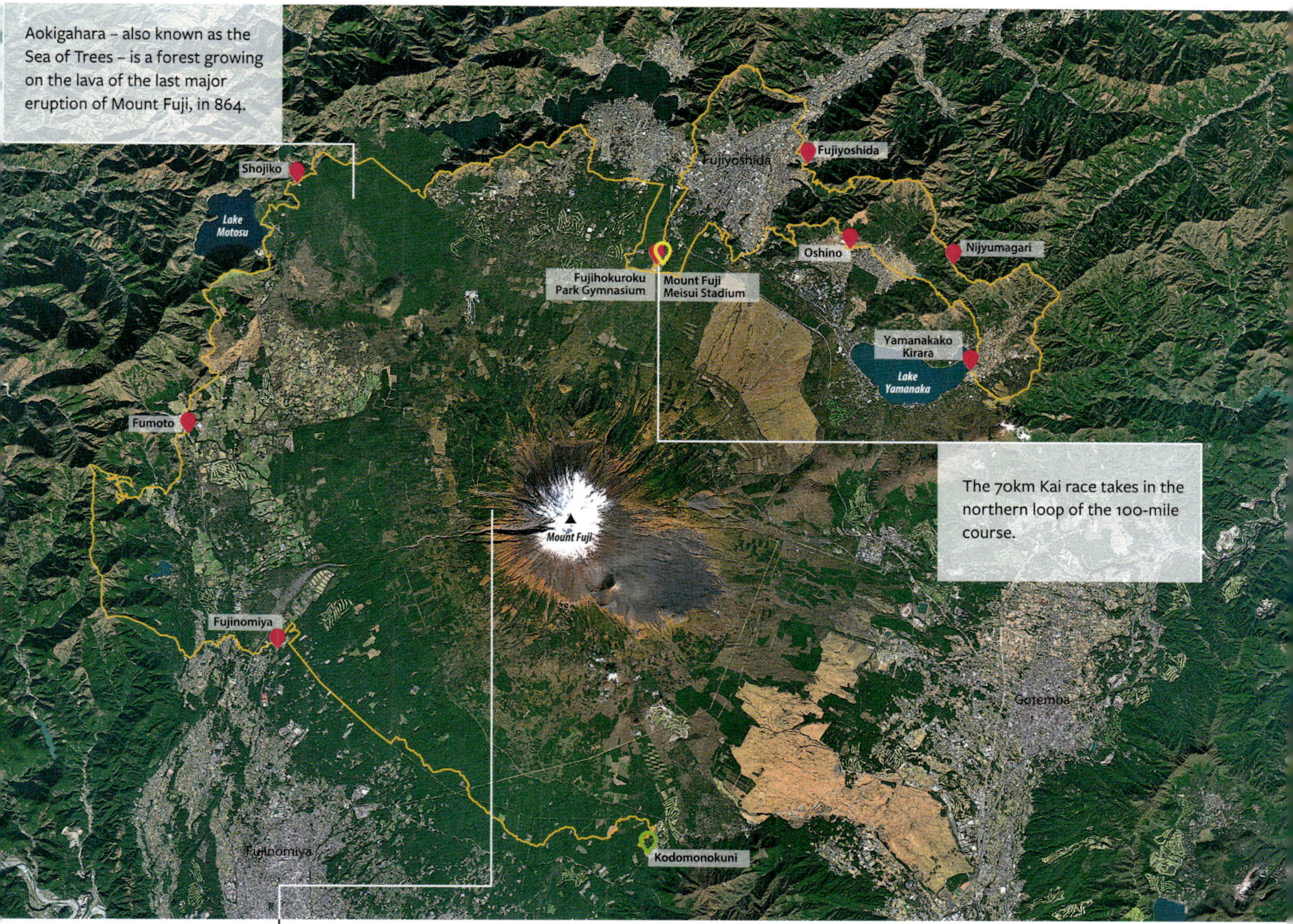

Aokigahara – also known as the Sea of Trees – is a forest growing on the lava of the last major eruption of Mount Fuji, in 864.

The 70km Kai race takes in the northern loop of the 100-mile course.

The race route encircles Mount Fuji, Japan's highest mountain at 3,776m (12,388ft).

ELEVATION PROFILE

835M (2,739FT)
500M (1,640FT)
1,567M (5,141FT)
1,009M (3,310FT)
0.00km/miles
82.53km (51 miles)
166.6km (103½ miles)

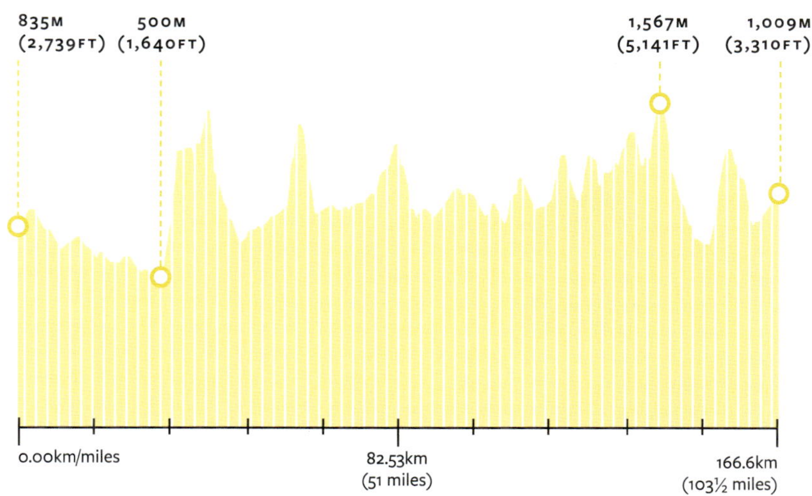

FAR LEFT The snow-capped peak of Mount Fuji provides an iconic backdrop to the race.

LEFT Courtney Dauwalter on her way to winning the women's race in 2024.

THE NORTH FACE
GranCanaria WORLD TRAIL MAJORS
Mt.FUJI 100
GranCanaria WORLD TRAIL MAJORS
THE NORTH FACE

OTHER DISTANCES

Kai: 70km (43½ miles); 3,500m (11,500ft) ascent
Asumi: 40km (25 miles); 1,481m (4,859ft) ascent

850 starters and establishing the race as a major player on the global ultrarunning stage.

The race is mainly on forest paths and tracks, traversing tranquil lakes and tackling technical steep climbs and descents mixed in with good, runnable trails. One of the forests that the race travels through, the Aokigahara, was formed after a volcanic eruption in the year 864; it has stood practically untouched for more than a thousand years. The race photos really capture the spirit of the place and the race – the magical landscape; courageous runners practising patience as they make their way through 100 miles; iconic, snow-capped Mount Fuji as a backdrop.

Following its inclusion in the new World Trail Majors series, the 2024 edition of Mount Fuji 100 put the race firmly back in the spotlight, with Courtney Dauwalter taking the women's win, finishing third overall and becoming the first woman to win the race twice.

For those looking for a shorter option to the full Mount Fuji 100, the Kai covers 70km (43½ miles) with 3,500m (11,500ft) of elevation gain and a generous 21-hour cut-off, following the route from the main aid station at around 97km (60 miles). Expect well-stocked aid stations serving traditional miso soup, rice balls, donuts and udon noodles – all fantastic for ultrarunning.

2024 saw the start times for both races moved to midnight, bringing in an extra level of challenge and need for strategic pre-race arrangements to avoid excessive sleep deprivation and/or the need for lengthy sleeps on the course.

In an article for *Ultrarunning* magazine, James Mallion, who ran the race for the first time in 2024, wrote: 'The Mount Fuji 100 and Kai are testaments to the spirit of ultra-trail running in Japan, uniting a passionate community from across the country and beyond. This 3,400-strong field, the largest I'd ever encountered, buzzed with international camaraderie, particularly with runners from neighboring Asian countries.'

ABOVE The 100-mile race loops three-quarters of the way around Mount Fuji, which provides a constant backdrop for runners.

BELOW China's Guomin Deng wins the Mount Fuji 100 in 2024.

OTHER ASIA HIGHLIGHTS

SOLANG SKYULTRA

SOLANG VALLEY, MANALI, INDIA

RACE STATISTICS

MONTH: October
DISTANCE: 100km (62 miles)
TOTAL ASCENT: 7,350m (24,114ft)
TIME ALLOWED: 32hr

WEBSITE:
thehellrace.com/the-hell-race/solang-sky-ultra/

This is a SkyUltra: the trails are steep and exposed, climbing and descending 7,350m (24,114ft) over the 100km (62 miles) distance on technical mountainous terrain. Underfoot will be a mixture of gravel, rock, snow and ice on the exposed upper slopes and more forgiving dirt and gravel trails through the valleys and forest. You'll experience the effects of altitude, starting at 2,500m (8,200ft), running down to 2,041m (6,696ft) and then climbing to the course highpoint of 4,187m (13,737ft).

Daytime temperatures range from 25°C to 10°C (77–50°F), but it will drop to between 10°C and 0°C (50–32°F) overnight. Of course, it may feel a lot colder on the high trails, especially if it's windy.

The 100km is the longest race at this event, but you can also run 60km (37¼ miles), 30km (18½ miles) or 14km (8¾ miles) trails. All the distances are tough with typically high DNF rates; to recognize the effort required to even start a race like this there are DNF certificates as well as finishers medals.

MOUNT EVEREST EXTREME ULTRA

EVEREST BASE CAMP–NAMCHE BAZAAR, NEPAL

RACE STATISTICS

MONTH: May
DISTANCE: 69.2km (43 miles)
TOTAL ASCENT: 3,549m (11,644ft)
TIME ALLOWED: 7.5hr to Pangboche, 13hr to Machhermo. No finish line cut-off.

WEBSITE: www.everestmarathon.com

The Tenzing Hillary Everest Marathon, Extreme Ultra and Half-marathon, is held on 29 May every year to commemorate the first ascent of Everest by Tenzing Norgay and Sir Edmund Hillary on 29 May 1953.

The Marathon and Extreme Ultra both start at Everest Base Camp (5,356m/17,572ft), making them the highest in the world. The 70km (43½ mile) ultra runs past glaciers and moraine, over five Himalayan passes and past sherpa villages, before it descends via Mongla towards Namche Bazaar at 3,440m (11,286ft).

Most competitors join a lodge package on a 19-day trip, which includes a guided trek from Lukla airport to Everest Base Camp, two nights at Base Camp, the race, then a guided trek from the finish back to the airport. Alternatively, you can run the classic Everest Marathon which follows a different, more direct course from base camp to Namche Bazaar.

RIGHT Amadablam Mountain (6,812m/22,349ft), overlooks a runner on the Mount Everest Extreme Ultra.

477

ANNAPURNA 100

POKHARA TO POON HILL, ANNAPURNA MASSIF, NEPAL

RACE STATISTICS

MONTH: October
DISTANCE: Approx. 100km (62 miles) for 2025
TOTAL ASCENT: Approx. 4,500m (14,764ft)
TIME ALLOWED: 24hr but not strictly enforced

WEBSITE: annapurna100.com

First run back in 1995, the Annapurna trail race has evolved from shorter distances and a multi-stage mountain race to the 100km (62 mile) event it is today. It was created to promote Nepali tourism and highlight the amazing trail running available in Nepal. The race pledges that all funds associated with the event will enter the Nepali economy.

Jan Turner, founder of Annapurna 100 says:

'The Annapurna 100 was Nepal's first Ultra, [it] was inspired by the ideas and efforts of the people that I met there and especially by the incredible spirit of the Nepalese people.'

The Annapurna 100 runs from Pokhara to Poon Hill and back. It follows trails past the Peace Pagoda and on to Bhadaure, Kande, Birethanti, Ghorepani and Poon Hill. This is an adventure run, the trail runs through Nepali villages, but long sections aren't accessible by road; runners need to be fairly self-sufficient, although there are checkpoints to top up your supplies.

GOBI MARCH

KARAKORUM REGION OF CENTRAL MONGOLIA

RACE STATISTICS

MONTH: June
STAGE RACE: Six stages in seven days
DISTANCE: 250km (155 miles)
TOTAL ASCENT: 4,461m (14,635ft)
TIME ALLOWED: approx. 63.5hr, actual stage times vary and are announced at the start of each stage

WEBSITE: www.racingtheplanet.com/gobimarch

This stage race starts in the Khar Bukh Balgas Fortress and races through the stunning Karakorum region of Central Mongolia. It is split into six stages: you'll cross the Mongolian Steppes and run on sand dunes, through huge rocky valleys and on beautiful grassland. You race across the ancient battlefields where Genghis Khan fought, pass through the Orkhon Valley, a UNESCO World Heritage Centre, and finish in the ancient city of Karakorum.

Most of the stages are between 35km (21¾ miles) and 45km (28 miles), but Stage 4 is 80km (49¾ miles) – it's known as the Long March. The last stage is just 10km (6¼ miles), allowing runners to finish in a fairly close group. There are checkpoints every 10km and an overnight checkpoint on the long day. The fastest runners take three to four hours to run 40km (25 miles), but cut-off times allow racers to fast walk.

ABOVE The descent from Ghorapani during the Annapurna 100.

ABOVE Sand dunes on the edge of the Gobi Desert in the Karakorum region, once the capital of the Mongol Empire. Stage 3 of the Gobi March in Mongolia.

FOUR SISTERS ULTRA TOUR ON MOUNT SIGUNIANG

MOUNT SIGUNIANG NATIONAL PARK, SICHUAN PROVINCE, CHINA

RACE STATISTICS

MONTH: October–November
DISTANCE: 100.5km (62½ miles)
TOTAL ASCENT: 4,711m (15,456ft)
TIME ALLOWED: 32hr
WEBSITE: www.foursistersultra.com

Mount Siguniang stands at 6,250m (20,505ft), the highest mountain in the Qionglai region of Western China; it's separate pointy summits are known locally as the Four Sisters. The 100km trail race reaches a lofty 4,537m (14,885ft), so high-elevation race experience is required to run here.

The 100km route is known as the Dream East Wall; it passes through the scenic Shuangqiao Valley, Haizigou and Changping Valley. There are amazing views, including the imposing south and north walls of Yaomei Peak, the highest point of Mount Siguniang. You'll be running on technical trails with narrow paths and a mixture of ice, snow and gravel underfoot. This, combined with the distance and altitude, means that the completion rate is quite low, sometimes below 25 per cent of starters.

There are also 75km, 50km and 35km races over the same weekend – all are challenging and at high altitude.

ABOVE Rou Ding, Ultra Trail Mount Siguniang 75km race.

HONG KONG 100 ULTRA MARATHON

PAK TAM CHUNG–TAI MO SHAN, HONG KONG

RACE STATISTICS

MONTH: January
DISTANCE: 103km (64 miles)
TOTAL ASCENT: 5,300m (17,389ft)
TIME ALLOWED: 30¼ hr
WEBSITE: www.hk100ultra.com

The HK100 course is based around Hong Kong's famous Maclehose Trail. It's a point-to-point trail, starting at Pak Tam Chung, and winds its way along pristine beaches, ancient forest and the UNESCO Global Geopark. For many visitors the highlights are the spectacular views of the contrasts between the city, the forests, mountains and islands and the South China Sea.

The start of the course runs along the coast of the Sai Kung peninsula. The second half of the course has most of the ascent; the trails are steep, technical in places and stepped. Watch out for Golden Hill at about 90km (miles), where the mischievous macaques will snatch your snack if you try to fuel! You finish with a descent from Tai Mo Shan, Hong Kong's highest peak (957m/ft) to the finish line party.

You can run the half (50km/31 miles) or the third (30km/ 18½ miles); both start in the same place as the 100. For the full experience, run all three distances over three consecutive days to complete The Grand Sam.

ABOVE Some of the seemingly endless steps, with Hong Kong lit up in the background.

5247

BORNEO ULTRA-TRAIL MARATHON

KIULU VALLEY NORTH OF KOTA KINABALU, BORNEO

RACE STATISTICS

MONTH: February
DISTANCE: 106km (66 miles)
TOTAL ASCENT: 5,216m (17,113ft)
TIME ALLOWED: 34hr
WEBSITE: **borneoultra.com/butm**

The Borneo Ultra-Trail course runs through dense jungle and cultural landscapes on trails, dirt tracks and back roads. There are sweeping views over the valleys, along the ridgelines and up towards Mount Kinabalu, the highest mountain in Borneo and Malaysia, at 4,095m (13,435ft).

The 106km (66 mile) course is a figure-of-eight around the central start and finish point in Kiulu. The first half (the 55km/34 miles course) has the most hill and is more technical underfoot, but run in daylight and with less fatigue. The second half is an extension of the 32km (20 miles) course. It follows a section of river – which a lot of competitors use as a chance to cool off – and finishes through bamboo and old rubber plantations.

Heat exhaustion is the biggest cause of a DNF at the Borneo Ultra-Trail. The temperature is likely to be around 28°C (82°F), and you'll be exposed to the sun when not under the cover of the jungle. It's recommended that you carry 3 litres (5¼ pints) of water, wear a hat that you can wet and take advantage of the streams and rivers to cool yourself en route.

The 106km category is designed for 'experts', there is a 55km or 32km course for intermediate runners and a 9km (5½ miles) race for juniors and those who would like to try out trail running.

These races require runners to be self-sufficient in terms of food and equipment. There are aid stations approximately every 10km (6¼ miles) where you can fill your water bottles. The 106km course has a drop bag at the halfway point.

LEFT Jungle trails during the Borneo Ultra-Trail Marathon.

RINJANI 100

MOUNT RINJANI NATIONAL PARK, LOMBOK, INDONESIA

RACE STATISTICS

MONTH: May
DISTANCE: 162km (100½ miles)
TOTAL ASCENT: 13,646m (44,770ft)
TIME ALLOWED: 55hr
WEBSITE: **fonesport.id/rinjani100**

Mount Rinjani (3,726m/12,224ft) is the second-highest volcano in Indonesia; it's classed as active, with the most recent eruptions recorded in 2016. To the peak's west lie a caldera and crater lake, evidence of larger eruptions in the past. The whole area is protected as part of the Gunung Rinjani National Park. The higher ground here is largely original forest, while the lower slopes have been extensively cultivated. The national park is home to a wide variety of plants and animals, including the endemic Rinjani scops owl.

The 100-miler starts at sea level on Belanting Beach and climbs up through savannah and volcanic ash into jungle and the mountains; it then runs a figure-of-eight shaped course with an additional out-and-back up the rocky trail to summit Mount Rinjani. You finish at Sembalun at 1,160m (3,806ft).

May is recognized as the best time to visit Lombok; it's normally dry with average temperatures of 21°C to 30°C (70–86°F). It will be much colder on the summits though, with temperatures likely to be around 5°C (41°F) and wind chill making it feel colder.

This event includes the Rinjani 162km (100 miles); the Senaru 60km (37¼ miles) or 100km (62 miles); and the classic 27km (16¾ miles) and 36km (22½ miles) routes. All the distances have impressive ascent-to-distance ratios.

91

AUSTRALASIA

AUSTRALASIA INTRODUCTION

Australia and New Zealand both boast strong ultrarunning communities and a wealth of ultramarathons, including many hundred milers – known simply as 'milers'. Australia has a long tradition in the sport: the Westfield Ultra Marathon was a well-known annual race between Sydney and Melbourne held between 1983 and 1991 and won by legendary Greek runner Yiannis Kouros five times. Kouros also set a new six-day world record in Australia at the Cliff Young six-day race in Colac, Victoria – one of the world's oldest six-day races, first held in 1983 and continuing today as the Australian Six Day Race. The Australian Ultra Runners Association (AURA) compiles a comprehensive list of race results and oversees race organization and records.

Australia in particular has seen rapid growth in ultrarunning events and participants in recent years, with many new events from 50km (31 miles) up to multi-day added to the calendar. Of these, the biggest and best-known is Ultra-Trail Australia by UTMB (see page 256), held in the Blue Mountains National Park in New South Wales and recently appointed the UTMB World Series Major for Oceania. Since it was first held in 2008, UTA has seen some big-name winners, including Pyrenean G.O.A.T. Kilian Jornet and Aussie ultrarunning legend Lucy Bartholomew.

Wilson's Prom (see page 260) is an institution in Aussie ultrarunning, billed as a challenge, not a race, that explores Wilson's Promontory National Park, the southernmost tip of mainland Australia, just 3.5 hours from Melbourne.

New Zealand's first ultramarathon was the Kepler Challenge (see page 272), first held in 1988 and still going strong today. Covering 60km (37 miles) through Fiordland National Park, it is one of the country's most popular races.

The Tarawera Ultra-Trail (see page 264) is held in February of each year, starting from the Bay of Plenty in the town of Rotorua on New Zealand's North Island. The inaugural edition was held in 2009 over a single distance of 85km (53 miles) with just a few hundred athletes taking part. Fifteen years on, the event is now part of the UTMB World Series and offers a range of distances drawing thousands of athletes each year – around 4,500 across the four distances between 23km and 162km (14½–100 miles).

As well as official ultramarathon races, New Zealand's Te Araroa (The Long Pathway) trail is a popular choice for those seeking adventure or a new Fastest Known Time (FKT). The trail stretches 3,000km (1,865 miles) through the length of the country's two main islands from Cape Reinga to Bluff, with an optional kayak between the two if conditions are favourable.

PPREVIOUS PAGE Nicole Paton on her way to 1st place at the 2024 Great Ocean Trail Ultra.

ABOVE Spectacular scenery on the Kepler Challenge, New Zealand.

Walkers generally take three to six months to complete the Te Araroa, but the FKT for runners stands at 31:19:41 for the men's supported record (Kare Sabbe in 2025) and 57:12:16 for the women's (Brooke Thomas in 2021).

Other Australasian highlights include the Great Ocean Trail Ultra (see page 277), which follows the full length of the Great Ocean Walk for 100km (62 miles) from Apollo Bay to the Twelve Apostles Visitor Centre. The Alpine Challenge (see page 278), which takes place in Australia's Victorian Alps, covers 159km (99 miles) including six big climbs, including Victoria's highest mountain Mount Bogong at 1,986m (6,516ft). The Cradle Mountain Run (see page 278) follows Tasmania's famous Cradle Mountain to Lake St Clair Overland track, traversing the alpine terrain of the Cradle Mountain Lake St Clair National Park and World Heritage Area. Lucky runners might spot echidnas, wombats and Tasmanian devils out on the route.

ULTRA-TRAIL AUSTRALIA BY UTMB

KATOOMBA, BLUE MOUNTAINS, AUSTRALIA

Ultra-Trail Australia by UTMB is Australia's biggest and best-known trail running event, held in the Blue Mountains National Park in New South Wales. Each event that takes place during race week is designed to make the most of this spectacular location, from the UTA11 on Thursday – a perfect introduction to the sport of trail running – right up to the UTA Miler, a new distance from 2025 and qualifier for UTMB Mont-Blanc, the 100-mile World Series Final in Chamonix.

UTA races honour the traditional custodians of country, with runners following in the footsteps of the Gundungurra who traversed these lands for thousands of years, immersing runners in indigenous culture from the traditional Welcome to Country on the start line to the incredible sounds of the yidaki out on Ironpot Ridge.

The race has a strong tradition in ultrarunning, and coveted UTA belt buckles based on their finishing times are awarded to runners as they cross the finish line:

Gold Buckle to the winning male and female.

Silver Buckle – Male sub 14 hours, Female sub 16 hours.

Bronze Buckle – Male between 14 and 20 hours, Female between 16 and 22 hours.

All finishers after 20 hours will receive a finisher medal.

RACE STATISTICS

MONTH: May
DISTANCE: 100km (62 miles)
TOTAL ASCENT: 4,300m (14,108ft)
HIGHEST POINT: 1,070m (3,511ft)
STARTERS 2024: 1,523 (293 female, 1,230 male)
FINISHERS 2024: 1,318 (241 female, 1,077 male)
TIME ALLOWED: 28hr
FEMALE COURSE RECORD: Anna McKenna 9:15:23 (2022)
MALE COURSE RECORD: Reece Edwards 8:10:11 (2022)
FIRST RUN: 2008
ENTRY FEE: $540

WEBSITE:
uta.utmb.world

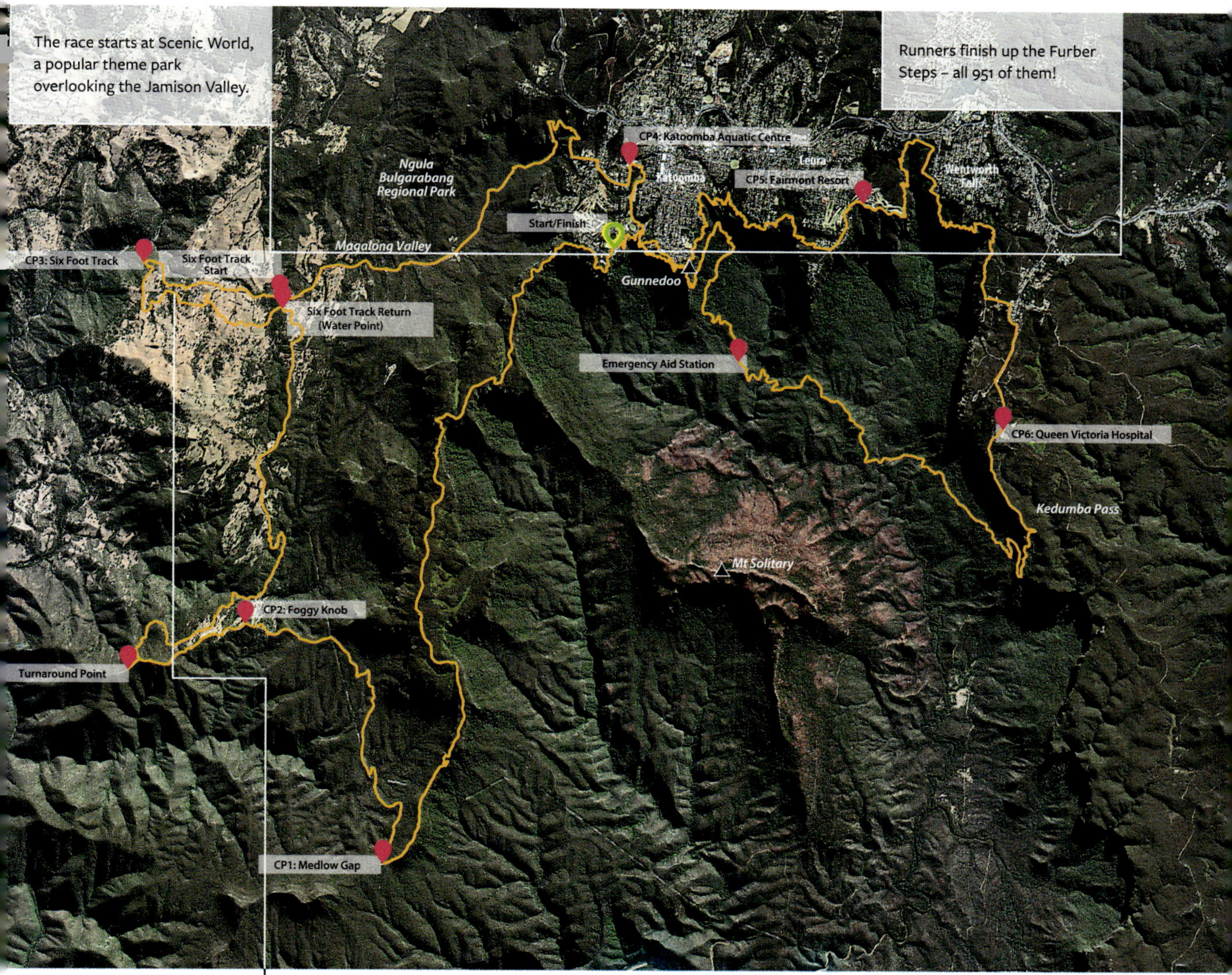

The race starts at Scenic World, a popular theme park overlooking the Jamison Valley.
Runners finish up the Furber Steps – all 951 of them!
CP4: Katoomba Aquatic Centre
Leura
Wentworth Falls
Katoomba
CP5: Fairmont Resort
Ngula Bulgarabang Regional Park
Start/Finish
Magalong Valley
CP3: Six Foot Track
Six Foot Track Start
Gunnedoo
Six Foot Track Return (Water Point)
Emergency Aid Station
CP6: Queen Victoria Hospital
Kedumba Pass
Mt Solitary
CP2: Foggy Knob
Turnaround Point
CP1: Medlow Gap

The Six Foot Track stretches from Katoomba to Jenolan Caves. Originally built as a bridle trail for horses, it's now a popular walking trail.

ELEVATION PROFILE

958M (3,143FT)
1,070M (3,511FT)
208M (682FT)
958M (3,143FT)
0.00km/miles
49.62km (30 miles)
100km (62 miles)

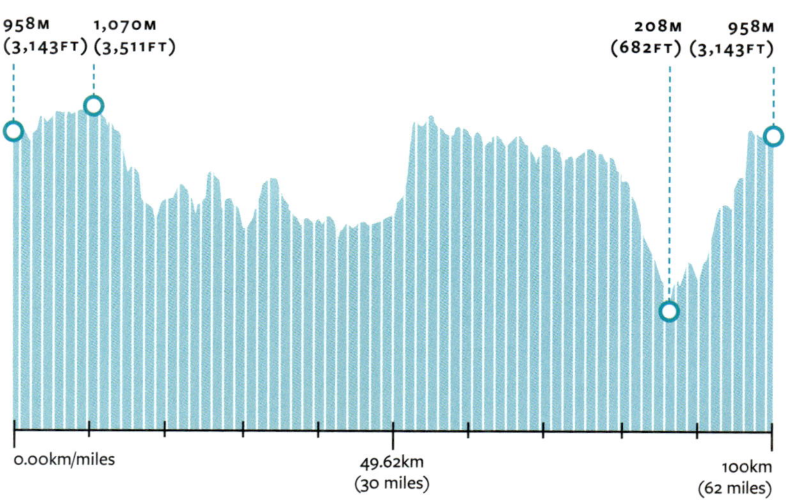

LEFT Well-maintained trails through the Blue Mountains National Park.

ABOVE The stepping stones on the National Pass Trail crossing Wentworth Falls.

As of 2025, Ultra-Trail Australia became the UTMB World Series Major for Oceania, meaning finishers receive double Running Stones, increasing their chances of gaining entry into the UTMB World Series Finals, should they wish to take part. 100-mile category finishers receive eight Stones; 100km category finishers receive six Stones; 50km category finishers receive four Stones and 25km category finishers receive two. UTA100 is also a Western States qualifying race, with finishers securing an entry into the WSER lottery.

Starting from the famous Scenic World in the idyllic town of Katoomba, the 100km (62 miles) route follows singletrack and wide trails through the World Heritage-listed national park of the Blue Mountains. Taking in 4,300m (14,100ft) of climbing, runners traverse rocky cliff-tops linked by narrow footbridges, descend into lush valleys where inviting singletrack winds through dense forest and follow scenic ridges with incredible, far-reaching views. Runners will discover the Golden Stairs walking track, the stunning Leura Forest and the picturesque Wentworth Falls as well as the beautiful landscape features at Narrow Neck, Ironpot Ridge and Kedumba Pass. The race finishes up the famous Furber Steps – all 951 of them – a unique challenge on tired legs fuelled by the camaraderie that the race is famous for.

The new 100-mile route, UTA Miler, visits landmarks including Grose Valley, Grand Canyon, Perrys Lookdown, Blue Gum Forest and Lockleys Pylon – new additions to the UTA adventure through the Blue Mountains National Park.

OTHER DISTANCES

UTA Miler: 164km (102 miles); 6,460m (21,194ft)
UTA50: 49km (30½ miles); 2,200m (7,200ft) ascent
UTA22: 22km (13½ miles); 1,200m (3,900ft) ascent
UTA11: 12km (7½ miles); 750m (2,460ft) ascent

The course also takes runners through some of the classic landmarks of the long-established UTA100, including Narrow Neck, Ironpot Ridge, Leura Forest, Wentworth Falls, Kedumba Pass and the infamous Furber Steps – names that have become trail running legend.

UTA Miler starts in Blackheath, heading through the dramatic Grose Valley and Grand Canyon before climbing to enjoy the views from the top of Lockleys Pylon. A scenic aid station at Hydro Majestic Hotel overlooks the beautiful Megalong Valley, and the way ahead for runners. The route joins with the existing UTA100 course at Narrow Neck Lookout, following a mix of terrain and trails through the Blue Mountains, including lush bushland, dramatic escarpments, soaring ridgelines and, at about 160km (99 miles), the first of the 951 steps that climb to the finish line at Scenic World.

For the future stars of trail and ultrarunning, the 1km-4-Kids race finishes under the UTA arch.

The UTA races have drawn many elite runners to the start line, including Kilian Jornet, who took the 2011 UTA100 title, and Aussie ultrarunning legend Lucy Bartholomew, who won the 2017 edition of UTA100 and finished second in both the 2023 and 2024 editions.

RIGHT The iconic Buttenshaw bridge, spanning the gap between Olympian Rock and Elysian Rock.

WILSON'S PROM

TIDAL RIVER, VICTORIA, AUSTRALIA

Australia's most spectacular coastal ultra explores Wilson's Promontory National Park, the southernmost tip of mainland Australia. Run along beaches and singletrack trails, with sand in your shoes, wind in your hair and (depending on the tide) water up to your waist!

Set entirely within the National Park, just 3.5 hours from Melbourne, Wilson's Prom, organized by Paul Ashton and his Running Wild team, offers 27km (16¾ miles), 47km (29¼ miles), 66km (41 miles) and 103km (64 miles) run loops on the Saturday, followed on the Sunday by the Darby River Half Marathon and 2km (1¼ miles), 5km (3 miles) and 10km (6 miles) fun run, as well as camping on site, making it a great weekend away for all the family.

Starting and finishing in the dark, the self-navigated 100km route predominantly follows singletrack, rocky trails and fire roads, crossing remote sandy beaches, with only approximately 10km on tarmac. Taking in a rough figure-of-eight, exploring the peninsula – and with out-and-back sections to visit the narrow, rugged headlands reaching out into the sea including South Point and South-East Point – it's an adventure that discovers the furthest reaches of the Wilson's Promontory. Throughout the event, runners are treated to spectacular coastal views and remote, often wild and windswept locations. Depending on the tide, some years it is necessary to wade across Growlers Creek at Oberon Beach.

RACE STATISTICS

MONTH: May
DISTANCE: 103.1km (64 miles)
TOTAL ASCENT: 3,498m (11,476ft)
HIGHEST POINT: 318m (1,043ft)
STARTERS 2024: 43 (9 female, 34 male)
FINISHERS 2024: 28 (7 female, 21 male)
TIME ALLOWED: 16hr
FEMALE COURSE RECORD: Nicole Paton 12:08:47 (2017)
MALE COURSE RECORD: Thomas Brazier 10:19:11 (2014)
FIRST RUN: 2001
ENTRY FEE: $120

WEBSITE: www.runningwild.net.au/coastal-runs/wilsons-prom-100.html

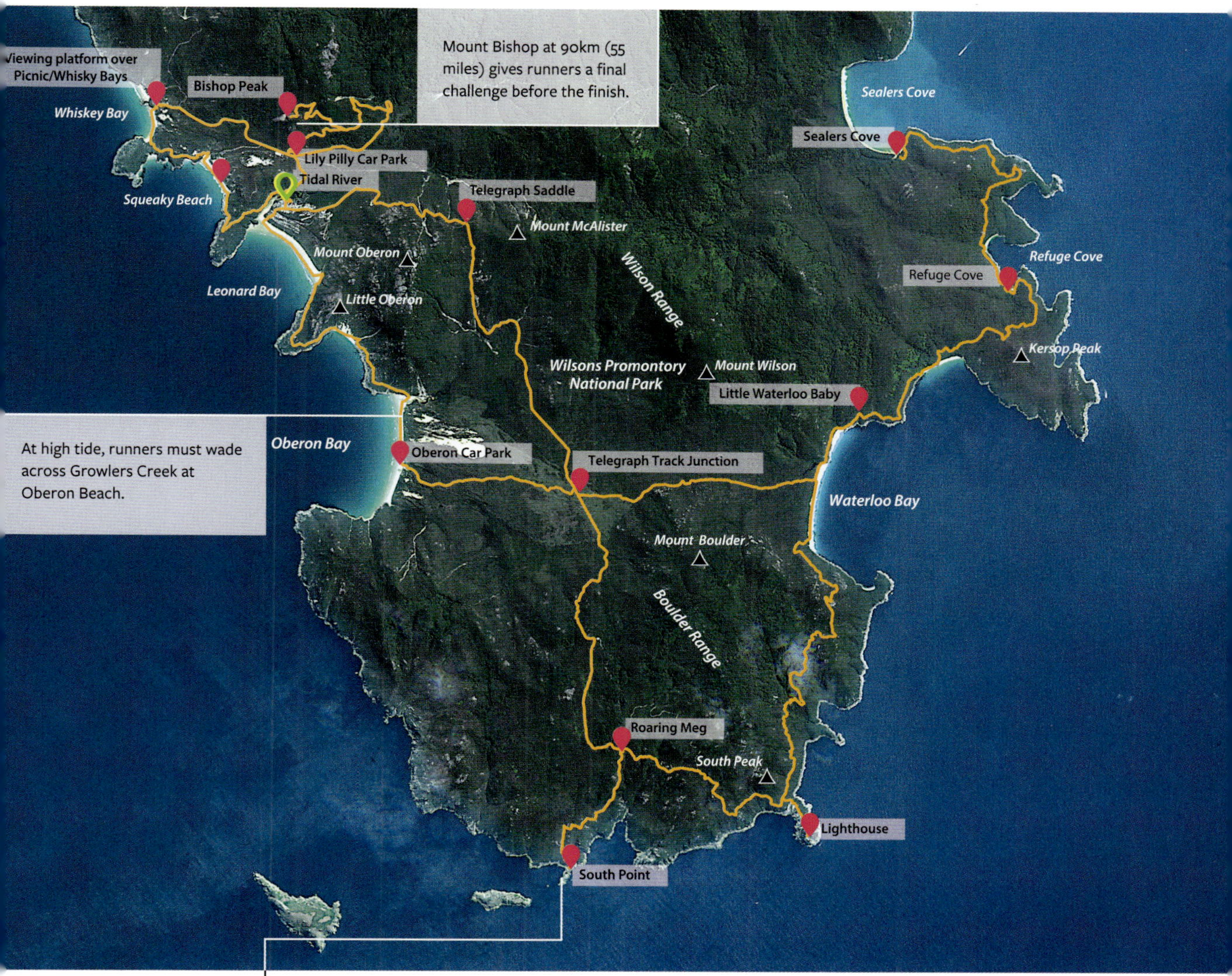

Viewing platform over Picnic/Whisky Bays
Bishop Peak
Whiskey Bay
Lily Pilly Car Park
Tidal River
Squeaky Beach
Telegraph Saddle
Mount McAlister
Mount Oberon
Leonard Bay
Little Oberon
Wilson Range
Sealers Cove
Sealers Cove
Refuge Cove
Refuge Cove
Kersop Peak
Wilsons Promontory National Park
Mount Wilson
Little Waterloo Baby
Oberon Bay
Oberon Car Park
Telegraph Track Junction
Waterloo Bay
Mount Boulder
Boulder Range
Roaring Meg
South Peak
Lighthouse
South Point

Mount Bishop at 90km (55 miles) gives runners a final challenge before the finish.

At high tide, runners must wade across Growlers Creek at Oberon Beach.

Runners take in an out-and-back to South Point – the most southerly point in mainland Australia.

ELEVATION PROFILE

3M (9FT)
0M
318M (1,043FT)
3M (9FT)
0.00km/miles
50.43km (31 miles)
103.1km (64 miles)

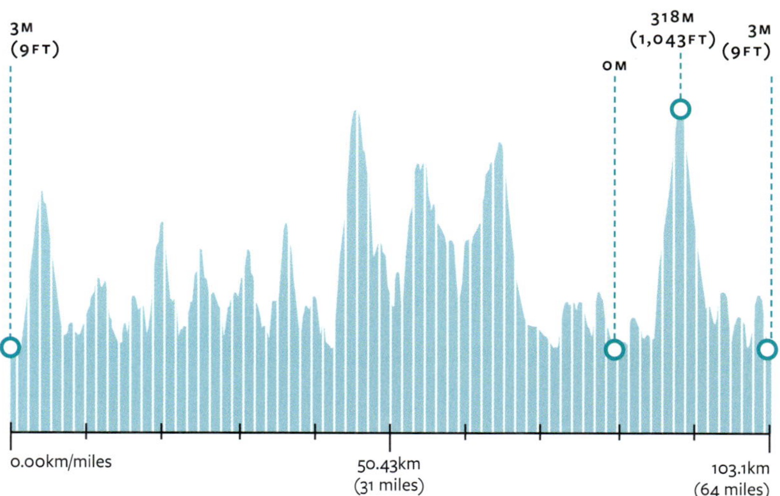

LEFT 60km runners on Squeaky Beach in 2022.

OTHER DISTANCES

66km (41 miles); 2,199m (7,215ft) ascent
47km (29¼ miles); 1,446m (4,744ft) ascent
27km (16¾ miles); 765m (2,510ft) ascent
Darby River Half Marathon 21km (13 miles); 783m (2,569ft) ascent

Runners cross the wonderfully named Squeaky Beach before heading out to Pillar Point, finishing with a beautiful last mile along the river. The climbs aren't long, but it's unrelentingly undulating, with the highest points being a little over 300m (984ft) high and around halfway and – the sting in the tail – is Mount Bishop at 90km (56 miles).

The Prom 100 is a self-supported run, not a race. Runners are fully responsible for their own safety and agree to support each other and offer assistance to other runners should they need it. Checkpoints with medical care are located at the junction of Telegraph Track and Waterloo Bay. Held in the Australian autumn, coastal weather conditions are unpredictable and can change rapidly, so could be cold, wet and windy when hypothermia is a risk for the unprepared.

The Prom 100 has strict entry criteria and should only be attempted by experienced trail runners with good navigation experience. As a minimum, runners attempting the 100km course must have successfully completed at least one 50km organized trail run or an 8+ hour rogaine (orienteering) event in the previous 24 months.

The race draws a strong women's field and, in 2024, winning woman Louise Clifton finished in third place overall, with the first three women all finishing in the top seven overall. In the 47km route that same year, women finished in third and fourth overall.

> 'Incredibly well organized, wonderfully supported by fabulous volunteers, and importantly, true to its word in being physically challenging, but oh so worth it!!! To be able to stand atop some of Victoria's highest coastal peaks, and be able to share these experiences with like-minded people is what draws [us] back to all of your events. The people as well as the wilderness, make your runs the best going around without a doubt.'
>
> JACQUI HANSEN

> 'Wilson's Prom is an amazing run – an incredible way to see gorgeous pristine bush and beaches, and amazingly relaxed, friendly and low-key. The organization and volunteers were terrific, and – as ever – the people I met on the trails were very friendly and generous.'
>
> CRAIG JEFFREY

ABOVE 80km race runners cross the Tidal River footbridge during the 2022 race.

BELOW Leaping across the creek at Squeaky Beach.

TARAWERA ULTRA-TRAIL BY UTMB

ROTORUA, NEW ZEALAND

Tarawera Ultra-Trail by UTMB is held in February of each year, based in the town of Rotorua on New Zealand's North Island. The inaugural edition was held in 2009, founded by Paul Charteris, when the race was a single distance ultramarathon, with just a few hundred athletes taking on 85km (53 miles) of spectacular trails throughout the Bay of Plenty.

Today, the event offers a variety of races and draws thousands of athletes each year – around 4,500 across the four distances of 23km (14¼ miles), 52km (32¼ miles), 103km (64 miles) and 162km (100 miles) – from around the world to this celebration of trail running.

In its 15th year, the event has rebranded to Tarawera Ultra-Trail by UTMB while continuing to honour its deep roots and connections with the local land and community. The new brand and identity were created in consultation with many stakeholders, including local iwi (Māori) groups.

'Our tohu, or our logo, represents Tarawera,' Mitch Murcott, Tarawera Ultra-Trail Race Director, states on the race website. 'A tara is a ray, or the sharp tip of a pounamu spear. Wera is warmth, a release of heat like the eruption of a volcano or the steam rising from the earth. Together, Tarawera represents the release of heat, the reciprocal sharing of warmth of our community and our event together to achieve something extraordinary.

RACE STATISTICS

MONTH: February
DISTANCE: 162km (100 miles)
TOTAL ASCENT: 3,700m (12,139ft)
HIGHEST POINT: 710m (2,329ft)
STARTERS 2024: 450 (134 female, 316 male)
FINISHERS 2024: 330 (91 female, 239 male)
TIME ALLOWED: 36hr
FEMALE COURSE RECORD: Lucy Bartholomew 17:13:27 (2023)

MALE COURSE RECORD: Zach Miller 14:41:41 (2023)
FIRST RUN: 2009
ENTRY FEE: NZ$965

WEBSITE: **tarawera.utmb.world**

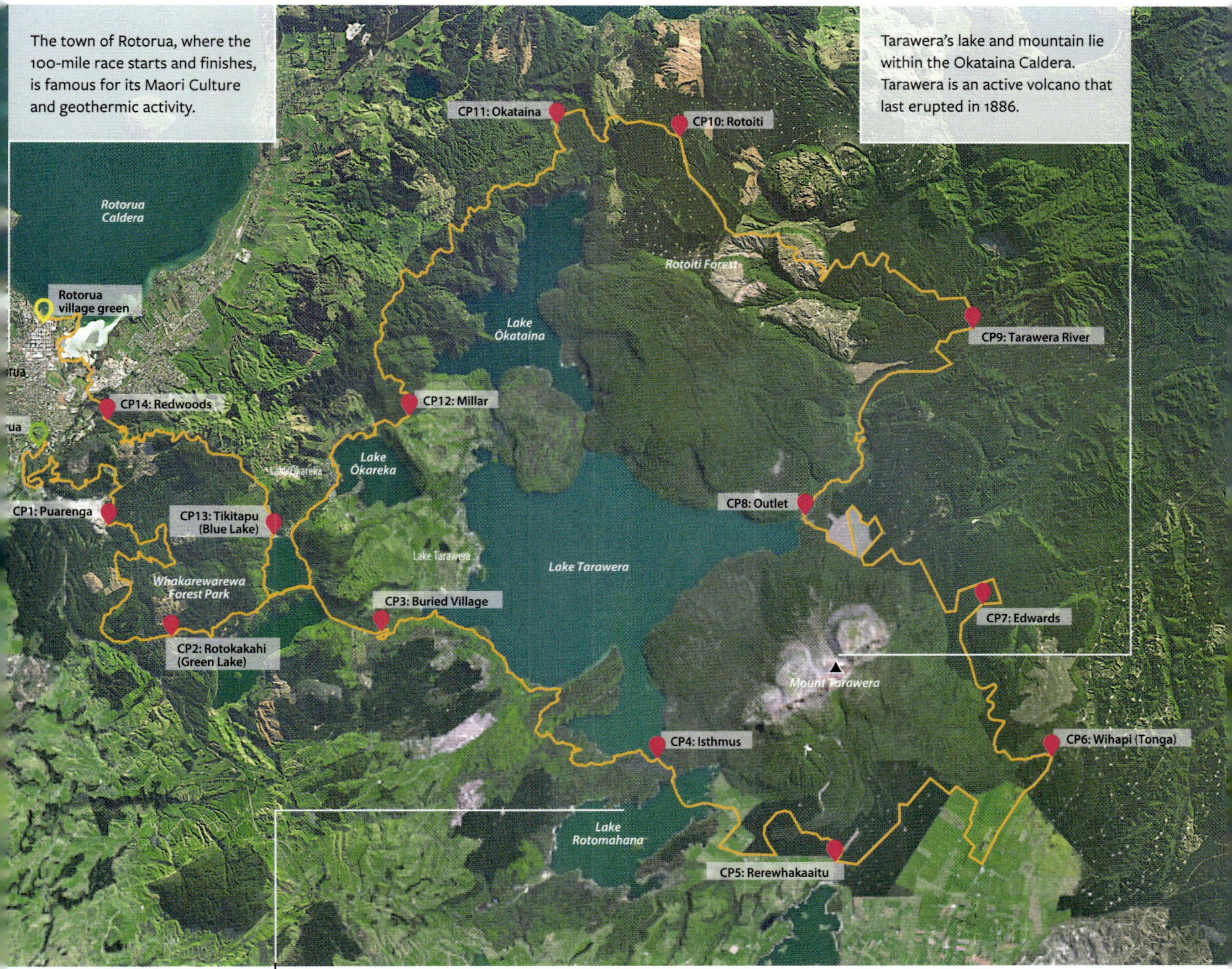

The town of Rotorua, where the 100-mile race starts and finishes, is famous for its Maori Culture and geothermic activity.

Tarawera's lake and mountain lie within the Okataina Caldera. Tarawera is an active volcano that last erupted in 1886.

Rotorua Caldera
Rotorua village green
CP11: Okataina
CP10: Rotoiti
Rotoiti Forest
CP9: Tarawera River
Lake Ōkataina
CP14: Redwoods
CP12: Millar
Lake Ōkareka
Lake Okareka
CP1: Puarenga
CP13: Tikitapu (Blue Lake)
CP8: Outlet
Lake Tarawera
Whakarewarewa Forest Park
CP3: Buried Village
CP7: Edwards
CP2: Rotokakahi (Green Lake)
Mount Tarawera
CP4: Isthmus
CP6: Wihapi (Tonga)
Lake Rotomahana
CP5: Rerewhakaaitu

Runners must cross Lake Rotomahana by boat.

ELEVATION PROFILE

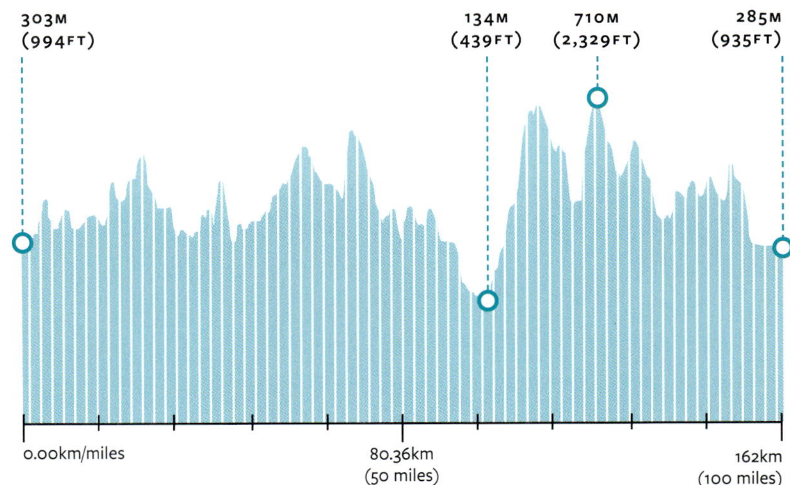

LEFT Runners line up at the start of the Tarawera Ultra-Trail.

While the event has grown, Tarawera was and still is all about the land, people, and connections. The warm energy of the land connects the community, bringing people in from all walks of life to experience trails full of Manaaki.'

Between 2009 and 2017 the course was 102km (63 miles) and ran from Rotorua to Kawerau, with records being set in 2017 by US ultrarunning royalty Camille Herron (8:56:00) and Jim Walmsley (7:23:32). The course changed direction in 2018, starting in Kawerau and finishing in Rotorua, and a 100-mile event – the TMiler – was added, becoming Tarawera's flagship race.

Other notable names with wins at the T102 race include Sage Canaday (2013 & 2014), Courtney Dauwalter (2019) and Tom Evans (2020). The 2024 race saw New Zealanders Ruth Croft and Dan Jones take the women's and men's T102 wins. New Zealand-based Japanese runner Konoka Azumi took the women's 100-mile win in 2024.

Each of the spectacular routes take in the most stunning scenery, including lakes, waterfalls, and lush native New Zealand forests. The feel is local and friendly and, despite being a 'by UTMB' race, meaning competitors can gain stones for entry into the World Series Finals at UTMB Mont-Blanc, the expo is nicely low-key. Courses are all point-to-point, on mostly non-technical runnable terrain, designed with the aim of seeing everyone succeed. The friendly aid stations, incredible volunteers and event crew cater to the runners' every needs.

The courses take runners on scenic and runnable trails through lush native bush and the towering Whakarewarewa Forest. Along the way they'll pass multiple lakes, waterfalls and evidence of geothermal activity, finishing at the Village Green by the lakeside in the heart of Rotorua.

The TMiler, the flagship 100-mile race, is a big loop around Lake Tarawera, starting at Te Puia in Rotorua and exploring the fascinating geothermal surroundings of the region. Runners cross eight different lakes – including crossing Lake Rotomahana by boat – and follow flowing singletrack trails that weave through dense forests with towering redwoods. The route takes runners past the waterfall on the Tarawera Falls track, through the archaeological site of Buried Village, alongside the trail at steamy Sulphur Point and around Mount Tarawera. It passes beneath the mighty maunga (the Māori word for a 'mountain', 'peak', or 'mount') of Tarawera, Ruawahia and Wahanga, before returning to Rotorua at the Lakefront Reserve. The majority of the climbing comes in the second half of the race, with the highest point at 710m (2,329ft), coming at around 120km (74½ miles). The TMiler has to be one of the most scenic 100-mile runs in the world.

The 103km (64 miles) event starts at Firmin Field in Kawerau – an hour east of Rotorua. From there runners must tackle 3,089m (10,134ft) of elevation gain, first heading southwards before joining the TMiler route to the northeast of Mount Tarawera, which they will then follow to the finish in Rotorua.

The T50 takes runners on a shorter loop around Rotorua, leaving Te Puia and heading southwards to Lake Rotokakahi and Lake Tikitapu before returning to the finish in Rotorua. It has a total elevation of 1,572m (5,157ft).

PREVIOUS PAGES Geysers at the Whakarewarewa thermal valley.

ABOVE Lush native forest trails.

BELOW Amanda Basham went on to finish within the top 10 at the 2023 TUM102.

Finally, the point-to-point T21 is a fast-and furious (for the race leaders, at least) 23km (14¼ miles) race with 734m (2,408ft) of elevation. Starting with a loop around Lake Tikitapu, runners will then race to the finish in Rotorua.

For those not running, or for runners wisely choosing to spend some time in the area before and/or after the race, Rotorua is a fantastic outdoor and adventure destination in its own right. Immerse yourself in hot springs and natural spas; experience the thrill of the area's great mountain biking trails; hit the trails for hiking and trail running; or go whitewater rafting on the mighty Kaituna River, including riding over Tutea Falls, the world's highest commercially rafted waterfall at 7m (23ft), crater walks and the opportunity to discover the local Maori culture.

ABOVE Sections of rough tracks wind through the forest, with big views of the lakes opening up between the trees.

RIGHT Tarawera Road, following the shore of Blue Lake.

OTHER DISTANCES
T102: 103km (64 miles); 2,200m (7,218ft) ascent
T50: 52km (32¼ miles); 1,150m (3,773ft) ascent
T21: 23km (14¼ miles); 400m (1,312ft) ascent

KEPLER CHALLENGE

FIORDLAND NATIONAL PARK, NEW ZEALAND

Fiordland National Park lies in the southwest of New Zealand's South Island. It's known for the glacier-carved fiords of Doubtful and Milford sounds, extensive beech forests, Mirror Lakes, and the Earl Mountains with stunning views of towering Mitre Peak. The Kepler Track was completed in 1988 to celebrate the centenary of National Parks in New Zealand. To mark its completion, three Fiordland College teachers decided to organize a one-off event and in December of that year, 149 people completed the first Kepler Challenge.

In the years since, with the support of the Department of Conservation and the local community, the Kepler Challenge has become New Zealand's premier mountain run.

With a limited field of fewer than 500 runners, the event balances competition with a supportive community feel. Elite runners will complete the 60km (37 miles) course in under five hours, but most will take much longer. Starting at the Control Gates, runners follow the Kepler Track, exploring spectacular scenery, traversing stunning ridgelines with glorious alpine views and winding through beech forested valleys before finishing along the banks of a fast-flowing river.

The Kepler Challenge and Luxmore Grunt – a 27km (16¾ miles) run up to Luxmore Hut and back – take place annually on the first Saturday in December.

RACE STATISTICS

MONTH: December

DISTANCE: 60km (37 miles)

TOTAL ASCENT: 2,200m (7,218ft)

HIGHEST POINT: 1,400m (4,593ft)

STARTERS 2024: 481 (162 female, 319 male)

FINISHERS 2024: 445 (150 female, 295 male)

TIME ALLOWED: 12hr

FEMALE COURSE RECORD: Nancy Jiang 4:59:46 (2020)

MALE COURSE RECORD: Martin Dent 4:33:37 (2013)

FIRST RUN: 1988

ENTRY FEE: NZ$375

WEBSITE: **www.keplerchallenge.co.nz**

Hanging Valley Shelter

Forest Burn Shelter

Mount Luxmore

Luxmore Hut

Luxmore Hut, on the way to the race high point at 1,400m (4,593ft), is a checkpoint, and the turnaround point on the 27km (16 mile) Luxmore Grunt.

Lake Te Anau

Iris Burn Hut

Brod Bay

Te Anau

Jackson Peaks

Te Anau

Rocky Point

Runners traverse the shores of Lake Manapouri, New Zealand's 2nd-deepest lake after Lake Hauroko, which also lies in the Fiordland National Park.

Moturau Hut

Shallow Bay

Rainbow Reach

Lake Manapouri

The race start and finish in the town of Te Anau is known as the gateway to the Fiordland National Park. The local community is an integral part of this race.

ELEVATION PROFILE

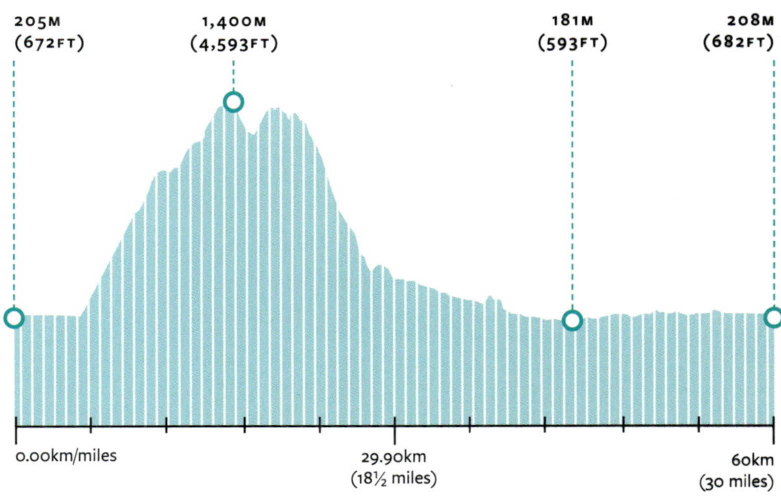

LEFT Running through the beech forest between Rainbow Reach and the control gates, near the end of the race.

Those wishing to take part must pre-register and then enter online at 6.30am (NZ time) on the first Saturday in July.

The Kepler Challenge remains a community-run event with everyone in Te Anau getting involved, creating a warm welcome for the runners and their supporters. Many runners return every year, with some earning 5-, 10- and even 20-year medals.

Dwight Grieve is a successful ultrarunner who comes from Fiordland. Here's his story of this special race:

'From a runner's perspective the Kepler Challenge is the original benchmark trail race in NZ, the very first real trail ultra in the country. When trail runners meet up around the country, they rate each other on their "Kepler time", it has endured at the top of the trail running "to do" list for runners of all abilities. It is so popular the race entries sell out in around three minutes. Getting in is a race inside a race.

'There are a few reasons for this, the Kepler Challenge caters to people of all ability, it is an amazing life achievement to make it over the mountains and complete the race, while also attracting the very top NZ athletes to earn the kudos of being the best in the country by winning the race. Over the history of the race the winners trophies are covered in the names of NZ's top trail runners; to have your name on there is to be at the pinnacle of the sport in NZ.

'What really sets the Kepler Challenge apart though is the race atmosphere; the race is held in the small tourist town of Te Anau and the whole community embraces the race, the whole town comes alive with runners and supporters, everyone all together for the whole weekend. It creates an atmosphere that has continued over the history of the event; it is not a race but a positive life experience. The race is not organized by a commercial operator and is still totally 100 per cent organized by the local community and any profits go back into the community.

'The experience is very much enhanced by the racecourse itself; it also caters for runners of all abilities. Being in the Fiordland National Park the pristine mountains and forests are protected and it is a privilege to experience the breathtaking world renown[ed] scenery. The trail itself is well maintained and easy to follow for the inexperienced, who also have the peace of mind of very well organized safety organization, and the famous Aid Stations who have their own competition each year to be the runners' "favourite"; don't be surprised to see everything from Santa to Where's Wally to even a whole supermarket Isle on the track.

'For the competitive runners the track creates interesting tactical racing; the main climb/descent is in the first half of the race with the back half containing constant undulation. It provides the opportunity for the lovers of mountains, and the fast flat to do well, all while trying to avoid the famous "Kepler Shuffle" as it is known in running circles; this is the name given when you blow up around the 50km [31 miles] mark and your running form goes.

OTHER DISTANCES

Luxmore Grunt: 27km (16¾ miles); 990m (3,248ft) ascent

ABOVE Descending the 'staircase' from Hanging Valley shelter to the bushline above the Iris Burn valley.

'I still remember my first Kepler Challenge, I was simply achieving life's challenges at that stage; I remember shedding a tear as I reached the finish line and was so proud to have made it, a true life experience. When a job opportunity came up after joining in the Kepler experience, I applied and got the job, a large reason for this was my family wanted to be part of the amazing local community that make up the Kepler Challenge. I can honestly say achieving the Kepler Challenge in my early days gave me the confidence to further myself personally, and as time has gone on also to further myself in my running; this has led me to being selected to represent NZ twice in mountain/trail running; looking back now the Kepler Challenge was an important step on that journey.'

OTHER AUSTRALASIA HIGHLIGHTS

THE BLACKALL 100

MAPLETON, SUNSHINE COAST, AUSTRALIA

RACE STATISTICS

MONTH: October
DISTANCE: 101.3km (63 miles)
TOTAL ASCENT: 3,407m (11,178ft)
TIME ALLOWED: 24hr

WEBSITE: www.runqld.com.au/blackall-100

The Blackall 100 follows sections of the Sunshine Coast Hinterland Great Walk and runs three different loops across the Blackall Range. Starting and finishing at the Queensland Conference and Camping Centres (QCCC) in Mapleton, you'll be running through ferny forests and areas of subtropical rainforest, past magnificent eucalyptus trees and waterfalls and through quiet local hamlets with stunning views of the Sunshine Coast.

There are six aid stations and four additional water stations en route; runners without crew can access a drop bag at several of the aid stations.

The race started in 2014 with course records set in 2017 by Charlie Boyle (9:08:06) and 2021 by Reesha Lewis (10:41:26). The majority of runners finish in around 17 hours. It's tradition that everyone who finishes rings the iconic Blackall Bell.

There is also a looped 50km race and a point-to-point 21km race on the same weekend.

BUFFALO STAMPEDE 100K

BRIGHT, VICTORIA, AUSTRALIA

RACE STATISTICS

MONTH: March
DISTANCE: 101.6km (63 miles)
TOTAL ASCENT: 5,131m (16,834ft)
TIME ALLOWED: 28hr

WEBSITE: www.buffalostampede.au

The Buffalo Stampede 100km (62 miles) follows an epic course from Bright, Australia's home of trail running, to the Horn, the highest point of the National Park, and back.

The first section of the trail runs on dirt roads and MTB singletrack, climbing over 1,000m (3,280ft) in the space of 10km (6¼ miles). You descend the long Snake Ridge and run a flatter section to reach Mount Buffalo National Park. Another big climb delivers you onto the Mount Buffalo Plateau, where remote trails pass plants endemic to the area. Summit the Horn at 1,723m (5,653ft), offering amazing panoramic views of the Australian Alps. Heading back to Bright there's one more big test, the Dingo Ridge Climb with a 757m (2,484ft) ascent over 6.3km (4 miles); it's a tough sting in the tail.

If you don't fancy racing solo, you can run the 100km as part of a team or race the 42km Sky Marathon, 20km Sky Run, 10km Sky Sprint or one of the family trail runs. Fancy a massive challenge? Take on the Ultra Grand Slam, running 10km on Friday, 100km on Saturday and 42km on Sunday.

RIGHT Sunrise for a solo runner on the 100km Surf Coast Century.

FAR RIGHT Stunning coastal trails on the Great Ocean Trail Ultra.

THE SURF COAST CENTURY

GREAT OCEAN ROAD REGION OF VICTORIA, AUSTRALIA

RACE STATISTICS

MONTH: September
DISTANCE: 99.3km (62 miles)
TOTAL ASCENT: 1,811m (5,942ft)
TIME ALLOWED: 19hr

WEBSITE: surfcoastcentury.rapidascent.com.au

The Surf Coast Century is a fast and easily runnable course, brilliant for a PB or a good choice as a first step into longer distances. It's fully waymarked, and well-supported with nine checkpoints. The crew do everything they can to live up its the slogan, the 'feel good ultra'!

You'll be running on a mixture of gravel trails and hard sandy beach, and occasionally along the intertidal zone with some technical terrain over reefs and rocks. You are very likely to get wet feet, and depending on the tide you may have to wade through deeper water. Some sections further on follow more technical singletrack trails through the bush with extended wildflower meadows. It's undulating rather than hilly, with the biggest hill coming at about 65km (40½ miles). The final section follows the sand back to the finish.

You can run the 100km solo or as a team of two, three or four runners – or try the 50km course which runs the first half of the 100km route.

GREAT OCEAN TRAIL ULTRA

APOLLO BAY, VICTORIA, AUSTRALIA

RACE STATISTICS

MONTH: October
DISTANCE: 100km (62 miles)
TOTAL ASCENT: 2,800m (9,186ft)
TIME ALLOWED: 20hr

WEBSITE: www.greatoceanultra.com

The Great Ocean Trail Ultra follows the full length of the Great Ocean Walk track from Apollo Bay to the Twelve Apostles Visitor Centre. You'll be running on a well-made trail through dense rainforest and along the beach; it stays close to the coast but does deviate inland in a couple of sections. The trail is undulating with a couple of bigger climbs, topping out at about 239m (784ft) at 14.5km (9 miles) and 285m (935ft) at 59km (36¾ miles).

The trail is quite fast, so there have been some good times since it started in 2009 (it was formerly known as the GOW100). Blake Hose set the men's record of 9:08:28 in 2014 and Gill Fowler holds the female record of 10:30:45, set in 2014 as well. Blake Hose also holds the team record, running 8:16:00 with David Byrne.

The trail is well signed, and the race organizers add some directions at confusing points, but it's officially a self-navigation race. There are five aid stations en route to refill your water. You can choose to run the 100km as a team of two or the 45km second half of the course solo.

ALPINE CHALLENGE

VICTORIAN ALPS, AUSTRALIA

RACE STATISTICS

MONTH: April
DISTANCE: 159km (99 miles)
TOTAL ASCENT: 7,600m (24,934ft)
TIME ALLOWED: 42hr

WEBSITE: runningwild.net.au/alpine-runs/alpine-challenge.html

The Alpine Challenge claims to be 'the toughest, most challenging, most spectacular and rewarding all mountain trail run in Australia'. The route packs a lot of ascent over six big climbs, including Victoria's highest mountain, Mount Bogong at 1,986m (6,516ft). The course is minimally marked so you need to navigate, but route finding is easy and the most important junctions are marked.

Bridie Temple, who finished first in the 100km female category, said: 'The course really took us through some of the most mind-blowing beautiful country in the southern hemisphere with just about every alpine biome and bush pocket; it just lights you up to run through.'

To add to the challenge, the alpine weather is unpredictable; expect sudden changes and anything from hot sunny days to rain, fog, high winds, sleet and snow. To combat this, the kit list helps you be prepared and includes mandatory cold or hot weather extras.

There are also 100km, 60km and 42km distances run in the same self-nav style, and 25km, 16km and 10km waymarked courses looping similar terrain.

CRADLE MOUNTAIN RUN

CRADLE MOUNTAIN–LAKE ST CLAIR NATIONAL PARK, TASMANIA

RACE STATISTICS

MONTH: February
DISTANCE: 78km (48½ miles)
TOTAL ASCENT: 2,195m (7,201ft)
TIME ALLOWED: 15hr

WEBSITE: www.cradlemtnrun.asn.au

The Cradle Mountain Run follows Tasmania's famous Cradle Mountain–Lake St Clair Overland Track. It traverses the alpine terrain of the Cradle Mountain–Lake St Clair National Park within the World Heritage-listed Tasmanian Wilderness Area. The park is made up of protected rainforest, heathland, alpine peaks and mountain lakes. The race climbs through the forest and spends much of the time above the treeline at over 1,000m (3,280ft). Look out for echidnas, wombats and Tasmanian devils on course.

Access is controlled in this environmentally sensitive area – only 60 runners are allowed to compete. If you want to train here, the area operates on a permit system to control user numbers.

LEFT Heading for Warby Corner at the end of Stage 1, enduring bad weather in the 2023 Alpine Challenge 100-miler.

RIGHT Runners on the Cradle Mountain Run approach Marion's Lookout early in the race, just before it gets steep. Crater Lake is in the background.

HUNUA HILLBILLY

HUNUA RANGES, AUCKLAND, NEW ZEALAND

RACE STATISTICS

MONTH: March
DISTANCE: 60km (37¼ miles)
TOTAL ASCENT: 3,000m (9,843ft)
TIME ALLOWED: 15hr

WEBSITE: www.hunuahillbilly.co.nz

The 60km (37¼ miles) course takes in all the best accessible trails in the Hunua Ranges. It's a big loop of the area, starting and finishing at the event base in the upper Mangatawhiri campground. Most of the trails are on 'grunty singletrack under the cover of stunning native bush', but you'll also run sections of gravel track, boardwalk, MTB trail and the odd dam. The sections that emerge from the bush offer some of the most amazing views in Auckland; the 688m (2,257ft) summit of Kohukohunui or K Trig is a highlight and viewpoint.

Dave Franks, event manager, says, '"Unapologetically Tough" is our "tag line" for the ultra – but as tough as the course is we certainly try and make the rest of the event weekend a really fun, festive feel.'

If you prefer, there is a marathon course or a 22km (13¾ miles) trail run/walk; the shorter routes run on similar terrain and start later on the same day.

OLD GHOST ULTRA

LYELL RANGE, SOUTH ISLAND, NEW ZEALAND

RACE STATISTICS

MONTH: February
DISTANCE: 85km (52¾ miles)
TOTAL ASCENT: 2,700m (8,858ft)
TIME ALLOWED: 13hr (to reach 67km/41½ miles)

WEBSITE: www.oldghostultra.com

This race follows the Old Ghost Road on a point-to-point adventure from Seddonville to Lyell. It's a long-forgotten gold miners' route, built in the 1870s and rediscovered in the 2000s. The first 30km (18½ miles) is fairly flat, which means the second half of the course is tough. There are two big climbs and despite starting and finishing at close to sea level the course spends around 15km (9¼ miles) over 1,000m (3,280ft), topping out at 1,340m (4,396ft) near 'Heaven's Door' in the mighty Lyell Range.

An added incentive to train well and work hard is the cut-off and drop-out procedure; after the first-aid station, the trail is very hard to access, so a helicopter is used. If you need to retire for non-life-threatening circumstances, including failure to meet the cut-off times, a maximum fee of $300 will be payable.

'What started as a humble fundraiser and opportunity to share some amazing backcountry through which we were privileged to build an 85km-long [52¾ miles] trail, is now an annual excuse to bring our local community together to host amazing people from all around the world, help them achieve new mental and physical limits, and make a whole lot of wonderful connections and memories in the process.' Phil Rossiter, Race Director

LEFT Celebrating at the finish gate at Hunua Hillbilly.

RIGHT Ben Kepes and Stu Cottam (both of New Zealand) running at 'Dam Wall' – a raised bund that separates Lake Grim and Lake Cheerful at 39.5km into the Old Ghost Ultra.

ULTRAMARATHON WORLD SERIES EVENTS CALENDAR

JANUARY

- **WINTER SPINE RACE** (see page 68)
- **ARC OF ATTRITION BY UTMB** (see page 104)
- **ARROWHEAD ULTRA 135** (see page 155)
- **BRAZIL 135 ULTRA** (see page 182)
- **HONG KONG 100 ULTRA MARATHON** (see page 249)

FEBRUARY

- **TRANSGRANCANARIA** (see page 58)
- **BLACK CANYON ULTRAS** (see page 126)
- **YUKON ARCTIC ULTRA** (see page 160)
- **LA MISIÓN** (see page 176)
- **ULTRA FIORD** (see page 181)
- **ULTRA X TANZANIA** (see page 210)
- **BORNEO ULTRA-TRAIL MARATHON** (see page 251)
- **TARAWERA ULTRA-TRAIL BY UTMB** (see page 264)
- **CRADLE MOUNTAIN RUN** (see page 278)
- **OLD GHOST ULTRA** (see page 280)

MARCH

- **LAPLAND ARCTIC ULTRA** (see page 92)
- **THE BARKLEY MARATHONS** (see page 138)
- **ATACAMA CROSSING** (see page 170)
- **ULTRA MARATHON CABALLO BLANCO** (see page 180)
- **ADDO ELEPHANT TRAIL RUN** (see page 213)
- **MUSTANG TRAIL RACE** (see page 228)
- **BUFFALO STAMPEDE 100K** (see page 276)
- **HUNUA HILLBILLY** (see page 280)

APRIL

- **MADEIRA ISLAND ULTRA-TRAIL** (see page 52)
- **ISTRIA 100 BY UTMB** (see page 101)
- **CANYONS ENDURANCE RUNS BY UTMB** (see page 152)
- **PATAGONIA RUN** (see page 182)
- **MARATHON DES SABLES** (see page 188)
- **ULTRA-TRAIL MOUNT YUN BY UTMB** (see page 234)
- **MOUNT FUJI 100** (see page 242)
- **ALPINE CHALLENGE** (see page 278)

MAY

- **ULTRA-TRAIL SNOWDONIA BY UTMB** (see page 82)
- **TRANSVULCANIA** (see page 103)
- **TRANSYLVANIA 100** (see page 103)
- **TIGER CLAW 50** (see page 155)
- **COCODONA 250** (see page 159)
- **THE JUNGLE ULTRA** (see page 166)
- **TRANS ATLAS MARATHON** (see page 208)
- **MOUNT EVEREST EXTREME ULTRA** (see page 246)
- **RINJANI 100** (see page 251)
- **ULTRA-TRAIL AUSTRALIA BY UTMB** (see page 256)
- **WILSON'S PROM** (see page 260)

JUNE

- **SWISS CANYON TRAIL** (see page 30)
- **LAVAREDO ULTRA TRAIL BY UTMB** (see page 34)
- **ZUGSPITZ ULTRATRAIL** (see page 44)
- **WEST HIGHLAND WAY RACE** (see page 88)
- **OH MEU DEUS ULTRA TRAIL** (see page 98)
- **MOZART 100 BY UTMB** (see page 103)
- **SOUTH DOWNS WAY 100** (see page 105)
- **WESTERN STATES ENDURANCE RUN** (see page 112)
- **CHICAMOCHA CANYON RACE** (see page 182)
- **COMRADES MARATHON** (see page 198)
- **GOBI MARCH** (see page 248)

JULY

- **LAKELAND 100** (see page 76)
- **BADWATER 135** (see page 118)
- **HARDROCK 100** (see page 134)
- **QUEBEC MEGA TRAIL** (see page 146)
- **VERMONT 100 ENDURANCE RACE** (see page 152)
- **GRAND MESA ULTRAS** (see page 154)
- **TAHOE RIM TRAIL** (see page 157)

AUGUST

- **UTMB MONT-BLANC** (see page 20)
- **GRAND RAID DES PYRENEES** (see page 100)
- **L'ÉCHAPPÉE BELLE** (see page 100)
- **SWISS PEAKS** (see page 98)
- **FIRE AND ICE ULTRA** (see page 106)
- **LEADVILLE TRAIL 100** (see page 130)
- **SELF-TRANSCENDENCE 3100** (see page 156)
- **SQUAMISH 50** (see page 110)
- **MONGOLIA SUNRISE TO SUNSET** (see page 224)

SEPTEMBER

- **TOR DES GÉANTS** (see page 38)
- **TRANSALPINE RUN** (see page 26)
- **SPARTATHLON** (see page 48)
- **ULTRA TOUR MONTE ROSA** (see page 101)
- **DRAGON'S BACK RACE** (see page 105)
- **THE KERRY WAY ULTRA** (see page 104)
- **ÖTILLÖ, THE SWIMRUN WORLD CHAMPIONSHIP** (see page 106)
- **GRAND TO GRAND ULTRA** (see page 154)
- **WASATCH FRONT 100 MILE ENDURANCE RUN** (see page 157)
- **SALT PANS ULTRA** (see page 194)
- **RUNYANGA ULTRA-TRAIL** (see page 211)
- **ULTRA X JORDAN** (see page 218)
- **THE SURF COAST CENTURY** (see page 277)

OCTOBER

- **ULTRA PIRINEU** (see page 64)
- **JAVELINA JUNDRED** (see page 122)
- **BIG DOG'S BACKYARD ULTRA** (see page 159)
- **GRAND RAID DE LA RÉUNION: LA DIAGONALE DES FOUS** (see page 202)
- **SOLANG SKYULTRA** (see page 246)
- **ANNAPURNA 100** (see page 248)
- **FOUR SISTERS ULTRA TOUR ON MOUNT SIGUNIANG** (see page 249)
- **THE BLACKALL 100** (see page 276)
- **GREAT OCEAN TRAIL ULTRA** (see page 277)

NOVEMBER

- **JFK 50 MILE** (see page 156)
- **LA TRANSTICA** (see page 181)
- **ULTRA MARATHON** (see page 210)
- **THE DESERT ULTRA** (see page 211)
- **RMB ULTRA-TRAIL CAPE TOWN** (see page 213)

DECEMBER

- **BOA VISTA ULTRA-TRAIL** (see page 208)
- **TRANS-INT 160 BY UTMB** (see page 238)
- **KEPLER CHALLENGE** (see page 272)

INDEX

PICTURE CREDITS

Octopus Publishing would like to thank all the photographers, agencies, race organisers and sponsors who have so kindly provided images for use in this book.

1 Montane, photo Jonas Palsson; 2-3 Ahansal Events, photo Christophe Angot; 4 David Miller; 7 courtesy Susie Chan; 9 Québec Mega Trail, photo Daniel Thibault; 10a Ultra Trail Cape Town, photo Zac Zinn; 10b ©Kailas Fuga; 13 Single Track Events, photo Sam Millington; 16 PLAN B, photo Andi Frank; 19 The North Face/Arista Eventos, photo Jose Miguel Munoze; 20 David Miller; 22, 23 ©Paul Brechu/Agence Zoom/UTMB® ; 24, 25a & b David Miller; 26, 28b PLAN B, photo Klaus Fengler; 28a & b PLAN B, photo Andi Frank; 30l MY Visual – Loukian Gindraux, Courtesy Swiss Canyon Trail, 30r, 32 MY Visual – Mathieu Vuilleumier, Courtesy Swiss Canyon Trail; 34, 36a & b ©Agence Zoom/UTMB®; 38l, 38r TORX, photo Stefano Coletta/Zzam! Agency; 40a & b, 43 TORX, photo Roberto Roux/Zzam! Agency; 41 TORX, photo Andrea Testa/Zzam! Agency; 44, 46 PLAN B, photo Andi Frank; 48l & r Spartathlon; 50a Lefteris Partsalis/IMAGO/Alamy Stock Photo; 50b Liu Yongqiu/Xinhua/Alamy Stock Photo; 52, 54-55 Clube de Montanha do Funchal, photo Paulo Abreu; 56, 57 Clube de Montanha do Funchal; 58 Arista Eventos, photo Ian Corless; 60-61 Arista Eventos, photo Matias Novo; 62 Arista Eventos, photo The Adventure Bakery; 63 Arista Eventos, Jose Miguel Munoze; 64 Ultra Pirineu, photo Sergi Colomé; 66a Ultra Pirineu, photo Borja Iban; 66b Ultra Pirineu, photo Jordi Costa; 68 grough.co.uk/Alamy Stock Photo; 70-71, 72, 75 Adam Jacobs - Wild Aperture Photography; 73 David Forster/Alamy Stock Photo; 76-81 David Miller; 82, 86 ©Gilly Photography/UTMB® ; 84-85, 87 ©Agence Zoom/UTMB®; 88 Duncan Watson 0002; 90l Adrian Stott; 90r Fiona Rennie; 91 Alan Young; 92 Montane, photo Swedish Lapland, 94-5, 97 Montane, photo Jonas Palsson; 99 Swisspeaks Trail, photo Christophe Angot; 100 Jen and Sim Benson; 101 ©Agence Zoom/UTMB®; 102 Jan Hetfleisch/Agence Zoom/UTMB®; 104 ©Evan Davies/UTMB®; © 105 Dragon's Back Race No Limits Photography Ourea Events; 106 Bailey-Cooper Photography/Alamy Stock Photo; 107 ÖTILLÖ, The Swimrun World Championship, photo by Jean-Marie Gueye; 108 Scott Rokis; 112-117 Facchino Photography; 111, 118-121 Ian Parker; Evanescent Light Photography; 122-124 Richard Staite; 126, 128 Scott Rokis; 130, 132a & b Daniel Petty/The Denver Post via Getty Images; 134-136 © Bare Photography; 138-145 David Miller; 146l Québec Mega Trail, photo Francis Fontaine; 146r, 150ar & b Québec Mega Trail, photo Sébastien Durocher; 148-149, 150al Québec Mega Trail, photo Daniel Thibault; 153 ©Agence Zoom/UTMB®; 154lAnastasia Wilde; 154r Anastasia Wilde/Alamy Stock Photo; 155 Arrowhead Ultra; 156 Andrew Mason; 157 Jacob Banta; 158 Scott Rokis; 161Ty Holtan Photo; 162 La Transtica; 165 Thiago Diz/RacingThePlanet Limited; 166, all 168 Adam Jacobs - Wild Aperture Photography; 170-174 Thiago Diz/RacingThePlanet Limited; 176-179 La Mision; 180 Ultra Marathon Caballo Blanco; 181 La Transtica; 183 Chicamocha Canyon Race; 184 Marathon des Sables, photo Antonio Miranda; 187 Gareth Roberts; 190-191, 193a Marathon des Sables; 193b Marathon des Sables, photo A. Deroeu; 194, 196 Gareth Roberts; 198 Comrades, photo Paul Henmman; 200a Rob Fenenga/Alamy Stock Photo; 200bl Comrades; 200br Comrades, photo Richard Dobbin; 202-205 imazpress.com/Grand Raid; 209 Ahansal Events, photo Christophe Angot; 210 UltraMARAthon, photo Finlay Marrian; 211 RuNyanga; 212 Ultra Trail Cape Town, photo Zac Zinn; 213 Live Adventure, photo Richard Pearce; 214 Onni Xiao/RacingThe Planet Limited; 217 ©Kailas Fuga, photo Allenfoto; 218-222 Ultra X, photo Benedict Tufnell; 224, 226a Konstantin Shishkin; 226b Braulio Romero; 228-233 Mustang Trail Race, photo Ananta Poudel; 234-241 ©Agence Zoom/UTMB®; 242-244 Mount Fuji 100; 247 Everest Marathon; 248l Annapurna 100; 248r Onni Xiao/RacingThePlanet Limited; 249l ©Kailas Fuga; 249r HK100 Ultra; 250 ©2024 Borneo Ultra Trails Sdn Bhd. All rights reserved. Photo: Magdalene Lucille Thien; 252 Tour de Trails/Aaron Collins; 255, 272 Trips and Tramps; 256-259 ©Tim Bardsley-Smith/Agence Zoom/UTMB®; 260-262 Ian and Velta Fellowes/The Eventurers; 264, 271 ©Cameron Mackenzie/Agence Zoom/UTMB®; 266-270 ©Graeme Murray/Agence Zoom/UTMB®; 275 Chris Watson - profocus.co.nz; 277l, 277r Tour de Trails/Aaron Collins; 278 Ian and Velta Fellowes, the Eventurers; 279 Tom Bryan; 280 Dave Franks; 281 Shakey Finger Photography; 282-283 Jack Yue/iStock.

AUTHORS' ACKNOWLEDGEMENTS

A huge THANK YOU to everyone who generously gave time and expertise towards putting this book together, with special mentions to: ultrarunning photographer David Miller; Gareth Roberts at the Salt Pans Ultra; Marie Cheng, Hayden Arrowsmith & Coralie Batte at UTMB; Christian and Sarah who we met serendipitously on the bus to Courmayeur at TDS by UTMB in 2024; Susie Chan; Pippa Ebel at Kailas; Sophie Seward; Renee McGregor; the Taylors. Thanks to the ace publishing team at Octopus, in particular Trevor Davies and Sybella Stephens. And, as always, our love and gratitude to Hugo and Eva for joining us on our many running, writing and life adventures.

First published in Great Britain in 2025 by Cassell, an imprint of Octopus Publishing Group Ltd
Carmelite House
50 Victoria Embankment
London EC4Y 0DZ
www.octopusbooks.co.uk

An Hachette UK Company
www.hachette.co.uk

The authorized representative in the EEA is Hachette Ireland, 8 Castlecourt Centre, Dublin 15, D15 XTP3, Ireland (email: info@hbgi.ie)

Distributed in the US by Hachette Book Group, 1290 Avenue of the Americas, 4th and 5th Floors, New York, NY 10104

Distributed in Canada by Canadian Manda Group
664 Annette St., Toronto, Ontario, Canada M6S 2C8

ISBN 9781788405775
A CIP catalogue record for this book is available from the British Library.

Printed and bound in Dubai.
10 9 8 7 6 5 4 3 2 1

Publisher: Trevor Davies
Senior Managing Editor: Sybella Stephens
Copy Editor: Chris Stone
Art Director: Yasia Williams
Designers: Peter Dawson and Ronja Rønning, www.gradedesign.com
Cartographer: Cosmographics
Picture Research Managers: Giulia Hetherington and Jennifer Veall
Senior Production Manager: Peter Hunt

Publisher's note
Ultramarathon races are usually standard distances (50km, 50 miles, 100km, 100 miles) but due to wild and often mountainous terrain and changing conditions, such as rockfall, exact distances can not be guaranteed and there may be discrepancies in the race distances provided.